工程力学专业英语

严波 皮文丽 编

清华大学出版社
北京

内 容 简 介

本书选编了工程力学专业涉及的科技英文文章,包括理论力学、材料力学、弹性力学、结构力学、振动力学、塑性力学、实验力学、计算力学、疲劳与断裂、复合材料力学和流体力学等内容,并注意纳入相应课程的新概念,覆盖面广。本书还分单元介绍了英文科技报告、学位论文、期刊论文写作技巧和英汉科技文章的翻译技巧,旨在培养学生科技论文写作和翻译的基本技能。各单元课文正文适用于教师精讲,第一篇阅读材料适用于本科生自学,或在教师指导下学习,第二篇阅读材料内容相对较深,主要适用于研究生学习参考。此外,每篇文章后面均列出了生词和短语,附录中列出了常用专业词汇和短语,便于读者查阅。

本书无论是在内容选材还是在内容编写上均具有特色,是一本适用于工程力学专业和力学类专业本科生的实用教材,也可供土木、机械、材料等相关工科专业的本科生、研究生及相关工程技术人员学习参考。

版权所有,侵权必究。举报: 010-62782989, beiqinquan@tup.tsinghua.edu.cn。

图书在版编目(CIP)数据

工程力学专业英语/严波,皮文丽编. —北京: 清华大学出版社,2012.8(2024.7重印)
ISBN 978-7-302-29648-5

Ⅰ. ①工… Ⅱ. ①严… ②皮… Ⅲ. ①工程力学－英语 Ⅳ. ①H31

中国版本图书馆 CIP 数据核字(2012)第 185115 号

责任编辑: 佟丽霞　赵从棉
封面设计: 常雪影
责任校对: 王淑云
责任印制: 丛怀宇

出版发行: 清华大学出版社
   网　　址: https://www.tup.com.cn, https://www.wqxuetang.com
   地　　址: 北京清华大学学研大厦 A 座　　邮　编: 100084
   社 总 机: 010-83470000　　邮　购: 010-62786544
   投稿与读者服务: 010-62776969, c-service@tup.tsinghua.edu.cn
   质量反馈: 010-62772015, zhiliang@tup.tsinghua.edu.cn
印 装 者: 涿州市般润文化传播有限公司
经　　销: 全国新华书店
开　　本: 185mm×260mm　　印　张: 16.25　　字　数: 390 千字
版　　次: 2012 年 8 月第 1 版　　印　次: 2024 年 7 月第 8 次印刷
定　　价: 46.00 元

产品编号: 044942-03

前　言

《工程力学专业英语》是在编者编写的《工程力学专业英语阅读教材》(讲义)的基础上改编而成。该讲义最初编写于1997年,于1998年开始在重庆大学工程力学本科专业使用,2002年编者根据教学使用的情况进行了一次修改,至今已经使用了十余年时间。本次正式出版前,编者对原讲义进行了全面的修改。

本书共分14个单元,每一单元包括一篇课文和两篇阅读材料,选材广泛,针对性强,内容新。所有文章均选自英文原文著作,内容涉及理论力学、材料力学、弹性力学、结构力学、振动力学、塑性力学、实验力学、计算力学、疲劳与断裂、复合材料力学和流体力学等工程力学专业主干课程和相关课程的基本概念和内容,并注意纳入了相应课程的新概念和新内容。各单元课文部分适用于教师精讲,第一篇阅读材料适用于本科生自学,第二篇阅读材料适用于研究生学习参考。为便于学生学习掌握工程力学专业英语词汇和概念,每篇文章后均列出了专业词语、词组和惯用语。

为了提高学生科技英文应用能力,书中分单元讲解了英文科技报告和论文的写作以及科技文章英汉翻译的基本技巧。这两部分内容主要参考国内外同类教材编写而成,讲解中尽量给出与力学专业相关的例句。

本书的编写得到重庆大学资源及环境科学学院万玲教授的大力支持,重庆大学工程力学系的部分教师和同学对本书内容提出了很多宝贵的意见和建议,使得本教材得以顺利完成。重庆大学工程力学系研究生崔伟同学认真仔细地描绘了书中所有示图,在此一并表示感谢。

由于编者的水平有限,不当和错误在所难免,恳望读者批评指正。

编　者
2012年5月于重庆大学

目 录

Unit One   Some Basic Concepts of Mechanics ·· 1
   Writing Skill of Experimental Research Report: INTRODUCTION (1) ············ 5
   Reading Material (1): Kinetic Energy and Work ·· 8
   Reading Material (2): The Lagrangian Method ·· 11
Unit Two   The Flexure Formula of Beams ··· 15
   Writing Skill of Experimental Research Report: INTRODUCTION (2) ············ 20
   Reading Material (1): Metals in Mechanical and Structural Design ················ 23
   Reading Material (2): Stability of Column ··· 28
Unit Three   What is Continuum Mechanics ··· 32
   Writing Skill of Experimental Research Report: INTRODUCTION (3) ············ 35
   Reading Material (1): Stress ··· 39
   Reading Material (2): Solid Mechanics ··· 42
Unit Four   Hooke's Law ··· 47
   Writing Skill of Experimental Research Report: METHOD and MATERIALS ········· 51
   Reading Material (1): Basic Equations of Elastic Homogeneous and Isotropic
      Bodies ·· 55
   Reading Material (2): Stress Waves in Solids ·· 57
Unit Five   Statically Indeterminate Structure ··· 61
   Writing Skill of Experimental Research Report: RESULTS and DISCUSSION ········ 65
   Reading Material (1): Basic Structural Elements ·· 70
   Reading Material (2): General Theory of Plane Trusses ································· 77
Unit Six   Free Vibrations: One Degree of Freedom ·· 84
   Writing Skill of Experimental Research Report: ABSTRACT ·························· 89
   Reading Material (1): Forced Harmonic Vibration ·· 91
   Reading Material (2): Response to Arbitrary, Step, and Pulse Excitations ········ 95
Unit Seven   Description of Elastoplastic Material Response under Uniaxial Case ········ 99
   科技英语翻译技巧：科技文章的特点 ·· 102
   Reading Material (1): Yield Criteria of Metals ·· 105
   Reading Material (2): Some Plasticity and Viscoplasticity Constitutive
      Theories ··· 108

目 录

Unit Eight   Experimental Stress Analysis 114
    科技英语翻译技巧：词义引申和词量增减 117
    Reading Material (1)：Strain Gage System 119
    Reading Material (2)：Perspectives in Experimental Solid Mechanics 122

Unit Nine   Direct Formulation of Finite Element Characteristics 128
    科技英语翻译技巧：词性的转换和句子成分转换 133
    Reading Material (1)：Variational Principle 137
    Reading Material (2)：Generalization of the Finite Element Concepts 139

Unit Ten   Fatigue of Materials 143
    科技英语翻译技巧：常见多功能词的译法 148
    Reading Material (1)：Linear Fracture Mechanics 152
    Reading Material (2)：Fracture Mechanics 155

Unit Eleven   Basic Terminology of Laminated Fiber-Reinforced Composite Materials 161
    科技英语翻译技巧：数词的译法和被动语态的译法 164
    Reading Material (1)：Macromechanical Behavior of a Lamina 167
    Reading Material (2)：Shape Memory Alloy and Smart Hybrid Composites
        Advanced Materials for the 21st Century 173

Unit Twelve   Fluid Mechanics 178
    科技英语翻译技巧：定语从句及同位语从句的译法 181
    Reading Material (1)：Constitutive Equations of Fluids 185
    Reading Material (2)：Finite Difference Method 187

Unit Thirteen   Rock Mechanics 194
    科技英语翻译技巧：状语从句的译法 199
    Reading Material (1)：Special Stress-Strain States of Rock 202
    Reading Material (2)：Soil Mechanics 205

Unit Fourteen   Structural Optimization 209
    科技英语翻译技巧：长句的译法 213
    Reading Material (1)：Research Directions in Computational Mechanics 215
    Reading Material (2)：New Directions in Mechanics 221

附录：常用专业词汇和用语汇总表 226

参考文献 250

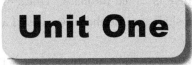

Some Basic Concepts of Mechanics[1,2]

Mechanics is a branch of physics concerned with motion or change in position of physical objects. It is sometimes further subdivideded into:

(1) Kinematics, which is concerned with the geometry of the motion;

(2) Dynamics, which is concerned with the physical causes of the motion;

(3) Statics, which is concerned with conditions under which no motion is apparent.

Some important basic concepts occurred in mechniacs are described in the following sections.

Mathematical Models

A mathematical description of physical phenomena is often simplified by replacing actural physical objects by suitable mathematical models. For example, in describing the rotation of the earth about the sun we can for many practical purposes treat the earth and sun as points.

Space, Time and Matter

From everyday experience, we all have some idea as to the meaning of each of the following terms or concepts. However, we would certainly find it difficult to formulate completely satisfactory definitions. We take them as undefined concepts.

(1) Space. This is closely related to the concepts of point, position, direction and displacement. Measurement in space involves the concepts of length or distance, with which we assume familiarity. Units of length are feet, meters, miles, etc. Here we assume that space is Euclidean, i. e. the space of Euclid's geometry.

(2) Time. This concept is derived from our experience of having one event taking place after, before or simultaneous with another event. Measurement of time is achieved, for example, by use of clocks. Units of time are seconds, hours, years, etc.

(3) Matter. Physical objects are composed of "small bits of matter" such as atoms and molecules. From this we arrive at the concept of a material object called a particle which can be considered as occupying a point in space and perhaps moving as time goes by. A

measure of the "quantity of matter" associated with a particle is called its mass. Units of mass are grams, kilograms, etc. Unless otherwise stated we shall assume that the mass of a particle does not change with time.

Length, mass and time are often called dimensions from which other physical quantities are constructed.

Scalars and Vectors

Various quantities of physics, such as length, mass and time, require for their specification a single real number (apart from units of measurement which are decided upon in advance). Such quantities are called scalars and the real number is called the magnitude of the quantity. A scalar is represented analytically by a letter such as t, m, etc.

Other quantities of physics, such as displacement, require for their specification a direction as well as magnitude. Such quantities are called vectors. A vector is represented analytically by a bold faced letter such as A in Fig. 1-1. Geometrically it is represented by an arrow PQ where P is called the initial point and Q is called the terminal point. The magnitude or length of the vector is then denoted by $|A|$ or A.

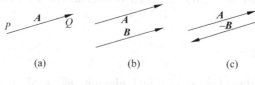

Fig. 1-1

Balancing Forces

A "static" situation is one where all the objects are motionless. If an object remains motionless, then $F=ma$ tells us that the total force acting on it must be zero. (The converse is not true, of course. The total force on an object is also zero if it moves with constant nonzero velocity. But we'll deal only with statics problems here.) The whole goal in a statics problem is to find out what the various forces have to be so that there is zero net force acting on each object. Since a force is a vector, this goal involves breaking the force up into its components. You can pick Cartesian coordinates, polar coordinates, or another set. It is usually clear from the problem which system will make your calculations easiest. Once you pick a system, you simply have to demand that the total force in each direction is zero.

There are many different types of forces in the world, most of which are large-scale effects of complicated things going on at smaller scales. For example, the tension in a rope comes from the chemical bonds that hold the molecules in the rope together (and these chemical forces are just electrical forces). In doing a mechanics problem involving a rope, there is certainly no need to analyze all the details of the forces taking place at the molecular scale. You simply call the force in the rope a "tension" and get on with the problem. Four types of forces come up repeatedly:

Tension. Tension is the general name for a force that a rope, stick, etc., exerts when it is pulled on. Every piece of the rope feels a tension force in both directions, except the end point, which feels a tension on one side and a force on the other side from whatever object is attached to the end.

In some cases, the tension may vary along the rope. The "Rope wrapped around a pole" example is a good illustration of this. In other cases, the tension must be the same everywhere. For example, in a hanging massless rope, or in a massless rope hanging over a frictionless pulley, the tension must be the same at all points, because otherwise there would be a net force on at least one tiny piece, and then $F=ma$ would yield an infinite acceleration for this tiny piece.

Normal force. This is the force perpendicular to a surface that the the surface applies to an object. The total force applied by a surface is usually a combination of the normal force and the friction force. But for frictionless surface such as greasy ones or ice, only the normal force exists. The normal force comes about because the surface actually compresses a tiny bit and acts like a very rigid spring. The surface gets squashed until the restoring force equals the force the object applies.

Remarks: For the most part, the only difference between a "tension" and a "normal force" is the direction of the force. Both situations can be modeled by a spring. In the case of a tension, the spring (a rope, a stick, or whatever) is stretched, and the force on the given object is directed toward the spring. In the case of normal force, the spring is compressed, and the force on the given object is directed away from the spring. Things like sticks can provide both normal forces and tension. But a rope, for example, has a hard time providing a normal force.

In practice, in the case of elongated objects such as stick, a compressive force is usually called a "compressive tension", or a "negative tension", instead of a normal force. So by these definitions, a tension can point either way. At any rate, it's just semantics. If you use any of these descriptions for a compressed stick, people will know what you mean.

Friction. Friction is the force parallel to a surface that a surface applies to an object. Some surfaces, such as sandpaper, have a great deal of friction. Some, such as greasy ones, have essentially no friction. There are two types of friction, called "kinetic" friction and "static" friction.

Kinetic friction deals with two objects moving relative to each other. It is usually a good approximation to say that the kinetic friction between two objects is proportional to the normal force between them. The constant of proportionality is called μ_k (the "coefficient of kinetic friction"), where μ_k depends on the two surfaces involved. Thus, $F=\mu_k N$, where N is the normal force. The direction of the force is opposite to the motion.

Static friction deals with two objects at rest relative to each other. In the static case, we have $F \leqslant \mu_s N$ (where μ_s is the "coefficient of static friction"). Note the inequality sign.

All we can say prior to solving a problem is that the static friction force has a maximum value equal to $F_{max} = \mu_s N$. In a given problem, it is most likely less than this. For example, if a block of large mass M sits on a surface with coefficient of friction μ_s, and you give the block a tiny push to the right (tiny enough so that it doesn't move), then the friction force is of course not equal to $\mu_s N = \mu_s Mg$ to the left. Such a force would send the block sailing off to the left. The true friction force is simply equal and opposite to the tiny force you apply. What the coefficient μ_s tells us is that if you apply a force larger than $\mu_s Mg$ (the maximum friction force on a horizontal table), then the block will speed up moving to the right.

Gravity. Consider two point objects, with masses M and m, separated by a distance R. Newton's gravitational force law says that the force between these objects is attractive and has magnitude $F = GMm/R^2$, where $G = 6.67 \times 10^{-11} \, m^3/(kg \cdot s^2)$. A sphere may be treated like a point mass located at its center. Therefore, an object on the surface of the earth feels a gravitational force equal to

$$F = m(GM/R^2) \equiv mg$$

where M is the mass of the earth, and R is its radius. This equation defines g. Plugging in the numerical values, we obtain (as you can check) $g \approx 9.8 \, m/s^2$. Every object on the surface of the earth feels a force of mg downward. If the object is not accelerating, then there must also be other forces present (normal forces, etc.) to make the total force equal to zero.

Words and Expressions

mechanics [mi'kæniks]	n.	力学
kinematics [ˌkinə'mætiks]	n.	运动学；动力学
dynamics [dai'næmiks]	n.	动力学；力学；动态
statics ['stætiks]	n.	静力学
scalar ['skeilə]	n.	数量；标量
vector ['vektə]	n.	矢量；向量
force [fɔːs]	n.	力；力量
Cartesian coordinate		笛卡儿坐标
polar coordinate		极坐标
tension ['tenʃən]	n.	张量，张力，拉力
acceleration [æk,selə'reiʃən]	n.	加速度
normal force		法向力
friction force		摩擦力
stretch [stretʃ]	vt. & vi.	伸展，拉紧，延伸
elongate ['iːlɔŋgeit]	vt. & vi.	拉长；伸长；延长
kinetic friction		动摩擦
static friction		静摩擦
sandpaper	n.	砂纸
gravitation force		引力；重力

Writing Skill of Experimental Research Report: INTRODUCTION (1)[32]

An *experimental research report* is a paper written by an investigator to describe a research study that he or she has completed. The purpose of the report is to explain to others in the field what the objectives, methods, and findings of the study were. The report may be published in a professional *journal*, it may appear as a *monograph* distributed by a research institution or publishing company, or it may be written in the form of a *thesis* or *dissertation* as part of the requirements for a university degree.

The organizational format for all experimental research reports is basically the same, regardless of the field of study in which the author is working. The major sections of a typical experimental research report in the order in which they are usually presented are

ABSTRACT
INTRODUCTION
METHOD
RESULTS
DISCUSSION

The *introduction* serves as an orientation for readers of the report, giving them the perspective they need to understand the detailed information coming in later sections.

Generally, the *introduction* of an experimental research report can be divided into the following five parts, or stages,

Stage I: General statement(s) about a field of research to provide the readers with a *setting* for the problem to be reported.

Stage II: More specific statements about the aspects of the problem *already studied* by other researchers.

Stage III: Statement(s) that indicate *the need for more investigation*.

Stage IV: Very specific statement(s) giving *the purpose/objectives* of the writer's study.

Stage V: Optimal statement(s) that give a *value or justification* for carrying out the study.

However, writers do not always arrange the stages of their *introduction* in this exact order. Sometimes a writer interrupts one stage with another, and then returns to the earlier stage. Sometimes Stage II, which is usually called "The Review of Literature", is completely separated from the rest of the *introduction*. In theses and dissertations, for example, it is often written as a separate chapter. Stage V is often omitted entirely. However, the general plan given here is very common and is the easiest for the beginning research writer to use.

INTRODUCTION: Establishing a Context

In stage I, the writer establishes a context, or frame of reference, to help readers understand how the research fits into a wider field of study.

(1) Information Conventions

(a) Inventing the Setting

You should write the setting (Stage I) of your ***introduction*** so that it provides your readers with the background necessary to see the particular topic of your research in relation to a general area of study. In order to do this, start with obvious, generally accepted statements about the area in which you are working. Then, step by step, move the readers to your specific topic. You may do this in just a few sentences or in several paragraphs.

You can think of this stage as a process of first, establishing a "universe" for your readers; then, isolating one "galaxy" within this universe; and finally, leading your readers to one "star" in the galaxy. That "star" is your specific topic.

- Begin with accepted statements of fact related to your *general area* (your "universe").
- Within the general area, identify one *subarea* (your "galaxy" which includes your topic).
- Indicate your *topic* (your "star").

(b) Linking Ideas through Old and New Information Order

To lead the readers smoothly through the ideas in Stage I, writers link sentences by making use of old and new information. This is done by placing old information—that is, information already known to the readers—at the beginning of sentences and placing new information at the end.

(2) Language Conventions

(a) General and Specific Noun Phrases

As we have seen, Stage I of the ***introduction*** usually begins with factual statements about the general area which includes your specific topic. When you write these kinds of general statements, it is conventional to use nouns that refer to objects or concepts at the highest possible level of generality. English offers several ways to construct these general nouns, which we examine in this section.

Statements in the setting of an ***introduction*** tend to be general in nature. Instead of referring to specific things, they often refer to *entire classes* of things. When you write sentences that contain nouns referring to an entire class of things, you should use *generic noun phrases* to carry this meaning. Generic noun phrase refer to all members of a particular class of living things.

In English there are different ways to write generic noun phrases. If the noun is *countable*, you can make it generic by adding the plural marker-s and omitting any article, or by using it in its singular form with the indefinite article *a* or *an*.

Example: *Composite materials* are widely used in engineering practices. (plural)

Example: The mechanical properties of *a new composite material* must be tested before its application in engineering. (singular, meaning "any new composite material")

When the noun you want to use is *uncountable*, you can make it generic by omitting any article.

Example: Thirty years later, *composite production* had more than doubled. (meaning "all composite production")

In addition, English has a fourth way of forming generic nouns you should learn to recognize and use. A *countable noun in its singular form* sometimes carries the generic meaning when used with the definite article *the*. This kind of generic noun phrase is often used when referring to living creatures or familiar machinery and equipment.

Example: The United States has experienced the integration of *the computer* into society. (meaning "computers in general")

We have seen that the first part of Stage I, the setting of the **introduction**, usually contains a large proportion of generic noun phrases. Later in the setting, you will probably find it necessary to refer to specific items and concepts in order to move the reader from the general area toward your specific topic. This requires the use of specific noun phrase—that is, nouns refer to particular, individual members of a class rather than to the class as a whole. In English, nouns with this meaning can be written in several ways.

- *Referring to assumed or shared information*. Use the definite article *the* if you assume your readers share knowledge of the specific thing you are referring to.

Example: In recent years the growth of application of the finite element software has been accelerating in *the world*.

- *Pointing back to old information*. Use the definite article *the* when referring to a specific thing which you have already mentioned (the first mentioned usually uses the indefinite article a/an).

Example: Professor Belytschko proposed a mesh-free method recently. *The new method* is very efficient to simulate the process of crack propagation.

- *Pointing forward to specific information*. Use the definite article *the* when the specific meaning is made clear in a following phrase or clause.

Example: *The load* which is carried by the beam must be less than 100N.

(b) Guidelines for Marking Generic and Specific Noun Phrases

If you are having difficulty determining which, if any, article to use before a noun or a noun phrase, ask yourself the following sequence of questions:

- Is the noun meant in a *general* or a *specific* sense? If it is *specific*, use "the" before the noun. If it is *general*, ask yourself a follow-up question:
- Is the noun *countable* or *uncountable*? If it is countable, use *a* or *an* (singular) or -s on the end (plural). If it is uncountable, use no article or -s ending.

(c) Expressing Old Information

There are several ways you can state old information to connect back to the information in a previous sentence. One way is to simply repeat a word or to use a derived form of the word.

Example: The idea of the finite element method (FEM) was originally proposed at the inception of the 20th century. It is a common knowledge that the FEM has to be carried out by coding a program.

Another way you can indicate old information is to use pronouns and pointing words.

Example: The concept of stress is the heart of our subject. *It* is the unique way continuum mechanics has for specifying the interaction between one part of a material body and another.

Sometimes you can assume the reader knows the old information without your having to state it explicitly.

Example: Buckling of pressure vessel may take place if the structure does not have enough stability to sustain internal pressure. *The accidents* [of buckling] usually give rise to big economic loss.

(3) **A Sample**

The following paragraph is adopted from the ***introduction*** of an academic paper [33], which may help the readers understand how to establish a context at the beginning of an ***introduction***.

Repairs of cracked components in aerospace structures are becoming more and more important due to the requirement of operation safety. The repair methods based on adhesively bonded fiber-reinforced polymer (FRP) composite patches have been demonstrated to be very promising to these cracked structures. FRP composite patches have the advantages of high ratios of stiffness and strength to weight, and are more structurally efficient and much less damaging to the repaired structures than fastened metallic patches. Although double-sided repair with FRP composite patches is more effective in reinforcement, single-sided repair plays a more important role because, in the most of practical repairs, it is difficult or even impossible to access both sides of the cracked structures that needed to be repaired. Fatigue crack growth behavior of cracked panels after being repaired decides the extension of fatigue life or service life of the repaired structures. Therefore, the evaluation of fatigue crack growth behavior of cracked panels repaired with a FRP composite patch becomes a focus in this research area.

◇◆◇◆◇◆◇◆◇◆◇◆◇◆◇◆◇◆◇◆◇◆◇◆

Reading Material (1): Kinetic Energy and Work[3]

As I have said, there are many different kinds of energy. Perhaps the most basic is kinetic energy (or KE), which for a single particle of mass m traveling with speed $\boldsymbol{v}$ is defined to be

$$T = \frac{1}{2} m \boldsymbol{v}^2 \tag{1}$$

Let us imagine the particle moving through space and examine the change in its kinetic energy as it moves between two neighboring points $\boldsymbol{r}_1$ and $\boldsymbol{r}_1 + \mathrm{d}\boldsymbol{r}$ on its path as shown in Figure 1. The time derivative of T is easily evaluated if we note that $\boldsymbol{v}^2 = \boldsymbol{v} \cdot \boldsymbol{v}$, so that

$$\frac{\mathrm{d}T}{\mathrm{d}t} = \frac{1}{2} m \frac{\mathrm{d}}{\mathrm{d}t}(\boldsymbol{v} \cdot \boldsymbol{v}) = \frac{1}{2} m (\dot{\boldsymbol{v}} \cdot \boldsymbol{v} + \boldsymbol{v} \cdot \dot{\boldsymbol{v}}) = m \dot{\boldsymbol{v}} \cdot \boldsymbol{v} \tag{2}$$

By the second law, the factor $m \dot{\boldsymbol{v}}$ is equal to the net force $\boldsymbol{F}$ on the particle, so that

$$\frac{dT}{dt} = \mathbf{F} \cdot \mathbf{v} \tag{3}$$

If we multiply both sides by dt, then since $\mathbf{v}dt$ is the displacement $d\mathbf{r}$, we find

$$dT = \mathbf{F} \cdot d\mathbf{r} \tag{4}$$

The expression on the right, $\mathbf{F} \cdot d\mathbf{r}$, is defined to be the **work done by the force $\mathbf{F}$** in the displacement $d\mathbf{r}$. Thus we have proved the **Work-KE theorem**, that the change in the particle's kinetic energy between two neighboring points on its path is equal to the work done by the net force as it moves between the two points.

So far we have proved the Work-KE theorem only for an infinitesimal displacement $d\mathbf{r}$, but it generalizes easily to larger displacements. Consider the two points shown as $\mathbf{r}_1$ and $\mathbf{r}_2$ in Figure 1. We can divide the path between these points 1 and 2 into a large number of very small segments, to each of which we can apply the infinitesimal result (4). Adding all of these results, we find that the total change in T going from 1 to 2 is the sum $\sum \mathbf{F} \cdot d\mathbf{r}$ of all the infinitesimal

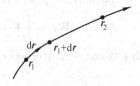

Figure 1 Three points on the path of a particle: $\mathbf{r}_1$ and $\mathbf{r}_1 + d\mathbf{r}$ (with $d\mathbf{r}$ infinitesimal) and $\mathbf{r}_2$

works done in all the infinitesimal displacements between points 1 and 2:

$$\Delta T \equiv T_2 - T_1 = \sum \mathbf{F} \cdot d\mathbf{r} \tag{5}$$

In the limit that all the displacements $d\mathbf{r}$ go to zero, this sum becomes an integral:

$$\sum \mathbf{F} \cdot d\mathbf{r} \rightarrow \int_1^2 \mathbf{F} \cdot d\mathbf{r} \tag{6}$$

This integral, called a **line integral**, is a generalization of the integral $\int f(x) dx$ over a single variable x, and its definition as the limit of the sum of many small pieces is closely analogous. If you feel any doubt about the symbol $\int_1^2 \mathbf{F} \cdot d\mathbf{r}$ on the right of (6), think of it as being just the sum on the left (with all the displacements infinitesimally small). In evaluating a line integral, it is usually possible to convert it into an ordinary integral over a single variable, as the following examples show. Notice that, as the name implies, the line integral depends (in general) on the path that the particle followed from point 1 to point 2.

The particular line integral on the right of (6) is called the work done by the force $\mathbf{F}$ moving between points 1 and 2 along the path concerned.

Example: Three Line Integrals

Evaluate the line integral for the work done by the two-dimensional force $\mathbf{F} = (y, 2x)$ going from the origin O to the point $P = (1, 1)$ along each of the three paths shown in Figure 2. Path a goes from O to $Q = (1, 0)$ along the x axis and then from Q straight up to P, path b

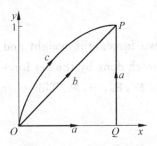

Figure 2 Three different paths, a, b, and c, from the origin to point $P = (1, 1)$

goes straight from O to P along the line $y=x$, and path c goes round a quarter circle centered on Q.

The integral along path a is easily evaluated in two parts, if we note that on OQ the displacements have the form $d\boldsymbol{r}=(dx,0)$, while on QP they are $d\boldsymbol{r}=(0,dy)$. Thus

$$W_a = \int_a \boldsymbol{F} \cdot d\boldsymbol{r} = \int_O^Q \boldsymbol{F} \cdot d\boldsymbol{r} + \int_Q^P \boldsymbol{F} \cdot d\boldsymbol{r} = \int_0^1 F_x(x,0)dx + \int_0^1 F_y(1,y)dy$$

$$= 0 + 2\int_0^1 dy = 2$$

On the path b, $x=y$, so that $dx=dy$, and

$$W_b = \int_b \boldsymbol{F} \cdot d\boldsymbol{r} = \int_b (F_x dx + F_y dy) = \int_0^1 (x+2x)dx = 1.5$$

Path c is conveniently expressed parametrically as

$$\boldsymbol{r} = (x,y) = (1-\cos\theta, \sin\theta)$$

where θ is the angle between OQ and the line from Q to the point (x, y), with $0 < \theta < \pi/2$. Thus on path c

$$d\boldsymbol{r} = (dx, dy) = (\sin\theta, \cos\theta)d\theta$$

and

$$W_c = \int_c \boldsymbol{F} \cdot d\boldsymbol{r} = \int_c (F_x dx + F_y dy)$$

$$= \int_0^{\pi/2} [\sin^2\theta + 2(1-\cos\theta)\cos\theta]d\theta = 2 - \pi/4 = 1.21$$

With the notation of the line integral, we can rewrite the result (5) as

$$\Delta T \equiv T_2 - T_1 = \int_1^2 \boldsymbol{F} \cdot d\boldsymbol{r} \equiv W(1 \to 2) \tag{7}$$

where I have introduced the notation $W(1\to 2)$ for the work done by $\boldsymbol{F}$ moving from point 1 to point 2. The result is the Work-KE theorem for arbitrary displacements, large or small: The change in a particle's KE as it moves between points 1 and 2 is the work done by the net force.

It is important to remember that the work that appears on the right of (7) is the work done by the net force $\boldsymbol{F}$ on the particle. In general, $\boldsymbol{F}$ is the vector sum of various separate forces

$$\boldsymbol{F} = \boldsymbol{F}_1 + \cdots + \boldsymbol{F}_n \equiv \sum_{i=1}^n \boldsymbol{F}_i$$

(For example, the net force on a projectile is the sum of two forces, the weight and air resistance.) It is a most convenient fact that to evaluate the work done by the net force $\boldsymbol{F}$, we can simply add up the works done by the separate forces $\boldsymbol{F}_1, \boldsymbol{F}_2, \cdots, \boldsymbol{F}_n$. This claim is easily proved as follows:

$$W(1 \to 2) = \int_1^2 \boldsymbol{F} \cdot d\boldsymbol{r} = \int_1^2 \sum_i \boldsymbol{F}_i \cdot d\boldsymbol{r}$$

$$= \sum_i \int_1^2 \boldsymbol{F}_i \cdot d\boldsymbol{r} = \sum_i W_i(1 \to 2) \tag{8}$$

The crucial step, from the first line to the second, is justified because the integral of a sum of n terms is the same as the sum of the n individual integrals. The Work-KE theorem can therefore be rewritten as

$$T_2 - T_1 = \sum_{i=1}^{n} W_i (1 \rightarrow 2) \tag{9}$$

In practice, one almost always uses the theorem in this way: Calculate the work W_i done by each of the n separate forces on the particle and then set ΔT equal to the sum of all the W_i.

If the net force on a particle is zero, then the Work-KE theorem tells us that the particle's kinetic energy is constant. This simply says that the speed v is constant, which, though true, is not very interesting, since it already follows from Newton's first law.

Words and Expressions

kinetic energy		动能
work [wə:k]	n.	功
derivative [di'rivətiv]	n.	导数
time derivative		时间导数
displacement [dis'pleismənt]	n.	位移
integral ['intigrəl]	n.	积分；整数
Newton's first law		牛顿第一定律

Reading Material(2): The Lagrangian Method[2]

Consider the problem of a mass on the end of a spring. We can solve this, of course, by using $F=ma$ to write down $m\ddot{x}=-kx$. The solutions to this equation are sinusoidal functions, as we well know. We can, however, solve this problem by using another method which doesn't explicitly use $F=ma$. In many (in fact, probably most) physical situations, this new method is far superior to using $F=ma$.

We will present our new method by first stating its rules (without any justification) and showing that they somehow end up magically giving the correct answer. We will then give the method proper justification.

Here is the procedure. Form the following seemingly silly combination of the kinetic and potential energies (T and V, respectively),

$$L \equiv T - V \tag{1}$$

This is called the Lagrangian. Yes, there is a minus sign in the definition (a plus sign would simply give the total energy). In the problem of a mass on the end of a spring, $T = m\ddot{x}^2/2$ and $V = kx^2/2$, so we have

$$L = \frac{1}{2}m\dot{x}^2 - \frac{1}{2}kx^2 \tag{2}$$

Now write

$$\frac{d}{dt}\left(\frac{\partial L}{\partial \dot{x}}\right) = \frac{\partial L}{\partial x} \quad (3)$$

This equation is called the Euler-Lagrange (E-L) equation. For the problem at hand, we have $\partial L/\partial \dot{x} = m\dot{x}$ and $\partial L/\partial x = -kx$, so Eq. (3) gives

$$m\ddot{x} = -kx \quad (4)$$

which is exactly the result obtained by using $F=ma$. An equation such as Eq. (4), which is derived from the Euler-Lagrange equation, is called an *equation of motion* (The term "equation of motion" is a little ambiguous. It is understood to refer to the second-order differential equation satisfied by x, and not the actual equation for x as a function of t, namely $x(t) = A\cos(\omega t + \phi)$ in this problem, which is obtained by integrating the equation of motion twice.)

If the problem involves more than one coordinate, as most problems do, we simply have to apply Eq. (3) to each coordinate. We will obtain as many equations as there are coordinates. Each equation may very well involve many of the coordinates (see the example below, where both equations involve both x and θ).

At this point, you may be thinking, "That was a nice little trick, but we just got lucky in the spring problem. The procedure won't work in a more general situation." Well, let's see. How about if we consider the more general problem of a particle moving in an arbitrary potential, $V(x)$ (we'll just stick to one dimension for now). Then the Lagrangian is

$$L = \frac{1}{2}m\dot{x}^2 - V(x) \quad (5)$$

The Euler-Lagrange equation, Eq. (3), gives

$$m\ddot{x} = -\frac{dV}{dx} \quad (6)$$

But $-dV/dx$ is simply the force on the particle. So we see that Eqs. (1) and (3) together say exactly the same thing that $F = ma$ says, when using a Cartesian coordinate in one dimension.

Note that shifting the potential by a given constant has no effect on the equation of motion, because Eq. (3) involves only derivatives of V. This, of course, is equivalent to saying that only differences in energy are relevant, and not the actual values, as we well know.

In a three-dimensional problem, where the potential takes the form $V(x, y, z)$, it immediately follows that the three Euler-Lagrange equations (obtained by applying Eq. (3) to x, y and z) may be combined into the vector statement,

$$m\ddot{\mathbf{x}} = -\nabla V \quad (7)$$

$-\nabla V = \mathbf{F}$, so we again arrive at Newton's second law, $\mathbf{F} = m\mathbf{a}$, now in three dimensions.

Let's now do one more example to convince you that there's really something nontrivial going on here.

Example (Spring pendulum): Consider a pendulum made out of a spring with a mass m

on the end (see Fig. 1). The spring is arranged to lie in a straight line (which we can arrange by, say, wrapping the spring around a rigid massless rod). The equilibrium length of the spring is l. Let the spring have length $l + x(t)$, and let its angle with the vertical be $\theta(t)$. Assuming that the motion takes place in a vertical plane, find the equations of motions for x and θ.

Fig. 1

Solution: The kinetic energy may be broken up into the radial and tangential parts, so we have

$$T = \frac{1}{2}m(\dot{x}^2 + (l+x)^2 \dot{\theta}^2) \tag{8}$$

The potential energy comes from both gravity and the spring, so we have

$$V(x,\theta) = -mg(l+x)\cos\theta + \frac{1}{2}kx^2 \tag{9}$$

The Lagrangian therefore equals

$$L \equiv T - V = \frac{1}{2}m(\dot{x}^2 + (l+x)^2\dot{\theta}^2) + mg(l+x)\cos\theta - \frac{1}{2}kx^2 \tag{10}$$

There are two variables here, x and θ. As mentioned above, the nice thing about the Lagrangian method is that we can simply use Eq. (3) twice, once with x and once with θ. Hence, the two Euler-Lagrange equations are

$$\frac{d}{dt}\left(\frac{\partial L}{\partial \dot{x}}\right) = \frac{\partial L}{\partial x} \Rightarrow m\ddot{x} = m(l+x)\dot{\theta}^2 + mg\cos\theta - kx \tag{11}$$

and

$$\frac{d}{dt}\left(\frac{\partial L}{\partial \dot{\theta}}\right) = \frac{\partial L}{\partial \theta} \Rightarrow \frac{d}{dt}(m(l+x)^2\dot{\theta}) = -mg(l+x)\sin\theta$$

$$\Rightarrow m(l+x)^2\ddot{\theta} + 2m(l+x)\dot{x}\dot{\theta} = -mg(l+x)\sin\theta$$

$$\Rightarrow m(l+x)\ddot{\theta} + 2m\dot{x}\dot{\theta} = -mg\sin\theta \tag{12}$$

Eq. (11) is simply the radial $F = ma$ equation, complete with the centripetal acceleration, $-(l+x)\dot{\theta}^2$. The first line of Eq. (12) is the statement that the torque equals the rate of change of the angular momentum.

After writing down the E-L equations, it is always best to double-check them by trying to identify them as $F = ma$ or $\tau = dL/dt$ equations. Sometimes, however, this identification is not obvious. For the times when everything is clear (that is, when you look at the E-L equations and say, "Oh, of course!"), it is usually clear only after you've derived them. The Lagrangian method is generally the safer method to use.

The present example should convince you of the great utility of the Lagrangian method. Even if you've never heard of the terms "torque", "centripetal", "centrifugal", or "Coriolis", you can still get the correct equations by simply writing down the kinetic and potential energies, and then taking a few derivatives.

At this point it seems to be personal preference, and all academic, whether you use the

Lagrangian method or the $F=ma$ method. The two methods produce the same equations. However, in problems involving more than one variable, it usually turns out to be much easier to write down T and V, as opposed to writing down all the forces. This is because T and V are nice and simple scalars. The forces, on the other hand, are vectors, and it's easy to get confused if they point in various directions. The Lagrangian method has the advantage that once you've written down $L \equiv T-V$ you don't have to think anymore. All you have to do is blindly take some derivatives.

Words and Expressions

Lagrange method		拉格朗日方法
sinusoidal function		正弦函数
potential energy		势能
Lagrangian [ləˈɡrɑːndʒiən]	*adj.*	拉格朗日的
Euler-Lagrange equation		欧拉-拉格朗日方程
Newton's second law		牛顿第二定律
pendulum [ˈpendjuləm]	*n.*	单摆,摆锤
equilibrium [ˌiːkwiˈlibriəm]	*n.*	平衡,均衡
centripetal acceleration		向心加速度
torque [tɔːk]	*n.*	转矩;力矩;扭矩
centrifugal [senˈtrifjuɡəl]	*adj.*	离心的
Coriolis acceleration		科氏加速度

The Flexure Formula of Beams[4]

Beams must be designed to be safe. When loads are applied perpendicular to the long axis of a beam, bending moments are developed inside the beam, causing it to bend. By observing a thin beam, the characteristically curved shape shown in Figure 1 is evident. The fibers of the beam near its top surface are shortened and placed in compression. Conversely, the fibers near the bottom surface are stretched and placed in tension.

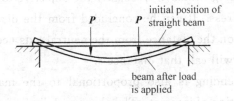

Figure 1 Example of a beam

Taking a short segment of the beam from Figure 1, we show in Figure 2 how the shape would change under the influence of the bending moments inside the beam. In part (a) the segment is in its initially straight form when it is not carrying a load. Part (b) shows the same segment as it is deformed by the application of the moments. Lines that were initially horizontal become curved. The ends of the segment, which were initially straight and vertical, remain straight. But now they are inclined, having rotated about the centroidal axis of the cross section of the beam. The result is that the material along the top surface has been placed under compression and consequently shortened. Also, the

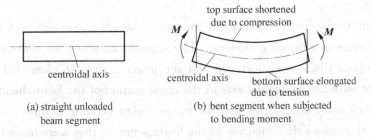

Figure 2 Influence of bending moment on beam segment

material along the bottom surface has been placed under tension and has elongated.

In fact, all of the material above the centroidal axis is in compression. But the maximum shortening (compressive strain) occurs at the top. Because stress is proportional to strain, then it can be reasoned that the maximum compressive stress occurs at the top surface. Similarly, all of the material below the centroidal axis is in tension. But the maximum elongation occurs at the bottom, producing the maximum tensile stress.

We can also reason that, if the upper part of the beam is in compression and the lower part is in tension, then there must be some place in the beam where there is no strain at all. That place is called the neutral axis and it will be shown later that it is coincident with the centroidal axis of the beam. In summary, we can conclude that: In a beam subjected to a bending moment of the type shown in Figure 2, material above the centroidal axis will be in compression with the maximum compressive stress occurring at the top surface. Material below the centroidal axis will be in tension with the maximum tensile stress occurring at the bottom surface. Along the centroidal axis itself, there is zero strain and zero stress due to bending. This is called the neutral axis.

In designing or analyzing beams, it is usually the objective to determine the maximum tensile and compressive stress. It can be concluded from the discussion above that these maximums are dependent on the distance from the neutral axis (centroidal axis) to the top and bottom surfaces. We will call that distance c.

The stress due to bending is also proportional to the magnitude of the bending moment applied to the section of interest. The shape and dimensions of the cross section of the beam determine its ability to withstand the applied bending moment. It will be shown later that the bending stress is inversely proportional to the moment of inertia of the cross section with respect to its horizontal centroidal axis.

We now state the flexural formula which can be used to compute the maximum stress due to bending.

$$\sigma_{max} = \frac{Mc}{I} \tag{1}$$

where σ_{max} is maximum stress at the outermost fiber of the beam; M is the bending moment at the section of interest; c is the distance from the centroidal axis of the beam to the outermost fiber; and I is the moment of inertia of the cross section with respect to its centroidal axis.

Refer again to Figure 2 showing the manner in which a segment of a beam deforms under the influence of a bending moment. The segment assumes the characteristic "bent" shape as the upper fibers are shortened and the lower fibers are elongated. The neutral axis, coincident with the centroidal axis of the cross section of the beam, bends but it is not strained. Therefore, at the neutral axis the stress due to bending is zero.

Figure 2 also shows that the ends of the beam segment that were initially straight and vertical remain straight. But as the bending moment is applied they rotate. The linear distance from a point on the initial vertical end line to the corresponding point on the rotated end line is an indication of the amount of strain produced at that point in the cross section. It can be reasoned, therefore, that there is a linear variation of strain with position in the cross section as a function of the distance away from the neutral axis. Moving from the neutral axis toward the top of the section results in greater compressive strain while moving downward toward the bottom results in greater tensile strain. For materials following Hooke's law, stress is proportional to strain. The resulting stress distribution, then, is as shown in Figure 3.

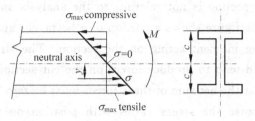

Figure 3 Stress distribution on a symmetrical section

If we desire to represent the stress at some point within the cross section, we can express it in terms of the maximum stress by noting the linear variation of stress with distance away from the neutral axis. Calling that distance y, we can write an equation for the stress, σ, at any point as,

$$\sigma = \sigma_{max} \frac{y}{c} \qquad (2)$$

The general form of the stress distribution shown in Figure 3 would occur in any beam section having a centroidal axis equidistant from the top and bottom surfaces. For such cases, the magnitude of the maximum compressive stress would equal the maximum tensile stress.

If the centroidal axis of the section is not the same distance from both the top and bottom surfaces, the stress distribution shown in Figure 4 would occur. Still the stress at the neutral axis would be zero. Still the stress would vary linearly with distance from the neutral axis. But now the maximum stress at the bottom of the section is greater than that at the top because it is farther from the neutral axis. Using the distances c_b and c_t, as indicated in Figure 4, the stresses would be

$$\sigma_{max} = \frac{Mc_b}{I} \text{(tension at the bottom)}$$

$$\sigma_{max} = \frac{Mc_t}{I} \text{(compression at the top)}$$

A better understanding of the basis for the flexure formula can be had by following the analysis used to derive it. The principles of static equilibrium are used here to show two concepts that were introduced earlier but that were stated without proof. One is that the neutral axis is coincident with the centroidal axis of the cross section. The second is the flexure formula itself and the significance of the moment of inertia of the cross section.

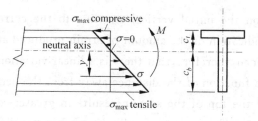

Figure 4　Stress distribution on a non-symmetrical section

Refer to Figure 3, which shows the distribution of stress over the cross section of a beam. The shape of the cross section is not relevant to the analysis and the I-shape is shown merely for example. The figure shows a portion of a beam, cut at some arbitrary section, with an internal bending moment acting on the section. The stresses, some tensile and some compressive, would tend to produce forces on the cut section in the axial direction. Equilibrium requires that the net sum of these forces must be zero. In general, force equals stress times area. Because the stress varies with position on the cross section, it is necessary to look at the force on any small elemental area dA and then sum these forces over the entire area using the process of integration. These concepts can be shown analytically as:

Equilibrium condition: $\sum F = 0$

Force on any element of area: $dF = \sigma dA$

Total force on the cross-sectional area:

$$\sum F = \int_A \sigma dA = 0 \qquad (3)$$

Now we can express the stress σ at any point in terms of the maximum stress by using Equation (2):

$$\sigma = \sigma_{max} \frac{y}{c}$$

where y is the distance from the neutral axis to the point where the stress is equal to σ. Substituting this into Equation (3) gives

$$\sum F = \int_A \sigma dA = \int_A \sigma_{max} \frac{y}{c} dA = 0$$

But σ_{max} and c are constants, they can be taken outside the integral sign.

$$\sum F = \frac{\sigma_{max}}{c} \int_A y dA = 0$$

Neither σ_{max} nor c is zero, so the other factor, $\int_A y dA$, must be zero. By definition,

$$\int_A y dA = \overline{Y}(A)$$

where $\overline{Y}$ is the distance to the centroid of the area from the reference axis and A is the total area. Again, A cannot be zero, so, finally, it must be true that $\overline{Y} = 0$. Because the reference axis is the neutral axis, this shows that the neutral axis is coincident with the centroidal axis of the cross section.

The derivation of the flexure formula is based on the principle of equilibrium, which requires that the sum of the moments about any point must be zero. Figure 3 shows that a bending moment M acts at the cut section. This must be balanced by the net moment created by the stress on the cross section. Moment is the product of force times the distance from the reference axis to the line of action of the force. As used above,

$$\sum F = \int_A \sigma \mathrm{d}A = \int_A \sigma_{\max} \frac{y}{c} \mathrm{d}A$$

Multiplying this by distance y gives the resultant moment of the force that must be equal to the internal bending moment M. That is,

$$M = \sum F(y) = \int_A \sigma_{\max} \frac{y}{c} \mathrm{d}A(y)$$

Simplifying, we obtain

$$M = \frac{\sigma_{\max}}{c} \int_A y^2 \mathrm{d}A$$

The last term in this equation is the moment of inertia I of the cross section with respect to its centroidal axis.

$$I = \int_A y^2 \mathrm{d}A$$

Then

$$M = \frac{\sigma_{\max}}{c} I$$

Solving for $\sigma_{\max}$ yields

$$\sigma_{\max} = \frac{Mc}{I}$$

This is the form of the flexure formula shown earlier as Equation(1).

Words and Expressions

flexure ['flekʃə]	n.	弯曲,曲率,挠度
formula ['fɔːmjulə]	n.	公式
beam [biːm]	n.	梁,桁,横梁
bending moment		弯矩
bend [bend]	vt. & vi.	弯曲,折弯
centroidal axis		形心轴,质心轴
cross section		横截面
stress [stres]	n.	应力
tensile stress		拉应力
compressive stress		压应力
bending stress		弯曲应力
stress distribution		应力分布
strain [stren]	n.	应变
neutral axis		中性轴

inertia [in'ə:ʃiə]	n.	惯性
moment of inertia		惯性矩
deform [di'fɔ:m]	vt. & vi.	变形
Hooke's law		胡克定律
static equilibrium		静力平衡
reference axis		参考坐标系

Writing Skill of Experimental Research Report: INTRODUCTION (2)[32]

INTRODUCTION: Reviewing Previous Research

In Stage I of your *introduction* you established a setting for your research topic. In Stage II you review the findings of other researchers who have already published in your area of interest. For this reason, Stage II is often called *review of literature*. It is essential an organized collection of references, or citations, to other works which are listed in a separate section at the end of your report.

The review of literature serves three important functions. First, it continues the process started in Stage I of giving your readers background information needed to understand your study. Second, it assures your readers that you are familiar with the important research that has been carried out in your area. Third, it establishes your study as one link in a chain of research that is developing and enlarging knowledge in your field.

(1) Information Conventions

(a) Citation Focus

When you cite the work of other author, you may choose to focus either on the *information* provided by that author, or on the *author him- or herself*. The first focus we call *information prominent* because the information is given primary importance. The author's name(s) and date of publication are parenthetically attached at the end of the sentence. More complete source information is found in an alphabetical list of references at the end of the paper.

Example: Based on good numerical experience, damping constants are set to represent equivalent viscous damping ratios of 2% critical for bare cables and 10% for iced cables (Roshan, 1998).

An alternate type of *information prominent* citation uses numbers between the parentheses (instead of author's name and date). The number refers to the alphabetic and numbered list of references at the end of the paper.

Example: However, a very fine mesh is still required for nonuniformly distributed loads, in which case curved elements having three nodes might be preferable [17-19, 24].

Information prominent citations are commonly used to signal the beginning of Stage II, where the citations refer to research in the general area of your study. (They may appear in Stage II as well.)

As the literature review continues, the citations refer to studies more closely related to your own. In this kind of citation, the author's name is given more emphasis. It serves as the subject of the sentence, followed by the date or citation number in parentheses, and then by the information. This kind of citation is called *author prominent*.

Example: Yamaguchi and Adhikari (1995) determined analytically the modal damping characteristics of single structural cable.

Example: Shibuya et al. [11] developed a three-layer model using Mindlin plate finite elements to analyze the fatigue crack growth of cracked aluminum panel repaired with a composite patch.

(b) Order of Citation

It is possible to arrange your Stage II citation in order from those *most distantly related* to your study to those *most closely related*. In addition, there are other ways to order your citations. For example, in a literature review describing the history of research in an area, you may arrange your citations in *chronological* order. Or, if you have a large number of citations to include in your literature review, as in a thesis or dissertation, you can group them according to the *different approaches* to the research problem taken by different authors. The citation within each group can then be ordered chronologically or from general to specific.

- Citations grouped by approach: One approach + Another approach + Still another approach +⋯
- Citations ordered from distant to close
- Citations ordered chronologically

(2) Language Conventions

(a) Citation Focus and Verb Tense

As we have seen, your decision whether to focus Stage II citations on the *information* or on the *author* determines the citation form you use. Similarly, this decision also helps to determine the *verb tense* you will use in each citation.

When the focus of your citation is on the information, you should write the citation in the *present tense*. The present tense is used when the information you are citing is generally accepted as *scientific fact*.

Example: Vibration *is* a common phenomenon in engineering and mechanical structures under the action of dynamic load (Chopra, 1995).

Example: The factors that control damping characteristics of a complex structure *are* poorly known [1].

The *present perfect tense* is used in citations where the focus is on the research area of several authors. This kind of citation is called *weak author prominent*.

Example: *Several* authors *have studied* the constitutive relation of this kind of composite materials (Madsen, 1999; Routh, 2000; Randall, 2003).

Example: Wave propagation phenomena in composite laminates *have been investigated* by several authors [3,7,14].

The *present perfect tense* is also used in general statements that describe the *level of research activity* in an area. These statements are often written without citations.

Example: Little research *has been done* on the parallel computation scheme for multi-scale dynamic systems.

Information prominent citations, weak author prominent citations, and general statements are usually written at the *beginning* of Stage II, or at transition points at the beginning of new sections within Stage II.

Later in Stage II, you use author prominent citations to report the *findings of individual studies* closely related to your own. In these citations the *simple past tense* is used in the verb of report.

Example: Biot (1983) *found(showed/ reported/ noted/ observed)* that there are two longitudinal waves and one transverse wave in fluid-saturated porous media.

(b) **Attitude and Tense in Reported Findings**

We have seen that the *focus* you choose helps to determine the tenses of the verbs in your literature review. Similarly, in author prominent citations your *attitude* towards the findings of the researchers also affects the complement verb forms in your Stage II sentences. You may feel that:

- the findings of a particular study aregenerally accepted as *fact*;
- the findings of a particular study are *limited to that study*, but are not to be accepted as true in all cases;
- the author(s) of the study you are citing may themselves feel *tentative* about their findings; or they may not be reporting findings at all but only making *suggestions* or *proposals*.

Depending on which attitude you take towards the findings of the researchers you cite, you may use the *present tense*, the *past tense*, or various *modal auxiliaries*.

When you believe the findings you are citing are *fact*, use the *present tense* in the complement verb (that is, the verb in the part of the sentence giving the findings).

Example: Biot [1] originally discussed the wave propagation problem in fluid-saturated elastic porous media consisting of two compressible constituents and concluded that there *are* two longitudinal waves traveling with different velocities, and one transverse wave in this kind of porous medium.

When you believe the findings are *restricted to the specific study you are citing*, use the *past tense* in the complement verb.

Example: Abramson (1974) reported that mobile students *had* lower academic performance.

Finally, if the findings you are citing were seen by the original authors as tentative, or were only suggestions or proposals rather than findings, use tentative verbs for the verb of report, and a modal auxiliary with the complement verb.

Example: Wang [5] proposed (suggested/ hypothesized) that the geometrical nonlinearity of the beam affects its dynamic response slightly.

Notice that in all three of these cases, the verb of report is always in the past tense, while the verb tense in the "findings" part of the sentence varies according to the author's attitude.

(3) A Sample

The folloing paragraphs are adopted from the ***introduction*** of an academic paper [33], which may help the readers understand how to write ***review of literature***.

Some analytical and experimental studies have investigated the fatigue crack growth behavior of cracked metallic panels repaired with a single-sided FRP composite patch [2-5]. So far, the numerical studies for this problem have mainly been focused on the determination of stress intensity factors in the cracked panels. The first numerical model proposed by Ratwani [6] used two-dimensional finite elements to represent cracked panel and shear spring elements to represent adhesive layer by neglecting the influence of out-of-plane bending, which may lead to large errors in the most of practical situations. Several authors have used Mindlin plate finite elements to represent cracked panels in the numerical analyses [7-13]. With Mindlin plate finite element method (FEM), it is impossible to determine accurately the crack front profiles and the distributions of stress intensity factors along crack fronts. To evaluate accurately the fatigue crack growth behavior of the repaired cracked panels, it is necessary to determine the crack front profiles during crack growth and the distributions of stress intensity factors along crack fronts. Three-dimensional modeling of the cracked panels is a prerequisite for this purpose.

The three-dimensional FEM has been used to analyze the single-sided repair problems by some authors [5,7,14]. However, these studies only dealt with the determination of stress intensity factors of cracked panels with a fixed crack length, no numerical simulation of the full process of fatigue crack growth has been performed.

A combined boundary element method and finite element method (BEM/FEM) has been developed by Young [15]. With this method, the cracked panel was represented by three-dimensional boundary elements including traction singular quarter-point elements, and the FRP composite patch was represented by finite elements. The nodes on the attachment surfaces of the two portions, respectively represented by the boundary elements and the finite elements, are linked by means of springs which are used to represent the adhesive layer. Using this method, the stress intensity factors along crack front can be determined accurately and directly by boundary elements.

◇▬◇▬◇▬◇▬◇▬◇▬◇▬◇▬◇▬◇▬◇▬◇▬◇▬◇

Reading Material(1): Metals in Mechanical and Structural Design[4]

Metals are most widely used for load-carrying members in buildings, bridges, machines, and a wide variety of consumer products. Beams and columns in commercial buildings are made of structural steel or aluminum. In automobiles, a large number of steels are used, including carbon steel sheet for body panels, free-cutting alloys for machined parts, and high-strength alloys for gears and heavily loaded parts. Cast iron is used in engine blocks, brake drums, and cylinder heads. Tools, springs, and other parts requiring high hardness and wear resistance are made from steel alloys containing a large amount of carbon. Stainless steels are used in transportation equipment, chemical plant products, and kitchen equipment where resistance to corrosion is required.

Aluminum sees many of the same applications as steel. Aluminum is used in many architectural products and frames for mobile equipment. Its corrosion resistance allows its use in chemical storage tanks, cooking utensils, marine equipment, and products such as highway signposts. Automotive pistons, trim, and die-cast housings for pumps and alternators are made of aluminum. Aircraft structures, engine parts, and sheet-metal skins use aluminum because of its high strength-to-weight ratio.

Copper and its alloys, such as brass and bronze, are used in electric conductors, heat exchangers, springs, bushings, marine hardware, and switch parts. Magnesium, one of the lightest metals, is often cast into truck parts, wheels, and appliance parts. Zinc sees similar service and may also be forged into machinery components and industrial hardware. Titanium has a high strength-to-weight ratio and good corrosion resistance, and thus is used in aircraft parts, pressure vessels, and chemical equipment.

Material selection requires consideration of many factors. Generally, strength, stiffness, ductility, weight, corrosion resistance, machinability, workability, weldability, appearance, cost, and availability must all be evaluated. Relative to the study of strength of materials, the first three of these factors are most important: strength, stiffness, and ductility.

Tensile Strength. Reference data listing the mechanical properties of metals will almost always include the *ultimate tensile strength* and *yield strength* of metal. Comparison of the actual stresses in a part with the ultimate or yield strength of the material from which the part is made is the usual method of evaluating the suitability of the material to carry the applied loads safely.

The ultimate tensile strength and yield strength are determined by testing a sample of the material in a tensile-testing machine such as the one shown in Figure 1-1. A round bar or flat strip is placed in the upper and lower jaws. Figure 1-2 shows a photograph of a typical tensile test specimen. A pulling force is applied slowly and steadily to the sample, stretching it until it breaks. During the test, a graph is made which shows the relationship between the stress in the sample and the strain or unit deformation.

A typical stress-strain diagram for a low-carbon

Figure 1-1 Universal testing machine for obtaining stress-strain data for materials.

steel is shown in Figure 1-3. It can be seen that during the first phase of loading, the plot of stress versus strain is a straight line, indicating that stress is directly proportional to strain. After point A on the diagram, the curve is no longer a straight line. This point is called the proportional limit. As the load on the sample is continually increased, a point called the elastic limit is reached, marked B in Figure 1-3. At stresses below this point, the material will return to its original size and shape if the load is removed. At higher stresses, the material is permanently deformed. The yield point is the stress at which a noticeable elongation of the sample occurs with no apparent increase in load. The yield point is at C in Figure 1-3, about 36000 psi (248 MPa). Applying still higher loads after the yield point has been reached causes the curve to rise again. After reaching a peak, the curve drops somewhat until finally the sample breaks, terminating the plot. The highest apparent stress taken from the stress-strain diagram is called the ultimate strength. In Figure 1-3 the ultimate strength would be about 53000 psi (365 MPa).

Figure 1-2 Tensile test specimen mounted in a holder.

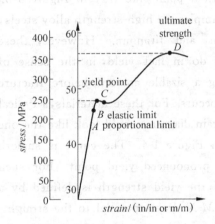

Figure 1-3 Typical stress-strain curve for steel.

The fact that the stress-strain curve in Figures 1-3 and 1-4 drops off after reaching a peak tends to indicate that the stress level decreases. Actually, it does not; the true stress continues to rise until ultimate failure of the material. The reason for the apparent decrease in stress is that the plot taken from a typical tensile test machine is actually load versus elongation rather than stress versus strain. The vertical axis is converted to stress by dividing the load (force) on the specimen by the original cross-sectional area of the specimen. When the specimen nears its breaking load, there is a reduction in diameter and consequently a reduction in the cross-sectional area. The reduced area required a lower force to continue stretching the specimen, even though the actual stress in the material is increasing. This results in the dropping curve shown in Figures 1-3 and 1-4. Because it is very difficult to monitor the decreasing diameter, and because experiments have shown that there is little difference between the true maximum stress and that found from the peak of the apparent stress versus strain curve, the peak is accepted as the ultimate tensile strength of the material.

A summary of the definitions of key strength properties of steels follows:

The proportional limit is the value of stress on the stress-strain curve at which the curve firstly deviates from a straight line.

The elastic limit is the value of stress on the stress-strain curve at which the material has deformed plastically; that is, it will no longer return to its original size and shape after removing the load.

The yield point is the value of stress on the stress-strain curve at which there is a significant increase in strain with little or no increase in stress.

The ultimate strength is the highest value of apparent stress on the stress-strain curve.

Many metals do not exhibit a well-defined yield point like that in Figure 1-3. Some examples are high-strength alloy steels, aluminum, and titanium. However, these materials do in fact yield, in the sense of deforming a sizable amount before fracture actually occurs. For these materials, a typical stress-strain diagram would look like the one shown in Figure 1-4. The curve is smooth with no pronounced yield point. For such materials, the yield strength is defined by a line like *M-N* drawn parallel to the straight-line portion of the test curve.

Point *M* is usually determined by finding that point on the strain axis representing a

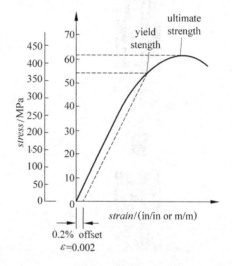

Figure 1-4 Typical stress-strain curve for aluminum.

strain of 0.002in/in. This point is also called the point of 0.2% offset. The point *N*, where the offset line intersects the curve, defines the yield strength of the material, about 55000 psi in Figure 1-4. The ultimate strength is at the peak of the curve, as was described before. Yield strength is used in place of yield point for these materials.

The units for the offset on the strain axis can be in any system. Recall that strain itself is sometimes called unit deformation, a ratio of the elongation of the material at a specific load to its original length in the unloaded condition. Thus strain is actually dimensionless. If measurements were being taken directly in the SI metric system, the strain would be m/m, meters of elongation per meter of original length. Or, mm/mm could be used.

The value of the offset, 0.2%, is typical for most commonly used metals. Other values may be used if 0.2% does not give reliable or convenient results. However, the value of 0.2% is assumed unless otherwise stated.

In summary, for many materials that do not exhibit a pronounced yield point, the definition of *yield strength* is,

The yield strength is the value of stress on the stress-strain curve at which a straight line drawn from a strain value of 0.002 in/in (or m/m) and parallel to the straight portion of the stress-strain curve, intersects the curve.

In most wrought metals, the behavior of the materials in compression is similar to that in tension and so separate compression tests are not usually performed. However, for cast materials and nonhomogeneous materials such as wood and concrete, there are large differences between the tensile and compressive properties, and compressive testing should be done.

Words and Expressions

member ['membə]	n.	构件
column ['kɔləm]	n.	柱体, 圆柱
carbon steel		碳钢
free-cutting alloy		易切削合金
high-strength		高强度
cast iron		铸铁
engine block		发动机缸体
brake drum		制动鼓；鼓式制动器
cylinder head		汽缸盖
hardness ['hɑːdnis]	n.	硬度, 硬性
wear resistance		耐磨性, 耐磨度
stainless steel		不锈钢
corrosion [kə'rəuʒən]	n.	腐蚀, 侵入
piston ['pistən]	n.	活塞
die-cast housing		压铸壳
pump [pʌmp]	n.	泵
alternator ['ɔːltəneitə]	n.	交流发电机
strength-to-weight ratio		比强度
brass [brɑːs]	n.	黄铜, 黄铜色
bushing ['buʃiŋ]	n.	绝缘套, 轴衬
magnesium [mæg'niːʃiəm]	n.	镁
zinc [ziŋk]	n.	锌
titanium [tai'teiniəm]	n.	钛
stiffness ['stifnis]	n.	刚度

ductility [dʌk'tiliti]	n.	韧性
corrosion resistance		耐蚀性；抗腐蚀性
machinability [məʃiːnə'biliti]	n.	可切削性；机械加工性
workability [ˌwəːkə'biliti]	n.	可使用性；施工性能；可加工性
weldability [weldə'biliti]	n.	焊接性；可焊性
appearance [ə'pirəns]	n.	出现，显露，外观
tensile strength		拉伸强度
ultimate tensile strength		最大拉伸强度
yield strength		屈服强度
tensile-testing machine		拉伸试验机
jaw [dʒɔː]	n.	虎钳
tensile test specimen		拉伸试样
stress-strain diagram		应力应变图
low-carbon steel		低碳钢
proportional limit		比例极限
elastic limit		弹性极限
yield point		屈服点
mount [maunt]	vt.	安装
holder ['həuldə]	n.	固定器；支架
stress-strain curve		应力应变曲线
apparent stress		表观应力
true stress		真实应力
dimensionless [də'menʃənləs]	adj.	无量纲
SI metric system		国际单位制
wrought [rɔːt]	adj.	锻造的；加工的；精细的
nonhomogeneous ['nɔnhɔmə'dʒiːnjəs]	adj.	非均质的；非齐次的；多相的
concrete ['kɔnkriːt]	n.	混凝土，凝结物

Reading Material(2)：Stability of Column[4]

A column is a relatively long, slender member loaded in compression. The failure mode for a column is called buckling, a common term for the condition of elastic instability, when the load on an initially straight column causes it to bend significantly. If the load is increased a small amount from the buckling load, the column would collapse suddenly—a very dangerous situation.

How do we determine when a compression member is long and slender?

How do we determine the magnitude of the load at which buckling would occur?

What kind of cross-sectional shapes are preferred for column?

What influence does the manner of holding the ends of a column have on the buckling load?

What industry standards apply to columns?

What examples have you found?

Now let's try to load one of these items with a direct axial compressive load. This means that the line of action of the load is in line with the long axis of the column. Just support it on a table or the floor and push down on it with your hand. Try to push straight down and not sideways at all, but don't hold it tight with your fingers. Be careful not to push too hard and break it!

What happened?

Here we describe the behavior of the wood meter stick. Loading it slowly, we find that it can support a very small load while remaining straight. But without much exertion, we can cause the stick to bend noticeably. This phenomenon is called buckling. Be careful! With just a modest increase in load after buckling occurs, the stick would break easily. Notice that the meter stick buckles about the thin dimension of its cross section. Figure 1 shows a sketch of what happened. You probably would have predicted that based on your own experience.

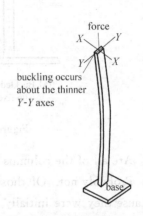

Figure 1   Illustration of buckling of a meter stick

Now let's change the procedure a bit. It appears that the meter stick tends to bow out near the middle, say at the 0.50m point. What if we provide some lateral support on the sides of the stick at that point? Try it yourself if you have a meter stick. Place your fingers lightly on either side to restrain the tendency for it to bow outward. Now push down on it again as you did before.

What happened?

Now we can apply a much higher load to the stick without it buckling. But there is a point where the load is high enough to see a quite different form of buckling. The lower half and the upper half of the stick buckle with one going one way and one going the other. In fact, it looks like the stick takes the form of a complete sine wave. We will discuss this observation later.

Let's change the procedure again. Grab both ends of the meter stick with a firm grip and try as hard as you can to keep the stick from rotating while simultaneously applying an axial load that will cause buckling.

What happened?

First, you should notice that it takes a much higher force to cause buckling. Also, you should notice that the shape of the buckled stick is different from that when you did not restrain the ends. Two factors are working here. Grabbing the stick with your fists effectively shortens the column by about 90mm (3.5 inches) on each end. Because the column is shorter, it takes a higher load to cause buckling. But also, your effort at keeping the ends from rotating caused the buckled shape to be similar to that shown in Figure 2(b).

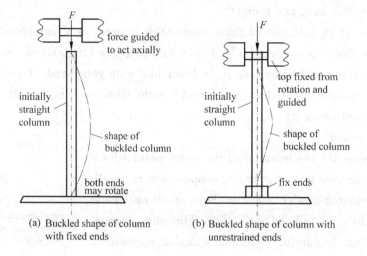

Figure 2 Comparison of shapes for buckled columns

Are all of the columns you found perfectly straight?

Probably not. Of those tested here, most tended to buckle in a particular direction because they were initially crooked. Pushing down on them had the additional effect of bending the crooked section even more in the same direction.

The examples discussed here are all items that were not meant to carry axial compressive loads. They do serve well as demonstrators for buckling.

What examples of columns can you find that are more substantial and that were designed to be sufficiently strong and stable to withstand sizable axial compressive loads?

You might not be able to carry all of these examples into a classroom, laboratory, or office, but here are a few.

- The vertical columns of a steel-framed building: The lower columns on a multi-story building must be strong and stiff enough to hold up all the weight above them. Even in a one-story building, they must hold the roof structure and, possibly, a snow load on top of that.
- The steel posts holding up the beam across the length of the basement of a home: The beam supports the joists from the floor above and all the weight of the furniture and the people there. The posts carry that load to the basement floor or the foundation. The posts are likely made from steel pipe or tubing.
- The cylinder rod of a hydraulic actuator: You may have seen these on a piece of construction equipment, agricultural machinery, or in an industial automation system. Some of these cylinder rods push with great force and they must be designed not to buckle as they extend out from the cylinder.

What others have you found?

Now summarize the observations so far.

- We have demonstrated that a long, slender member tends to buckle when subjected to an axial compressive load. But when does a member become long and slender? We define the term slenderness ratio later to quantify that. It is a function of the length of the column, how its ends are held, and the shape and size of the cross section of the column.
- We demonstrated that a column can take some magnitude of axial load before buckling begins. Then the onset of buckling is quite sudden.
- We demonstrated that the way the ends of the column are held affects the buckling load. We elaborate on that later using the term end fixity.
- The columns we found were made from different materials, such as steel, aluminum, wood, or plastic. What effect does the material have on its tendency to buckle? We show that the material's modulus of elasticity, E, has a major effect on the tendency for a long column to buckle. For shorter columns, the yield strength is also a factor.
- Some of the columns we found were initially crooked. It seemed that they buckled at a lower load than the straight ones and always in the direction of the initial crookedness.

Words and Expressions

stability [stə'biliti]	n.	稳定,稳定性
failure ['feiljə]	n.	破坏,失效
buckle ['bʌkl]	vi.	屈曲
instability [,instə'biliti]	n.	不稳定
collapse [kə'læps]	vi.	破坏,塌陷
crook [kruk]	vi.	弯曲,成钩状
steel-framed		钢架
post [pəust]	n.	柱
modulus of elasticity		弹性模量
crookedness ['krukidnis]	n.	弯曲;扭曲
sine wave		正弦波

What is Continuum Mechanics[5]

Our objective is to learn how to formulate problems and how to reduce vague questions and ideas to precise mathematical statements.

Let us consider a few such questions: an airplane is flying above us. The wings must be under strain in order to support the passengers and freight. How much strain are the wings subjected to? If you were flying a glider and an anvil cloud appears, the thermal current would carry the craft higher. Dare you fly into the cloud? Have the wings sufficient strength? Ahead you see the Golden Gate Bridge. Its cables support a tremendous load. How does one design such cable? The cloud contains water and the countryside needs that water. If the cloud were seeded, would that produce the rain? And would it fall where needed? Would the amount of rainfall be adequate and not produce a flood? In the distance there is a nuclear reactor power station. How is the heat transported in the reactor? What kind of thermal stresses are there in the reactor? How does one assess the safety of the power station against earthquake? What happens to the Earth in an earthquake? Thinking about the globe, you may wonder how the continents float, move, or tear apart. And how about ourselves: how do we breathe? What changes take place in our lungs if we do a yoga exercise and stand on our heads?

Interestingly, all these questions can be reduced to certain differential equations and boundary conditions. By solving such equations we obtain precise quantitative information. In continuum mechanics we deal with the fundamental principles that underlie such differential equations and boundary conditions. Although it would be a pleasure to solve these equations once they are formulated, we shall not become involved in discussing their solutions in detail. Our objective is formulation: the formal reduction of general ideas to a mathematical form. These mathematical problems may not be easy to solve. Many scientific and engineering disciplines devise special methods to solve problems quickly and efficiently. A generation ago students of science and engineering spent countless hours learning the techniques needed for solving differential equations. Today the task is made much easier by using computers.

In the first, what is mechanics? Mechanics is the study of the motion of matter and the forces that cause such motion. Mechanics is based on the concepts of time, space, force, energy, and matter. Knowledge of mechanics is needed for the study of all branches of physics, chemistry, biology, and engineering.

To consider all aspects of mechanics would be too great a task for us. Instead, in continuum mechanics, we shall study only the mechanics of continua. We shall concern ourselves with the basic principles common to fluids and solids.

The concept of a continuum is derived from mathematics. We say that the real number system is a continuum. Between any two distinct real numbers there is another distinct real number, and therefore there are infinitely many real numbers between any two distinct real numbers. Intuitively we feel that time can be represented by a real number system t and that a three-dimensional space can be represented by three real number systems x, y, z. Thus we identify time and space as a four-dimensional continuum.

Extending the concept of continuum to matter, we speak of a continuous distribution of matter in space. This may be best illustrated by considering the concept of density. Let the amount of matter be measured by its mass, and let us assume that a certain matter permeates a certain space v_0, as in Fig. 1. Let us consider a point P in v_0, and a sequence of subspaces v_0, $v_1, v_2, \cdots$, converging on P:

$$v_n \subset v_{n-1}, P \in v_n, \quad n = 1, 2, \cdots \tag{1}$$

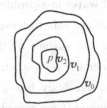

Fig. 1   A sequence of spatial domains converging on P.

Let the volume of v_n be V_n and the mass of the matter contained in v_n be M_n. We form the ratio M_n/V_n. Then if the limit of M_n/V_n exists as $n \to \infty$, and $V_n \to 0$, the limiting value is defined as the density of the mass distribution at the point P, and is denoted by $p(P)$:

$$p(P) = \lim_{\substack{n \to \infty \\ V_n \to 0}} \frac{M_n}{V_n} \tag{2}$$

If the density is well defined everywhere in v_0, the mass is said to be continuously distributed.

A similar consideration can be used to define the density of momentum, the density of energy, and so on. A material continuum is a material for which the densities of mass, momentum, and energy exist in the mathematical sense. The mechanics of such a material continuum is continuum mechanics.

Continuum mechanics has wide applications to problems of the physical world. But because it is a mathematical abstraction, the question of applicability deserves a careful consideration. In particular, since matter is conceived in modern physics as structures of elementary particles, there is a need to reconcile the particle point of view with the continuum point of view. Obviously, if water is considered as a structure of elementary particles, then water is not a continuum. If we try to define the density of water according to the definition, we shall encounter an obvious difficulty when the dimension of v_n is reduced to the order of the atomic radius. Thus, if v_n and v_{n+1} differ by a neutron, the ratio M_n/V_n will have a finite difference from M_{n+1}/V_{n+1}. It is easy to see that as the particles move about, the limit M_n/V_n either does not exist or fluctuates with time and space. To rescue this situation, we shall apply a smoothing process as follows. We consider the ratio M_n/V_n. Let v_n become smaller and smaller but always remain so large that it contains a large number of particles in it. If the ratio M_n/V_n tends to a definite limit $p(P)$ within this added restriction, then $p(P)$ is defined as the density of the matter. In other words, corresponding to the real material, we define a mathematical continuum which has the same density $p(P)$ in the strict sense of (2). Further analysis of the mechanics of the material can then be based on the mathematical model.

In practice, there is little difficulty in applying such a smoothing procedure. The molecular dimension of water is about $1\text{Å}(10^{-8}\text{cm})$; hence, if we are concerned about the liquid water in a problem in which we never have to consider dimensions less than say 10^{-6} cm, we are safe to treat water as a continuum. The mean free path of the molecules of the air on the surface of the earth at room temperature is about 5×10^{-6} cm; hence, if we consider the flow of air about an airplane, we may treat air as a continuum. The red blood cell in our body has a diameter about 8×10^{-4} cm; hence, we can treat our blood as a continuum if we consider the flow in arteries of diameter, say, 0.5cm.

These arguments can be made rigorous statistically. The kinetic theory of gases is the best known example. The motion of molecules of a gas is separated into "random" and "systematic" parts. The former contributes zero resultant momentum but has a finite kinetic energy, which is identified with thermal energy and is related to the absolute temperature. On the other hand, the systematic part (the local mean value) contributes to the systematic motion of the body of gas as conceived in continuum mechanics.

Thus the concept of a material continuum as a mathematical idealization of the real world is applicable to problems in which the fine structure of matter can be ignored. When the fine structure attracts our attention, we should return to particle physics and statistical mechanics. The duality of continuum and particles helps us to understand the physical world as a whole, in a manner which was made famous by modern optics, in which light is treated sometimes as particles and sometimes as waves.

Words and Expressions

continuum mechanics		连续介质力学
mathematical statement		数学表达式，数学描述
strength [streŋθ]	n.	强度
seed [siːd]	vt.	催(云)化雨
thermal stress		热应力
differential equation		微分方程
boundary condition		边界条件

discipline ['disiplin, 'disəplin]	n.	学科
momentum [məu'mentəm]	n.	动量,冲量
mean free path		平均自由程
red blood cell		红血球
resultant [ri'zʌltənt]	adj.	合成的,组合的
resultant momentum		合力矩
absolute temperature		绝对温度

Writing Skill of Experimental Research Report：INTRODUCTION（3）[32]

INTRODUCTION：Advancing to Present Research

After you have presented a contextual setting and discussed the previous work of other researchers, you use the final part of the ***introduction*** to focus on the attention of the readers on the ***specific research problem*** you will be dealing with in the body of your report. This is done in three additional stages, which we designate as III, IV and V. Stage III indicates an area that is *not treated* in the previous literature, but that is important from the point of view of your own work; Stage IV formally announces the *purpose* of your research; and Stage V indicates possible *benefits or applications* of your work.

（1）**Information Conventions**

（a）**Ordering Your Information**

The kind of information contained in Stages III, IV and V are sequenced in order to move the readers logically from the literature review to the purpose of your study. We examine each stage individually to see how the information is presented.

（b）**Writing Stage III：Missing Information**

StageIII serves to signal the readers that the literature review is finished. It sums up the review by pointing out a *gap* —that is, an important research area not investigated by other authors. Usually Stage III is accomplished in only one or two sentences. Here are three alternatives you can choose from in writing your Stage III statement.

- You may indicate that the previous literature described in Stage II is *inadequate* because an important aspect of the research area has been ignored by other authors.
- You may indicate that there is an *unresolved conflict* among the authors of previous studies concerning the research topic. This may be a theoretical or methodological disagreement.
- You may indicate that an examination of the previous literature *suggests* an *extension* of the topic, or raise a *new research question* not previously considered by other workers in your field.

In indicating some kind of gap left by earlier studies, Stage III prepares the readers for your own study.

Example: However, a few investigations have been reported on the determination of stress intensity factors of three dimensional cracks.

(c) **Writing Stage IV: The Statement of Purpose**

Stage IV serves to state as concisely as possible the specific objective(s) of your research report. This stage, *the statement of purpose*, thus follows directly from Stage III because it answers the need expressed in Stage III for additional research in your area of study.

You may write the statement of purpose (Stage IV) from one of two alternative orientations:

- The orientation of the statement of purpose may be towards the report itself—that is, it may refer to the paper (thesis, dissertation, or report) that communicates the information about the research.

Example: The purpose of this thesis (The aim of the present paper/ The objective of this report) is to find an efficient way to measure the residual stress in the cracked composite laminate.

- Or the orientation of the statement of purpose may be towards the research activity, in other words the study itself, rather than the written report.

Example: The purpose of this study (this investigation/ this research/ the research reported here) was to determine if the maximum Mises stress in the bending component exceeds the yield strength of the material.

(d) **Writing Stage V: The Statement of Value**

In Stage V you justify your research on the basis of some possible value or benefit the work may have to other researchers in the field or to people working in practical situations. We can call this stage the *statement of value*.

Stage V is not included in every introduction. You should include Stage V in your *introduction* when you write a thesis, dissertation, or a thesis proposal. The statement of value is also commonly included in research reports written to describe a project conducted with money from outside sources. In reports written up as journal articles, Stage V is often omitted.

You may write Stage V from either of the two alternative points of view.

- The statement of value may be written from the point of view of the practical benefits which may result from applying the findings of your research.

Example: The results obtained in this study could be used to improve the design of the air-conditioner compressors used in automobile.

- Or you may write the statement of value to emphasize the theoretical importance of your study in advancing the state of knowledge in your specific area of research.

Example: Both of the two factors under investigation may be of importance in explaining the path of crack propagation.

(2) **Language Conventions**

(a) **Signal Words and Verb Tense in Stages III, IV and V**

As we have seen, when you write each of the last three stages to your *introduction*, you have several choices in determining the kind of focus you wish to give to your information. The choices you make in each case will determine the vocabulary and grammatical structures you will need in order to write these stages.

(b) Stage III: Signal Words

Special signal words are commonly used to indicate the beginning of Stage III. Connectors such as *however* are used for this purpose. The connector is followed immediately by a *gap statement* in the present or present perfect tense, which often contains modifications such as *few*, *little*, or *no*.

Example: However, (But) *few studies* have been done on (*little literature* is available on/ *very little* is known about/ *no work* has been done on) the constitutive relations of ceramics in high strain rate.

Subordinating conjunctions like *although* and *while* can also be use to signal Stage III. If you use these kinds of signals, you must write a complex sentence, using modifiers such as *some*, *many*, or *much* in the first clause, and modifiers like *little*, *few*, or *no* in the second clause.

Example: Although (While) *some* literature is available on X (*many* studies have been done on X/ *much* research has been devoted to X), *little information* is available on Y.

Notice that nouns like *literature*, *research*, and *work* are uncountable and are therefore followed by singular verb forms.

(c) Stage IV: Orientation and Tense

We have already seen that Stage IV, the statement of purpose, can be written from either of two points of view, *a research* or *a report* orientation. If you choose the research orientation you should use the *past tense*, because the research activity has been completed.

Example: The purpose of this study *was* to investigate the damage evolution law in debonded composite laminates.

On the other hand, if you choose to use the *report* orientation, use the *present* or *future* tense.

Example: This paper *describes* (*presents*) the results of surveys conducted in the Southwest of China to determine the distribution of collapse accidents of transmission line towers caused by strong wind.

Example: This thesis *will deal with* (*discuss*) the effects of both material damping and structural damping on the dynamic response of the system.

Notice that in both research and report orientation, phrases like *this study* and *the present paper* reinforced the fact that Stage IV refers to your work, not the work of the other authors mentioned earlier.

(d) Stage IV and Your Research Question

Your statement of purpose (Stage V) should be directly related to the research question upon which you based your study. Although you may not need to include the research question *explicitly* in your report, the statement of purpose should be written so that your readers can infer the research question behind your study.

If the implied research question is a *yes* or *no* question, the connecting words *whether* or *if* are used in Stage IV, and a modal auxiliary like *would* or *could* accompanies the verb.

Example: The purpose of this thesis is to determine *if* an automatic measurement system would be suitable for classroom and laboratory demonstrations.

When the implied question is an information question, *if/whether* is omitted and an infinitive or noun phrase is used.

Example: This paper reports the results of surveys conducted in order to *determine* the safety of power supply system in operation.

(e) **Stage V - Modal Auxiliaries and Tentativeness**

Stage V, the statement of value, is usually written in a way that suggests an attitude of tentativeness or modesty on the part of the author. When reporting your own study, you should not sound too sure of the benefits, either practical or theoretical, of your work. It is conventional to sound more cautious. This is accomplished in Stage V by using modal auxiliaries, principally *may*.

Example: The application of the algorithm described here *may*(*should*) *enhance* the computational efficiency.

Example: The system described here *could* serve as the basis for a study of automatic measurement systems in an instrumentation course.

Example: This study *may* lead to a better understanding of elasto-plastic property of the special aluminum alloy.

Selecting the most appropriate modal auxiliary is often a problem because the meanings of some these words differ only slightly from one another. The following examples may help you choose the best modal auxiliary when you are writing these stages.

Example: The data contained in this report *will* supplement that presented in our earlier publication. (*no doubt about the future*)

Example: The purpose of this study was to determine if the use of stiffners *would* improve the strength of this kind of plate structure. (*no doubt about the future, assuming certain conditions*)

Example: This alterative method *should* simplify the analysis procedure. (*reasonable expectation about the future*)

Example: Both of the factors studied here *may* be of importance in explaining the occurrence of this accident. (*some doubt about the future*)

Example: Results of this study *could* have considerable impact on estimates of reliability of the system. (*more doubt about the future*)

(3) **A Sample**

The following paragraph is adopted from the ***introduction*** of an academic paper [33], which may help the readers understand how to advance to present research as writing ***introduction*** section.

Effective numerical investigation of fatigue crack growth behavior of cracked aluminum panels repaired with a FRP composite patch needs to simulate the fatigue crack growth process. However, except a few papers, e. g. [12], most of the works aforementioned focused on the determination of stress intensity factors of the repaired cracked panels at a certain crack length, but the crack growth process. In Ref. [12], stress intensity factors at the midplane of the cracked panel, which are calculated by Mindlin plate elements, have been used in the prediction of fatigue crack growth at the unpatched side, which may lead to some errors. This study, therefore, investigates numerically the fatigue crack growth behavior of cracked aluminum panels repaired with a FRP composite patch. Based on the facts that the stress intensity factors determined with the boundary element method (BEM) are more accurate than those with the FEM, when the number of the elements used in both models is the same, and the FEM is more powerful to analyze FRP composite laminates, the combined BEM/FEM with an effective method of automatic remeshing is adopted in the numerical simulation. Fatigue tests were performed to determine the material constants of fatigue crack growth and to provide the data for comparison with the results of numerical simulation. It has been found that the present numerical technique can appropriately evaluate the fatigue crack growth behavior of cracked aluminum panels repaired with an adhesively bonded FRP composite patch.

Reading Material(1): Stress[5]

The concept of stress is the heart of our subject. It is the unique way continuum mechanics has for specifying the interaction between one part of a material body and another. We shall examine the idea of stress and the method of describing it. It will be shown that the specification of the state of stress at any point in a body requires nine numbers, called the components of stress. These nine numbers can be arranged to form a matrix. Under the assumption that the body-moment and the couple-stress do not exist, it is shown that the stress-matrix is symmetric, so that three pairs of stress components are equal, and six independent components fully describe the state of stress at any point. A change in the frames of reference changes the values of the stress components. Examination of the rules of the change of stress components under rotation of the frame of reference shows that the rule is a tensor-transformation rule. Therefore the stress is a tensor.

One must be able to compute the stress vector acting on any surface when the stress tensor is known. This relation is furnished by Cauchy's formula.

The Idea of Stress

In particle mechanics, we study two types of interaction between particles: by collision and by action at a distance. In considering a system of particles we must specify exactly the manner in which one particle is influenced by all the others. In a similar way, in continuum mechanics, we have to consider the interaction between one part of the body and another. However, since a continuum is a mathematical abstraction of the real material, for which even the smallest volume contains a very large number of particles, it would be futile to approach the interaction problem through the particle concept. A new method of description is necessary.

The new concept that evolved is the stress. Consider a material continuum B occupying a spatial region V at some time (Fig. 1). Imagine a closed surface S within B. We would like to express the interaction between the material outside S and that in the interior. This interaction can be divided into two kinds: one, due to the action-at-a-distance type of forces such as the gravitation and the electromagnetic force, which can be expressed as force per unit mass, and are called the body forces; and another, due to the action across the

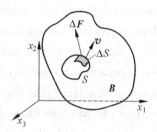

Fig. 1 Stress principle

boundary surface S, called the surface force. To express the surface force, let us consider a small surface element of area ΔS on our imagined surface S. Let us draw, from a point on ΔS, a unit vector v normal to ΔS, with its direction outward from the interior of S. Then we can distinguish the two sides of ΔS according to the direction of v. Let the side to which this normal vector points be called the positive side. Consider the part of material lying on the positive side. This part exerts a force ΔF on the other part which is situated on the negative side of the normal. The force ΔF depends on the location and size of the area and the orientation of the normal. We introduce the assumption that as ΔS tends to zero, the ratio $\Delta F/\Delta S$ tends to a definite limit dF/dS, and that the moment of the force acting on the surface ΔS about any point within the area vanishes in the limit. The limiting vector will be written as

$$T^v = \frac{dF}{dS} \tag{1}$$

where a superscript v is introduced to denote the direction of the normal v of the surface ΔS.

The limiting vector T^v is called the traction, or the stress vector, and represents the force per unit area acting on the surface.

The assertion that there is defined upon any imagined closed surface S in the interior of a continuum a stress vector field whose action on the material occupying the space interior to S is equipollent to the action of the exterior material upon it, is the stress principle of Euler and Cauchy. This principle is well accepted, and it seems to meet all the needs of conventional fluid and solid mechanics. However, this statement is no more than a basic simplification. For example, there is no a priori justification why the interaction of the material on the two sides of the surface element ΔS must be momentless. Indeed, some people who do not like the restrictive idea "...that the moment of the forces acting on the surface ΔS about any point within the area vanishes in the limit" have proposed a generalization of the stress principle of Euler and Cauchy to say that "across any infinitesimal surface element in a material the action of the exterior material upon the interior is equipollent to a force and a couple." The resulting theory requires the concept of couple-stress and is much more complex than the conventional theory. So far no real application has been found for the couple-stress theory.

Notation for Stress Components

Consider a special case in which the surface ΔS_k, $k=1,2$, or 3, is parallel to one of the coordinate planes. Let the normal of ΔS_k be in the positive direction of the x_k-axis. Let the stress vector acting on ΔS_k be denoted by $\boldsymbol{T}^k$, with three components T_1^k, T_2^k, T_3^k along the direction of the coordinate axes x_1, x_2, x_3, respectively; the index i of T_i^k denoting the components of the force, and the symbol k indicating the normal (x_k-axis) to the surface on which the force acts. In this special case, we introduce a new set of symbols for the stress components,

$$T_1^k = \tau_{k1}, \quad T_2^k = \tau_{k2}, \quad T_3^k = \tau_{k3} \tag{2}$$

If we arrange the components of tractions acting on the surfaces ΔS_k, $k=1,2$, and 3, in a square matrix, we obtain

	Components of stress		
	1	2	3
Surface normal to x_1	τ_{11}	τ_{12}	τ_{13}
Surface normal to x_2	τ_{21}	τ_{22}	τ_{23}
Surface normal to x_3	τ_{31}	τ_{32}	τ_{33}

(3)

This is illustrated in Fig. 2. The components τ_{11}, τ_{22}, τ_{33} are called normal stresses, and the remaining components τ_{12}, τ_{13}, etc., are called shearing stresses. Each of these components has the dimension of force per unit area, or M/LT^2.

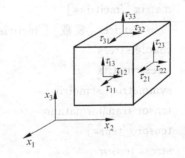

Fig. 2 Notation of stress components

A great diversity in notations for stress components exists in the literature. The most widely used notations in American literature are, in reference to a system of rectangular Cartesian coordinates x,y,z,

$$\begin{matrix} \sigma_x & \tau_{xy} & \tau_{xz} \\ \tau_{yx} & \sigma_y & \tau_{yz} \\ \tau_{zx} & \tau_{zy} & \sigma_z \end{matrix} \tag{4}$$

or

$$\begin{matrix} \sigma_{xx} & \sigma_{xy} & \sigma_{xz} \\ \sigma_{yx} & \sigma_{yy} & \sigma_{yz} \\ \sigma_{zx} & \sigma_{zy} & \sigma_{zz} \end{matrix} \tag{5}$$

Love writes X_x, Y_x for σ_x and τ_{xy}, and Todhunter and Pearson use xx, xy. Since the reader is likely to encounter all these notations in the literature, we shall not insist on uniformity and would use (3) or (4) or (5), whichever happens to be convenient. There should be no confusion.

It is important to emphasize again that a stress will always be understood to be the force (per unit area) that the part lying on the positive side of a surface element (the side on the positive side of the outer normal) exerts on the part lying on the negative side. Thus, if the outer normal of a surface element points in the positive direction of the x_2-axis and τ_{22} is positive, the vector representing the component of normal stress acting on the surface element will point in the positive x_2-direction. But if τ_{22} is positive while the outer normal points in the negative x_2-axis direction, then the stress vector acting on the element also points to the negative x_2-axis direction (see Fig. 3).

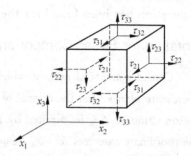

Fig. 3　Senses of positive stress components

Similarly, positive values of τ_{21}, τ_{23} will imply shearing stress vectors pointing to the positive x_1-, x_3-axes if the outer normal agrees in sense with x_2-axis, whereas the stress vectors point to the negative x_1-, x_3-directions if the outer normal disagrees in sense with the x_2-axis, as illustrated in Fig. 3. A careful study of the figure is essential. Naturally, these rules agree with the usual notions of tension, compression, and shear.

Words and Expressions

matrix ['meitriks]	*n.*	矩阵
matrices [复数] ['meitrisi:z]		
couple-stress		偶应力
stress-matrix		应力矩阵
symmetric [si'metrik]	*adj.*	对称的
tensor-transformation		张量转换
tensor ['tensə]	*n.*	张量
stress tensor		应力张量
collision [kə'liʒən]	*n.*	相撞,碰撞
action-at-a-distance		远距离作用
gravitation [ˌgrævi'teiʃən]	*n.*	(万有)引力；重力；地心吸力
body force		体力
surface force		表面力

Reading Material (2): Solid Mechanics[6]

The application of the principles of mechanics to bulk matter is conventionally divided into the mechanics of fluids and the mechanics of solids. The entire subject is often called continuum mechanics, particularly when we adopt the useful model of matter as being continuously divisible, making no reference to its discrete structure at microscopic length scales well below those of the application or phenomenon of interest. Solid mechanics is concerned with the stressing, deformation and failure of solid materials and structures. What, then, is a solid? Any material, fluid or solid, can support normal forces. These are forces directed perpendicular, or normal, to a material plane across which they act. The force per unit of area of that plane is called the normal stress. Water at the base of a pond, air in an automobile tire, the stones of a Roman arch, rocks at base of a mountain, the skin of a pressurized airplane cabin, a stretched rubber band and the bones of a runner all support force in that way (some only when the force is compressive). We call a material solid rather than fluid if it can also support a substantial shearing force over the time scale of some natural process or technological application of interest. Shearing forces are directed parallel, rather than perpendicular, to the material surface on which they act; the force per unit of area is called shear stress. For example, consider a vertical metal rod that is fixed to a support at its upper end and has a weight attached at its lower end. If we consider a horizontal surface through the material of the rod, it will be evident that the rod supports normal stress. But it also supports shear stress, and that becomes evident when we consider the forces carried across a plane through the rod that is neither horizontal nor vertical. Thus, while water and air provide no long term support of shear stress, normally granite, steel, and rubber do so, and are called solids. Materials with tightly bound atoms or molecules, like the crystals formed below melting temperature by most substances or simple compounds, or the amorphous structures formed in glass and many polymer substances at sufficiently low temperature, are usually considered solids.

The distinction between solids and fluids is not precise and in many cases will depend on the time scale. Consider the hot rocks of the Earth's mantle. When a large earthquake occurs, an associated deformation disturbance called a seismic wave propagates through the adjacent rock and the whole earth is set into vibrations which, following a sufficiently large earthquake, may remain detectable with precise instruments for several weeks. We would then describe the rocks of the mantle as solid. So would we on the time scale of, say, tens to thousands of years, over which stresses rebuild enough in the source region to cause one or a few repetitions of the earthquake. But on a significantly longer time scale, say of order of a million years, the hot rocks of the mantle are unable to support shearing stresses and flow as a fluid. Also, many children will be familiar with a substance called silly putty, a polymerized silicone gel. If a ball of it is left to sit on a table at room temperature, it flows and flattens on a time scale of a few minutes to an hour. But if picked up and tossed as a ball against a wall, so that large forces act only over the short time of the impact, it bounces back and retains its shape like a highly elastic solid.

In the simple but very common case when such a material is loaded at sufficiently low temperature and/or short time scale, and with sufficiently limited stress magnitude, its deformation is fully recovered upon unloading. We then say that the material is elastic. But substances can also deform permanently, so that not all deformation is recovered. For example, if you bend a metal coat hanger substantially and then release the loading, it springs back only partially towards its initial shape, but does not fully recover and remains bent. We say that the metal of the coat hanger has been permanently deformed and in this case, for which the permanent deformation is not so much a consequence of long time loading at sufficiently high temperature, but more a consequence of subjecting the material to large stresses (above the yield stress), we describe the permanent deformation as plastic deformation, and call the material elastic-plastic. Permanent deformation of a sort that depends mainly on time of exposure to a stress, and that tends to increase significantly with time of exposure, is called viscous or creep deformation and materials which exhibit that, as well as tendencies for elastic response, are called viscoelastic solids (or sometimes visco-plastic solids when we focus more on the permanent strain than on the tendency for partial recovery of strain upon unloading).

Who uses solid mechanics? All those who seek to understand natural phenomena involving the stressing, deformation, flow and fracture of solids, and all those who would have knowledge of such phenomena to improve our living conditions and accomplish human objectives, have use for solid mechanics. The latter activities are, of course, the domain of engineering and many important modern sub fields of solid mechanics have been actively developed by engineering scientists concerned, for example, with mechanical, structural, materials, civil or aerospace engineering. Natural phenomena involving solid mechanics are studied in geology, seismology and tectonophysics, in materials science and the physics of condensed matter, and in parts of biology and physiology. Further, because solid mechanics poses challenging mathematical and computational problems, it (as well as fluid mechanics) has long been an important topic for applied mathematicians concerned, for example, with partial differential equations and with numerical techniques for digital computer formulations of physical problems.

Here is a sampling of some of the issues addressed using solid mechanics concepts: How do flows develop in the earth's mantle and cause continents to move and ocean floors to slowly subduct beneath them? How do mountains form? What processes take place along a fault during an earthquake, and how do the resulting disturbances propagate through the earth as seismic waves, and shake, and perhaps collapse, buildings and bridges? How do landslides occur? How does a structure on a clay soil settle with time, and what is the maximum bearing pressure which the footing of a building can exert on a soil or rock foundation without rupturing it? What materials do we choose, and how do we proportion and shape them and control their loading, to make safe, reliable, durable and economical structures, whether airframes, bridges, ships, buildings, chairs, artificial heart valves, or computer chips, and to make machinery such as jet engines, pumps, bicycles, and the like? How do vehicles (cars, planes, ships) respond by vibration to the irregularity of surfaces or media along which they move, and how are vibrations controlled for comfort, noise reduction and safety against fatigue failure? How rapidly does a crack grow in a cyclically loaded structure, whether a bridge, engine, or airplane wing or fuselage, and when will it propagate catastrophically? How do we control the deformability of structures during impact so as to design crash worthiness into vehicles? How do we form the materials and products of our technological civilization, e. g. , by extruding metals or polymers through dies, rolling material into sheets, punching out complex shapes, etc. ? By what microscopic processes do plastic and creep strains occur in polycrystals? How can we fashion different materials together, like in fiber reinforced composites, to achieve combinations of stiffness and strength needed in applications? What is the combination of material properties and overall response needed in downhill skis or in a tennis racket? How does the human skull respond to impact in an accident? How do heart muscles control the pumping of blood in the human body, and what goes wrong when an aneurysm develops?

Words and Expressions

solid mechanics		固体力学
mechanics of fluids		流体力学
granite ['grænit]	n.	花岗岩,花岗石
amorphous [ə'mɔːfəs]	adj.	无定性的;非晶形的,无一定方向的
polymer ['pɔlimə]	n.	聚合物
seismic wave		地震波
silly putty		弹性橡胶泥
silicone gel		硅凝胶
unload ['ʌn'ləud]	vt. & vt.	卸载
elastic [i'læstik]	adj.	弹性的
permanent deformation		永久变形
plastic ['plæstik]	adj.	塑性的
elastic-plastic		弹塑性的
viscous ['viskəs]	adj.	粘性的
creep [kriːp]	vi.	蠕变
	n.	蠕变
visco-elastic		粘弹性的
visco-plastic		粘塑性的
flow [fləu]	vi.	流动
civil engineering		土木工程
aerospace engineering		航空工程
geology [dʒi'ɔlədʒi]	n.	地质学,地质情况
seismology [saiz'mɔlədʒi]	n.	地震学

tectonophysics [ˌtektənəuˈfiziks]	n.	构造物理学，地壳构造物理学
partial differential equation		偏微分方程
fault [fɔːlt]	n.	断层
landslide [ˈlændslaid]	n.	滑坡
clay soil settle		粘土土层沉降
soil foundation		土基础
rock foundation		岩石基
artificial heart valve		人工心脏瓣膜
vibration [vaiˈbreiʃən]	n.	振动，震动
fatigue [fəˈtiːg]	n.	疲劳
crack [kræk]	vt. & vi.	裂开，爆裂，断裂
	n.	裂纹
catastrophically [ˌkætəˈstrɔfikli]	adv.	灾难性地
die [dai]	n.	冲模，钢模
punch [pʌntʃ]	vt.	钻孔
	n.	冲头
microscopic [ˈmaikrəˈskɔpik]	adj.	显微的，微观的
fiber reinforced composite		纤维增强复合材料
fashion [ˈfæʃən]	vt.	制造，使成形
	n.	时尚
aneurysm [ˈænjurizəm]	n.	动脉瘤

Unit Four

Hooke's Law[7]

Linear relations between the components of stress and the components of strain are known generally as Hooke's law. Imagine an elemental rectangular parallelopiped with the sides parallel to the coordinate axes and submitted to the action of normal stress σ_x uniformly distributed over two opposite sides, as in the tensile test. The unit elongation of the element up to the proportional limit is given by

$$\varepsilon_x = \frac{\sigma_x}{E} \tag{1}$$

in which E is the modulus of elasticity in tension. Materials used in engineering structures have moduli which are very large in comparison with allowable stresses, and the unit elongation (1) is a very small quantity. In the case of structural steel, for instance, it is usually smaller than 0.001.

This extension of the element in the x direction is accompanied by lateral strain components (contractions)

$$\varepsilon_y = -v\frac{\sigma_x}{E}, \quad \varepsilon_z = -v\frac{\sigma_x}{E} \tag{2}$$

in which v is a constant called Poisson's ratio. For many materials Poisson's ratio can be taken equal to 0.25. For structure steel it is usually taken equal to 0.3.

Equations (1) and (2) can be also used for simple compression. The modulus of elasticity and Poisson's ratio in compression are the same as in tension.

If the above element is submitted simultaneously to the action of normal stresses σ_x, σ_y, σ_z, uniformly distributed over the sides, the resultant components of strain can be obtained from Eqs. (1) and (2). If we superpose the strain components produced by each of the three stresses, we obtain the equations

$$\begin{cases} \varepsilon_x = \frac{1}{E}[\sigma_x - v(\sigma_y + \sigma_z)] \\ \varepsilon_y = \frac{1}{E}[\sigma_y - v(\sigma_x + \sigma_z)] \\ \varepsilon_z = \frac{1}{E}[\sigma_z - v(\sigma_x + \sigma_y)] \end{cases} \tag{3}$$

which have been found consistent with very numerous test measurements.

In our further discussion we shall often use this method of superposition in calculating total deformations and stresses produced by several forces. It is legitimate as long as the deformations are small and the corresponding small displacements do not affect substantially the action of the external forces. In such cases we neglect small changes in dimensions of deformed bodies and also small displacements of the points of application of external forces and base our calculations on initial dimensions and initial shape of the body. The resultant displacements will then be obtained by superposition in the form of linear functions of external forces, as in deriving Eqs. (3).

There are, however, exceptional cases in which small deformations cannot be neglected but must be taken into consideration. As an example of this kind, the case of the simultaneous action on a thin bar of axial and lateral forces may be mentioned. Axial forces alone produce simple tension or compression, but they may have a substantial effect on the bending of the bar if they are acting simultaneously with lateral forces. In calculating the deformation of bars under such conditions, the effect of the deflection on the moment of the external forces must be considered, even though the deflections are very small. Then the total deflection is no longer a linear function of the forces and cannot be obtained by simple superposition.

In Eqs. (3), the relations between elongations and stresses are completely defined by two physical constants E and v. The same constants can also be used to define the relation between shearing strain and shearing stress.

Let us consider the particular case of deformation of the rectangular parallelepiped in which $\sigma_z = \sigma, \sigma_y = -\sigma$ and $\sigma_x = 0$. Cutting out an element $abcd$ by planes parallel to the x axis and at 45° to the y and z axes (Fig. 1), it may be seen from Fig. 1(b), by summing up the forces along and perpendicular to bc, that the normal stress on the sides of this element is zero and the shearing stress on the sides is

$$\tau = 1/2(\sigma_z - \sigma_y) = \sigma$$

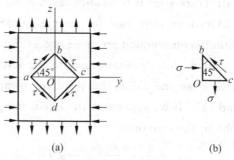

Fig. 1

Such a condition of stress is called pure shear. The elongation of the vertical element Ob is equal to the shortening of the horizontal elements Oa and Oc, and neglecting a small quantity of the second order we conclude that the lengths ab and bc of the element do not change during deformation. The angle between the sides ab and bc changes, and the corresponding magnitude of shearing strain γ may be found from the triangle Obc. After deformation, we have

$$\frac{Oc}{Ob} = \tan\left(\frac{\pi}{4} - \frac{\gamma}{2}\right) = \frac{1+\varepsilon_y}{1+\varepsilon_z}$$

Substituting, from Eq. (3),

$$\varepsilon_z = \frac{1}{E}(\sigma_z - v\sigma_y) = \frac{(1+v)\sigma}{E}, \quad \varepsilon_y = -\frac{(1+v)\sigma}{E}$$

and noting that for small γ

$$\tan\left(\frac{\pi}{4} - \frac{\gamma}{2}\right) = \frac{\tan\frac{\pi}{4} - \tan\frac{\gamma}{2}}{1 + \tan\frac{\pi}{4}\tan\frac{\gamma}{2}} = \frac{1 - \frac{\gamma}{2}}{1 + \frac{\gamma}{2}}$$

we find

$$\gamma = \frac{2(1+v)\sigma}{E} = \frac{2(1+v)\tau}{E} \tag{4}$$

Thus the relation between shearing strain and shearing stress is defined by the constants E and v. Often the notation

$$G = \frac{E}{2(1+v)} \tag{5}$$

is used. Then Eq. (4) becomes

$$\gamma = \frac{\tau}{G}$$

The constant G, defined by Eq. (5), is called the modulus of elasticity in shear, or the modulus of rigidity.

If shearing stresses act on all the sides of an element, as shown in Fig. 1, the distortion of the angle between any two intersecting sides depends only on the corresponding shearing stress component. We have

$$\gamma_{xy} = \frac{1}{G}\tau_{xy}, \quad \gamma_{yz} = \frac{1}{G}\tau_{yz}, \quad \gamma_{zx} = \frac{1}{G}\tau_{zx} \tag{6}$$

The elongations (3) and the distortions (6) are independent of each other. The general case of strain, produced by three normal and three shearing components of stress, can be obtained by superposition: on the three elongations given by Eqs. (3) are superposed three shearing strains given by Eqs. (6).

Equations (3) and (6) give the components of strain as functions of the components of stress. Sometimes the components of stress expressed as functions of the components of strain are needed. These can be obtained as follows. Adding Eqs. (3) together and using the notations

$$\begin{cases} e = \varepsilon_x + \varepsilon_y + \varepsilon_z \\ \theta = \sigma_x + \sigma_y + \sigma_z \end{cases} \tag{7}$$

we obtain the following relation between the volume expansion e and the sum of normal stresses:

$$e = \frac{1-2v}{E}\theta \tag{8}$$

In the case of a uniform hydrostatic pressure of the amount p we have

$$\sigma_x = \sigma_y = \sigma_z = -p$$

and Eq. (8) gives

$$e = -\frac{3(1-2v)p}{E}$$

which represents the relation between unit volume expansion e and hydrostatic pressure p. The quantity $E/3(1-2v)$ is called the modulus of volume expansion.

Using notations (7) and solving Eqs. (3) for $\sigma_x, \sigma_y, \sigma_z$, we find

$$\begin{cases} \sigma_x = \dfrac{vE}{(1+v)(1-2v)}e + \dfrac{E}{1+v}\varepsilon_x \\ \sigma_y = \dfrac{vE}{(1+v)(1-2v)}e + \dfrac{E}{1+v}\varepsilon_y \\ \sigma_z = \dfrac{vE}{(1+v)(1-2v)}e + \dfrac{E}{1+v}\varepsilon_z \end{cases} \tag{9}$$

or using the notation

$$\lambda = \frac{vE}{(1+v)(1-2v)} \tag{10}$$

and Eq. (5), these become

$$\begin{aligned}\sigma_x &= \lambda e + 2G\varepsilon_x \\ \sigma_y &= \lambda e + 2G\varepsilon_y \\ \sigma_z &= \lambda e + 2G\varepsilon_z\end{aligned} \tag{11}$$

Words and Expressions

parallelopiped [ˌpærəle'lepiped]	n.	平行六边形
component [kəm'pəunənt]	n.	分量;构成要素;零件;成分
modulus ['mɔdjuləs];	n.	模量,系数
moduli [复数] ['mɔdʒəˌlai]		
allowable stress		许用应力
elongation [ˌiːlɔŋ'geiʃən]	n.	伸长,延长
structural steel		结构钢
Poisson's ratio		泊松比
superposition [ˌsjuːpəpə'ziʃən]	n.	叠加,重叠,叠合
deformation [ˌdiːfɔː'meiʃən]	n.	变形
displacement [dis'pleismənt]	n.	位移
external force		外力
axil force		轴向力
lateral force		横向力

deflection [di'flekʃən]	n.	弯曲；挠曲；挠度
shearing stress		剪切应力
shearing strain		剪切应变
pure shear		纯剪切
hydrostatic pressure		静水压力
modulus of volume expansion		体积膨胀模量

Writing Skill of Experimental Research Report: METHOD and MATERIALS[32]

METHOD

After the introduction, the second major section of the experimental research report, often labeled *method*, describes the steps you followed in conducting your study and the materials you used at each step. The *method* section is useful to readers who want to know how the methodology of your study may have influenced your results, or who are interested in replicating or extending your study.

(1) **Information Conventions**

The main part of the *method* section is a description of the *procedural steps* used in your study and the *materials* employed at each step. However, other elements are commonly described in this section as well.

(a) **Ordering Your Information**

The elements included in the *method* section and the order in which they are presented are not fixed. However, the list in the following is conventional and provides you with a good model.

Overview of the Experiment
Population/Sample
Location
Restrictions/ Limiting Conditions
Sampling Technique
Procedures (*always included*)
Materials (*always included*)
Variables
Statistical Treatment

(b) **Writing the Procedural Description**

The description of the steps you followed in conducting your study should be written clearly so that a reader in your field could accurately replicate your procedure. Of course, the best way to describe a procedure is step-by-step, or chronologically.

(2) **Language Conventions**

Several grammatical conventions govern the *method* section. We concentrate on those conventions governing the *procedure description*. These concern choosing the correct *verb* tense and *verb voice*.

(a) **Choosing the Correct Verb Tense in Procedural Descriptions**

The procedures you used in carrying out your study should usually be described in the *simple past tense*. Sentences included under **method** that are not written in the past tense usually do not refer to the procedures used in the study being reported. Instead, they may describe standard procedures that are commonly used by others.

Example: The study *was carried out* on a marine laboratory research vessel.

Note: In a few fields of study, procedural descriptions can sometimes be written in the *simple present tense*. You should check journals in your field or ask professors in your university department to determine which convention to use.

(b) **Choosing the Appropriate Verb Voice—Active or Passive**

You can use either the *active* or *passive voice* when you describe the procedure used in your project. Examples of both voices are given in the following.

Example: We *applied* load to the rubber segments in gradually increasing increments.

Example: Load *was applied* (by the investigator) to the rubber segments in gradually increasing increments.

Your decision whether to use the active or passive voice in procedural statements should be made with the following considerations:

- The passive voice is conventionally used to describe procedure in order to *depersonalize* the information. The passive construction allows you to omit the agent (usually "I" or "we"), placing the emphasis on the procedure and how it was done. However, your professor or editor may specifically ask you not to use the passive voice because he or she prefers a *more personal style* with frequent use of the pronouns "I" or "we".

- In addition to questions of style, your choice of the active or passive voice should place *old information* near the beginning of the sentences and *new information* at the end.

(c) **Using Short Passive Forms to Describe Procedure**

In technical and scientific English, there is a tendency to *shorten* certain kinds of passive constructions. Three such kinds of sentences are commonly used in procedural descriptions. The first type is a compound sentence with two identical subjects and two or more verbs in the passive. To shorten this kind of sentence, omit the *subject* and the *be* auxiliary in the second part of the sentence.

Example: The data were collected and they were analyzed. (*Full form*)

Example: The data were collected and analyzed. (*Shorten form*)

The second type of sentences is also compound, but in this case there are two different subjects, each with different verbs in the passive voice. To shorten this kind of sentence, omit the *be* auxiliary before the second verb.

Example: The data were collected and correlations were calculated. (*Full form*)

Example: The data were collected and correlations calculated. (*Shorten form*)

The third type of sentence has a *which* clause containing a passive verb form. In this case, you can shorten the clause by dropping the conjunction *which* and the *be* auxiliary.

Example: The data which were obtained were subjected to an analysis of variance. (*Full form*)

Example: The data obtained were subjected to an analysis of variance. (*Shorten form*)

MATERIALS

Although the second major section of the experimental research report is often called "method", it is sometimes titled ***materials and method***. This combined title indicates that researchers generally describe these two aspects together when they write up their research. That is, they simultaneously describe any equipment or other materials they used with each step in their procedure.

(1) Information Conventions

By materials we mean any items used to carry out a research project. They may fall into any of the following categories:

Laboratory equipment; Field equipment; Human or animal subjects; Natural substances; Fabricated materials; Surveys, Questionnaires and tests; Computer models; Mathematical models.

(a) **Ordering Your Information**

If the materials you used are well-known to researchers in your field, it is conventional to identify them only. However, if you used specially designed or unconventional materials in your experiment, it is common to write a detailed description of them in the report. In this case, you should include the following information, in the order of three steps given below.

Step1. *Overview*: This step consists of one or two sentences that give a general idea of the material and the purpose for which it is intended.

Step2. *Description of principal parts*: Here, each major part or characteristics of the material is described in logical sequence.

Step3. *Functional description*: This last step shows how the various features described in Step 2 function together.

(b) **Ordering the Description of Principal Parts-Step 2**

In Step 2 you describe the principal features of the material used in your study. There are two main organizing plans that you can use in this step, depending on your material.

- *Spatial arrangement*: Describe the features from top to bottom, front to back, left to right, from the center to the outside, or in some other spatial way. This arrangement is especially useful for describing equipment consisting of various connected parts.

- *Functional arrangement*: Describe the principal features in the order in which they function, from beginning to end. This arrangement is best for describing parts that operate in a fixed sequence.

(c) **Integrating Materials with Procedure**

The materials used in a study are sometimes described separately from the procedures. This arrangement may be used when several different pieces of conventional laboratory equipment are used to carry out a routine procedure.

More commonly, however, materials and methods are described in an integrated form, often with both elements mentioned in each sentence.

(2) **Language Conventions**

There are also some grammatical conventions you should know in order to describe materials clearly in your report. These conventions mainly involve choosing the correct *verb tense* and *voice*.

(a) **Choosing Verb Tense — Samples and Populations**

Sentences describing the subjects or materials used in a study require either the *past* or the *present tense*. When we describe the sample used in a study we commonly use the *past tense*.

Example: The transducer was attached on the upper surface of the component to sense the strain.

However, when describing the *general population* from which the sample subjects were selected, the *present tense* is normally used.

Example: All students who apply for admission to the department of engineering mechanics of Chongqing University for graduate program *take* the examination of comprehensive knowledge related to mechanics.

(b) **Use of Tense with Conventional and Specially Designed Materials**

If you use equipment in your study which is standard or conventional in your field and probably familiar to most other researchers, you should describe it using the *present tense*.

Example: A round bar or flat strip is placed in the upper and lower jaws of the tensile-testing machine.

On the other hand, descriptions of *specially designed* materials with which other workers in your field may not be familiar are usually written in the *past tense*. Common devices that you modified in some special way for use in your study are also sometimes described in the *past*.

Example: In this test, the strain gage bonded on the surface of the shaft *was covered* with water-proof sheet to protect it from short curcuit.

(c) **Using Active and Passive Voice in Describing Materials**

Both active and passive voice verb constructions are used in describing experimental materials. Your decision to use active or passive voice depends partly on whether the verb is *transitive* or *intransitive*. Only *transitive verbs* can be used in the passive voice.

If the verb is transitive, follow these rules to determine which voice to use:
- The *passive voice* is usually used when a human agent (the experimenter) is manipulating the materials.

Example: The temperature inside the chamber *was increased* from 0℃ to 20℃. (The researcher increased the temperature.)
- The *active voice* is usually used when no human is directly responsible for manipulating the materials - that is, when the materials operate "by themselves".

Example: Control gauges *monitored* air pressure inside the chamber.
- The passive voice may be used to describe an action involving a nonhuman agent, but a *phrase* must be included to indicate the agent.

Example: Power *was supplied* by 14 generators with capacities ranging from 90 to 300 kW.

Reading Material(1): Basic Equations of Elastic Homogeneous and Isotropic Bodies[5]

A Hookean body has a unique natural state, to which the body returns when all external loads are removed. All strains and particle displacements are measured from this natural state: Their values are counted as zero in that state.

Let $u_i(x_1, x_2, x_3, t)$, $i=1,2,3$, describe the displacement of a particle located at x_1, x_2, x_3 at time t from its position in the natural state. Various strain measures can be defined for the displacement field. The Almansi strain tensor is expressed in terms of $u_i(x_1, x_2, x_3, t)$ according to Eq. (5.3-4):

$$e_{ij} = \frac{1}{2}\left[\frac{\partial u_j}{\partial x_i} + \frac{\partial u_i}{\partial x_j} + \frac{\partial u_k \partial u_k}{\partial x_i \partial x_j}\right] \quad (12.1\text{-}1)$$

The particle velocity v_i is given by the material derivative of the displacement,

$$v_i = \frac{\partial u_i}{\partial t} + v_j \frac{\partial u_i}{\partial x_j} \quad (12.1\text{-}2)$$

The particle acceleration a_i is given by the material derivative of the velocity, Eq. (10.3-7),

$$a_i = \frac{\partial v_i}{\partial t} + v_j \frac{\partial v_i}{\partial x_j} \quad (12.1\text{-}3)$$

The conservation of mass is expressed by the equation of continuity (10.5-3),

$$\frac{\partial \rho}{\partial t} + \frac{\partial (\rho v_i)}{\partial x_i} = 0. \quad (12.1\text{-}4)$$

The conservation of momentum is expressed by the Eulerian equation of motion (10.6-7),

$$\rho a_i = \frac{\partial \sigma_{ij}}{\partial x_j} + X_i \quad (12.1\text{-}5)$$

Hooke's law for a homogeneous isotropic material is

$$\sigma_{ij} = \lambda e_{kk} \delta_{ij} + 2G e_{ij}, \quad (12.1\text{-}6)$$

where λ and G are Lame constants.

Equations (12.1-1) through (12.1-6) together describe a theory of elasticity. If we compare these equations with the corresponding equations for a viscous fluid as shown in Sec. 11.1, we see that the theoretical structure is similar except that we have a nonlinear strain-and-displacement-gradient relation (12.1-1), in contrast to the linear rate-of-deformation-and-velocity-gradient relation (6.1-3) for the fluid. Hence, the theory of elasticity is more deeply involved in nonlinearity than the theory of viscous fluids.

The nonlinear problem is so wrought with mathematical complexities that a general theory is not available. The solutions of even relatively simple problems usually require extensive numerical treatment. For this reason it is common to simplify the theory by introducing a severe restriction that *the displacements and velocities are infinitesimal* so that Eq. (12.1-1) to (12.1-3) can be linearized. Such a linearized theory is amenable to mathematical treatment. A phenomenon described by a set of linear equations is easier to understand; the principle of superposition applies, and more complex solutions can be obtained by superposition of the simpler ones. In any case, the linearized theory provides a foundation on which the nonlinear theory can be built. One tries to learn as much as possible about the linearized theory and then proceed to discover what special features are introduced by the nonlinearities.

Little can be said about the nonlinear theory at the elementary level. Hence, we shall *linearize* the equations by restricting ourselves to values of u_i, v_i so small that the nonlinear terms in Eq. (12.1-1) through (12.1-3) may be neglected. Thus,

$$e_{ij} = \frac{1}{2}\left(\frac{\partial u_i}{\partial x_j} + \frac{\partial u_j}{\partial x_i}\right), \tag{12.1-7}$$

$$v_i = \frac{\partial u_i}{\partial t}, \quad \alpha_i = \frac{\partial v_i}{\partial t} \tag{12.1-8}$$

Equations (12.1-4) through (12.1-8) together are 22 equations for the 22 unknowns $\rho, u_i, v_i, \alpha_i, e_{ij}, \sigma_{ij}$. We may eliminate σ_{ij} by substituting Eq. (12.1-6) into Eq. (12.1-5) and using Eq. (12.1-7) to obtain the well-known *Navier's equation*,

$$G\nabla^2 u_i + (\lambda + G)\frac{\partial e}{\partial x_i} + X_i = \rho \frac{\partial^2 u_i}{\partial t^2}, \tag{12.1-9}$$

where e is the divergence of the displacement vector **u**,

$$e = \frac{\partial u_j}{\partial x_j} = \frac{\partial u_1}{\partial x_1} + \frac{\partial u_2}{\partial x_2} + \frac{\partial u_3}{\partial x_3} \tag{12.1-10}$$

∇^2 is the *Laplace operator*. If we write x, y, z instead of x_1, x_2, x_3, we have

$$\nabla^2 = \frac{\partial^2}{\partial x^2} + \frac{\partial^2}{\partial y^2} + \frac{\partial^2}{\partial z^2} \tag{12.1-11}$$

If we introduce the Poisson's ratio ν as in Eq. (9.6-9), we can write Navier's equation (12.1-9) as

$$G\left(\nabla^2 u_i + \frac{1}{1-2\nu}\frac{\partial e}{\partial x_i}\right) + X_i = \rho \frac{\partial^2 u_i}{\partial t^2} \tag{12.1-12}$$

This is the basic field equation of the linearized theory of elasticity.

Navier's equation (12.1-9) must be solved for appropriate boundary conditions, which are usually one of two kinds:

(1) *Specified displacements*. The components of displacement are prescribed on the boundary.

(2) *Specified surface tractions*. The components of surface traction $\hat{T}_i$ are assigned on the boundary.

In most problems of elasticity, the boundary conditions are such that over part of the boundary the displacements are specified, whereas over another part the surface tractions are specified. In the latter case Hooke's law may be used to convert the boundary condition into prescribed values of a certain combination of the first derivatives of u_i.

Words and Expressions

homogeneous [ˌhɔməˈdʒiːnɪəs]	adj.	同质的，均匀的，齐次的
isotropic [ˌaisəˈtrɔpik]	adj.	各向同性的
anisotropic [ænˌaisəˈtrɔpik]	n.	各向异性的
Almansi strain		阿曼西应变
material derivative		物质导数
equation of continuity		连续性方程
conservation of momentum		动量守恒
Lame constants		拉梅常数
gradient [ˈgreidiənt]	n.	梯度，倾斜度
nonlinearity [ˌnɔnliniˈæriti]	n.	非线性
infinitesimal [ˌinfiniˈtesiməl]	adj.	无限小的
linearized theory		线性化理论
Navier's equation		纳维方程
divergence [daiˈvəːdʒəns]	n.	散度，分歧，分离
Laplace operator		拉普拉斯算符
specified displacement		给定位移
specified surface traction		给定面力
surface traction		表面力

Reading Material(2): Stress Waves in Solids[8]

The subject of wave propagation in elastic solids has a long and distinguished history. The early theoretical work is associated with names such as Navier, Poisson, Stokes, Rayleigh and Kelvin. At the beginning of this century, with the exception of seismological studies, which were largely concerned with the application of earlier theory to rather complex physical situations, very little new work was done. During the last two or three decades there has been a remarkable revival of interest in the field. A large and growing number of original papers on both the experimental and the theoretical aspects of the subject is appearing in the scientific literature, and two international conferences solely concerned with stress-wave propagation have been held during the last five years.

There are a number of reasons for this revival of interest, of which the most important are: first, the availability of experimental apparatus with which stress waves can be produced and detected; second, the practical engineering need for data on the behaviour of materials at very high rates of loading when stress waves are inevitably generated; third, the growing interest in the structure of solids, where high frequency stress waves provide a powerful experimental tool for investigating the microscopic processes which take place in a solid when it is deformed; and last (and unfortunately, not least) the universal increase in armament research where the investigation of the response of structures to large forces maintained for very short times plays such a prominent part.

One class of investigation in which there has been considerable and continuing interest is that of the propagation of pulses of high frequency sinusoidal oscillations of very small amplitude. This has in fact become a subject of its own, known as Ultrasonics, and in the present article it is not proposed to consider in any detail either the many and important results on the structure of solids and fluids which have been achieved by the use of this technique, or the use of such pulse techniques for flaw detection in engineering components. The purpose of this paper is instead to review the recent experimental and theoretical advances in the propagation of waves of larger amplitude and arbitrary shape through elastic and anelastic solids, to attempt to outline the problems on which present efforts are being directed and to predict probable lines of future development.

From a theoretical standpoint the subject falls naturally into two parts which correspond to whether or not the medium through which the stress wave is being propagated can be considered to obey Hooke's Law. The experimental techniques used are generally similar whether elastic or anelastic solids are being investigated, but the purpose of carrying out experiments is often quite different in the two types of investigation. Thus, in principle, any elastic wave problem can be treated theoretically when the values of the elastic constants of the medium are known. In practice very few such problems indeed can be solved, and experiments are carried out either to test the validity of approximate theories or to obtain information about the behaviour of systems which are far too complicated for theoretical studies even to be attempted. Such experimental investigations are then the dynamic counterpart of the experimental stress analysis of engineering structures.

In the second type of investigation, where the solid through which the waves are being propagated cannot be assumed to obey Hooke's Law, experiment plays a different role as in nearly every case an "exact" theoretical treatment is of very limited validity since it depends on a mathematical model of the anelastic behaviour of the solid. Now, for many materials Hooke's Law is an extremely close approximation to the actual mechanical behaviour of the solid when the deformations are sufficiently small, and the law is of the same form, i. e. a linear one, for all elastic solids. In contrast, the various mathematical representations of anelastic behaviour which have been used are approximate ones, which describe specific solids, are of very limited validity, and often would appear to have no physical validity at all. Thus experimental investigations are generally the only possible method of determining the real behaviour of the materials, and theory can, at best, act only as a general guide to the type of behaviour which may be expected.

Departures from Hooke's Law may manifest themselves in two ways: first, the stress-strain relation may depart from linearity and also be different for loading and unloading; such behaviour is characteristic of metals strained "plastically" beyond their proportional limit; second, the stress-strain relation may depend on the rate of straining so that the material behaves in a manner analogous to that of a viscous fluid; such materials are called viscoelastic, and viscoelastic effects are most clearly seen in high polymers such as rubber and the many different plastics. As will be described later, many such viscoelastic materials are "linear" in the sense that although they do not obey Hooke's Law, their behaviour can be described by linear differential equations involving the stress, the strain, and their derivatives with respect to time. This division into non-linear behaviour, which does not depend on strain-rate, and linear viscoelastic behaviour, which does not depend on amplitude, is convenient although often somewhat artificial. Under some conditions many anelastic materials behave both in a non-linear and in a time-dependent manner so that the stress-strain relation, or the constitutive equation, as it is often called, must be expressed in the form of a non-linear differential equation involving stress, strain and time and is often of considerable complexity.

However, since on the one hand the mechanical behaviour of metals is generally not highly rate-dependent, and on the other hand most unfilled polymers and rubbers are linearly viscoelastic for small deformations, theoretical studies in which the non-linearity and the time-dependence are dealt with separately have considerable practical justification. Waves travelling in a rate-dependent solid are termed viscoelastic waves, whilst waves travelling in a solid which shows the phenomenon of yield, so that the stress-strain curve is concave towards the strain axis, are termed plastic waves. When the stress-strain curve is non-linear but curves towards the stress axis, i. e. becomes "stiffer" for large stresses than for smaller ones, the nature of wave propagation is radically different from that of either viscoelastic waves or of plastic waves.

When a mechanical pulse is propagated through such a medium, the velocity of propagation is greatest for those parts of the wave whose amplitudes are greatest, and consequently the front of the disturbance becomes steeper and steeper as the pulse progresses through the medium. The final shape of the wave is then determined by dissipative processes which take place because of the intense stress gradients produced in the wave front, and often also depends on the microscopic structure of the medium. Such waves, which are called shock waves, of course also occur in fluids.

Words and Expressions

stress wave		应力波
seismological [ˌsaizmə'lɔdʒikl]	adj.	地震学上的
apparatus [ˌæpə'reitəs]	n.	仪器；装置
oscillation [ˌɔsi'leiʃən]	n.	振荡
amplitude ['æmplitjuːd]	n.	幅值
ultrasonics [ˌʌltrə'sɔniks]	n.	超声波，超声学
anelastic [ˌænil'æsti]	adj.	滞弹性的
strain rate		应变率
rate-dependent		率相关的
stress gradient		应力梯度
elastic wave		弹性波
viscoelastic wave		粘弹性波
plastic wave		塑性波
shock wave		冲击波；激波

Unit Five

Statically Indeterminate Structures[9]

Statically indeterminate structures are called the structures for which all reactions and internal forces cannot be determined solely using equilibrium equations. Redundant constraints (or excess) are constraints, which are not necessary for geometrical unchangeability of a given structure.

Degree of redundancy, or statical indeterminacy, equals to the number of redundant constraints whose elimination leads to the new geometrically unchangeable and statically determinate structure. Thus, degree of statical redundancy is the difference between the number of constraints and number of independent equilibrium equations that can be written for a given structure.

Primary unknowns represent reactions (forces and/or moments), which arise in redundant constraints. Unknown internal forces may be treated as primary unknowns. Primary system (principal or released structure) is such structure, which is obtained from the given one by eliminating redundant constraints and replacing them by primary unknowns.

Let us consider some statically indeterminate structures, the versions of primary systems, and the corresponding primary unknowns. A two-span beam is presented in Fig. 1(a). The total number of constraints, and as result, the number of unknown reactions, is four. For determination of reactions of this planar set of forces, only three equilibrium equations may be written. Therefore, the degree of redundancy is $n=4-3=1$, where four is a total number of reactions, while three is a number of equilibrium equations for given structure. In other words, this structure has one redundant constraint or statical indeterminacy of the first degree.

Four versions of the primary system and corresponding primary unknowns are shown in Fig. 1 (b)-(e). The primary unknown X_1 in cases (b) and (c) are reaction of support B and C, respectively. The primary unknown in cases (d) and (e) are bending moments. In case (d), the primary unknown is the bending moment at any point in the span, while in case (e), the primary unknown is the bending moment at the support B. Each of the primary systems is geometrically unchangeable and statically determinate; the structure in

Fig. 1(d) is a Gerber-Semikolenov beam; in case (e), the primary system is a set of simply supported statically determinate beams. The constraint which prevents the horizontal displacement at support A cannot be considered as redundant one. Its elimination leads to the beam on the three parallel constrains, i. e. , to the geometrically changeable system. So the structure in Fig. 1(f) cannot be considered as primary system. The first condition for the primary system geometrically unchangeable is the necessary condition. The second condition—statical determinacy—is not a necessary demand; however, here we will consider only statically determinate primary systems.

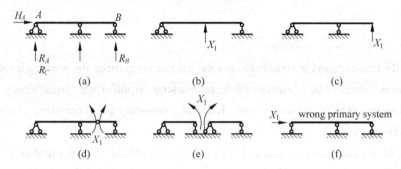

Figure 1 (a) Design diagram of a beam; (b-e) The different versions of the primary system; (f) Wrong primary system

The statically indeterminate frame is presented in Fig. 2(a). The degree of redundancy is $n=4-3=1$. The structure in Fig. 2(b) presents a possible version of the primary system. Indeed, the constraint which prevents horizontal displacement at the right support is not a necessary one in order to provide geometrical unchangeability of a structure (i. e. , it is a redundant constraint) and it may be eliminated, so the primary unknown presents the horizontal reaction of support. Other version of the primary system is shown in Fig. 2(c); in this case the primary unknown presents the bending moment at the rigid joint.

The system shown in Fig. 2(d) is geometrically changeable because three remaining support bars would be incapable of preventing rotation of the frame with respect to the left pinned support. Indeed, the constraint which prevents vertical displacement at the right support is a necessary constraint in order to provide a geometrical unchangeability of a structure (i. e. , it is not a redundant one). It means that the system shown in Fig. 2(d) cannot be accepted as a version of primary system.

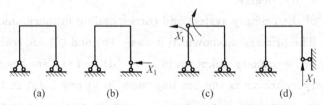

Figure 2 (a) Design diagram of a portal frame; (b-c) The different versions of the primary system; (d) Wrong primary system

Another statically indeterminate frame is presented in Fig. 3(a). The degree of redundancy is $n=6-3=3$.

One version of the primary system and corresponding primary unknowns is shown in Fig. 3(b). The primary unknowns are reactions of support. The structure shown in Fig. 3(c) presents the primary system where primary unknowns are internal forces (axial force X_1, shear X_2, and moment X_3), which appear in pairs. Figure 3(d) presents another version of the primary system. In this case, we eliminate two constraints which prevent two displacements (horizontal and angular) at support and one constraint which prevents mutual angular displacement, i. e. , the primary unknowns are a combination of reactions X_1 and X_2 and internal moment X_3. Is it obvious that three-hinged frame (Fig. 3(e)) can be adopted as the primary system?

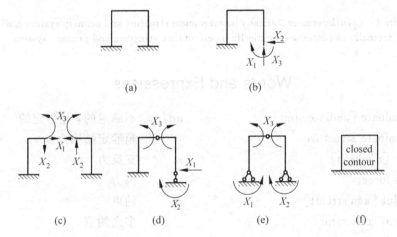

Figure 3 (a) Statically indeterminate frame; (b-e) The different versions of the primary system; (f) A concept of closed contour

The structure shown in Fig. 3(a) can also be considered as a system with closed contour (Fig. 3(f)). One closed contour has three degrees of redundancy, and primary system can be similar as in Fig. 3(c).

More complicated statically indeterminate frame is presented in Fig. 4(a). This structure contains three support bars and one closed contour. All reactions of supports may be determined using only equilibrium equations, while the internal forces in the members of the closed contour cannot be obtained using equilibrium equations. Thus, this structure is externally statically determinate and internally statically indeterminate. The degree of redundancy is $n=3$. The primary unknowns are internal forces as shown in Fig. 4(b). They are axial force X_1, shear X_2, and bending moment X_3.

The frame in Fig. 4(c) contains five support bars and one closed contour. So this structure is externally statically indeterminate in the second degree and internally statically indeterminate in the third degree. A total statical indeterminacy is five. Primary unknowns may be chosen as shown in Fig. 4(d).

Degree of statical indeterminacy of structures does not depend on a load. It is evident that inclusion of each redundant constraint increases the rigidity of a structure. So the displacements of statically indeterminate structures are less than the displacements of corresponding structures without redundant constraints.

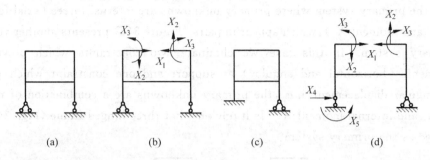

Figure 4 (a,b)Internally statically indeterminate structure and primary system and(c, d) Externally and internally statically indeterminate structure and primary system

Words and Expressions

indeterminate [ˌindi'tə:minit]	adj.	不确定的,超静定的
indeterminate structure		超静定结构
reaction [ri'ækʃən]	n.	支反力
internal force		内力
constraint [kən'streint]	n.	约束
redundant constraint		多余约束
degree of redundancy		冗余度
statical indeterminancy		静不定
determinate [di'tə:minit]	adj.	确定的,静定的
determinate structure		静定结构
equilibrium equation		平衡方程
primary unknowns		主要未知量
primary structure		主要结构
principal ['prinsəpəl]	adj.	主要的,首要的
two-span beam		双跨梁
simply supported beam		简支梁
frame [freim]	n.	框架
support [sə'pɔ:t]	n.	支撑
rotate [rəu'teit]	vi.	转动,旋转
rotation [rəu'teiʃən]	n.	转动,旋转
contour ['kɔntuə]	n.	轮廓,等高线
externally statically determinate		外部静定
internally statically indeterminate		内部静不定

Writing Skill of Experimental Research Report: RESULTS and DISCUSSION[32]

RESULTS

Now we examine the third major section of the experimental research report, called *results*, in which you present the findings of your study and briefly comment on them. Some writers call this section "Results and Discussion", thus indicating more extensive comments on the findings of the study. Before you write this part of your report, check with your professor or editor to find out which organizational format you should follow.

(1) Information Conventions

The *results* section of the report presents the findings of the study in both *figures* and in written *text*. Figures (graphs, tables, and diagrams) present the complete findings in numerical terms, while the accompanying text helps the reader to focus on the most important aspects of the results and to interpret them.

(a) Ordering Your Information

Typical *results* sections in research reports consist of three basic elements of information.

Element 1: a statement that *locates* the *figure(s)* where the results can be found.

Element 2: statements that *present the most important findings*.

Element 3: statements that *comment* on the results.

(b) Alternative Short Form

Another ordering system for the results section is a *short form* of the ordering system, in which the three elements are reduced to two kinds of statements.

Element 1 and 2 combined: statements that *present the most important results* and indicate in parentheses *the figure where* they can be found;

Element 3: statements that *comment* on the results.

Examples: Furthermore, the longitudinal wave propagates faster than the transverse one in porous media, which is reflected by the elliptic shape of disturbance as shown in Fig. 8. It is coincident with that indicated by Biot [5].

(c) Commenting on Results-Two Patterns

There are two possible ways to order *comment statements* (Element 3). You may put a short comment (one or two sentence) after each significant result you mention, or you may leave your comments until all the results have been mentioned.

Alternative Pattern: Result 1 + Comment 1; Result 2 + Comment 2; Result 3 + Comment 3

Sequential Patten: Result 1 + Result 2 + Result 3 + Comment

The *alternating pattern* is best if you have many individual results with specific comments about each result. The *sequential pattern* is used when there are several individual results to which one general comment applies. (Your professor or editor may ask you to put *all* comments in a separate section called "Discussion")

(d) Functions of Comments

The *comments* in **results** sections may serve a variety of different functions. Some of the most common functions are

- *generalize* from the results;
- *explain* possible reasons for the results;
- *compare* the results with results from other studies.

(2) Language Conventions

The language conventions we look at in the **results** section of the report will help you to choose the appropriate *verb tense* or *modal auxiliary* for each element of information. We also examine some special words and expressions you can use to report different types of findings.

(a) Choosing Verb Tense for Results

In using the three-step format to write your **results** section, you should observe the following verb tense conventions. In Element 1, use the *present tense* to locate your data in a figure.

Example: The obtained curves of relationships between stress and strain *are shown* in Fig. 1.

Example: Table 4 *summarizes* the test results of stress analyses.

Notice in the examples that locational statements can be written in either the *active or passive voice*, but in both cases the *present tense* is used.

When you report your findings (Element 2), use the *past tense*.

Example: The fatigue life of the rotational shaft *was found* to be 2×10^5 cycles of alternating load.

Note: In some field such as engineering and economics, authors may present their findings in the *present tense*.

When *commenting* on the findings (Element 3), it is conventional to use the *present tense* or *modal auxiliaries*.

When the comment *compares* your results with the results of other studies, use the *present tense*.

Example: This is consistent with earlier findings indicating that the stress concentrator increases with the decrease of radius of the hole.

When the comment gives a *possible* explanation for the result, use a *modal auxiliary*.

Example: These results may be explained by considering the friction between the two parts.

When the comment *generalizes* from the results, use *may*.

Example: The ratios of stiffness and strength to weight of this kind of composite material may be generally higher than those of aluminum.

In your Element 3 comments you may also use *tentative verbs* in the *present tense* instead of modal auxiliaries to generalize from results.

Example: It *seems*(*appears* / *is likely*) that the fatigue life of this aluminum alloy is longer than that of steel.

Example: These results *suggest* that the Young's modulus of a metal is generally higher than that of a polymer.

(b) **Element 2**: **Presenting Different Types of Findings**

There are three different types of findings that you may need to report, depending on the kind of study you do. Specific words and expressions are used in writing about each type.

- In some studies the findings involve a *comparison* among group, often one or more experimental groups with a control group. In these cases Element 2 statements are often written using *comparative* or *superlative* expressions.

Example: Q345 carbon steel has *higher* yeilding strength *than* Q235 steel. (Group 1 + Comparison + Group 2)

Example: The *highest* strength was found *among* nanomaterials. (Superlative + Group 1)

- In other studies the findings show the tendency of a variable to fluctuate over time. To report these kinds of results, use expressions of variation or special verbs of variation in your Element 2 statements.

Example: The stress tends to *increase proportionally* in the first 10 seconds. (Variable + Verb + Phrase of variation + Time period)

Example: The thermal stress *rose*(*fell* / *increased* / *decreased* / *dropped* / *remained constant* / *declined*) over the period studied. (Variable + Verb + Time period)

- Findings of a third type show the relationship of one variable with another, or relationships among variables. When you report these kinds of results, it is common to use verbs of correlation or association in Element 2.

Example: Choice of test scheme was *correlated with* (*negatively correlated with* / *associated with*) the configuration and material properties of the structures.

Example: The propagation rate of the crack was not *highly*(*significantly* / *closely*) *related* to ambient temperature.

DISCUSSION

Usually titled ***discussion***, it is the last major section of the report, followed by the list of references. In the ***discussion*** section you step back and take a broad look at your findings and your study as whole. As in the introduction, researchers use the discussion section to examine their work in the larger context of their field.

Sometimes this section is called "**conclusions**" instead of "discussion". In either cases the writing conventions reflects some common features.

(1) **Information Conventions**

This section moves the readers back from the *specific information* reported in the methods and the results sections to a more *general view* of how the findings should be interpreted.

(a) Ordering Your Information

The information that you include in this section depends greatly on the findings of your study; however, the specific-to-general movement is a convention that most writers follow. The kinds of information that you can include in your **discussion** section are not fixed. However, the first elements are typically those that refer *most directly* to the study and its findings. They include:

- A *reference* to the *main purpose* or *hypothesis* of the study;
- A *review* of the most important *findings*, whether or not they support the original hypothesis, and whether they agree with the findings of other researchers;
- Possible *explanations* for or *speculations* about the findings;
- *Limitations* of the study that restrict the extent to which the findings can be *generalized*.

As the discussion section continues, the writer moves the reader's attention away from the specific results if the study and begins to focus *more generally* on the importance that the study may have for other workers in the field.

- *Implications* of the study (generalization from the results);
- *Recommendations* for future research and practical applications.

Note: The order of discussion elements shown here is not strictly followed by all authors. However, the progressive move from specific to more general information elements is conventional.

(b) Researcher's Position towards the Findings

In the **discussion** section more than any other place in the report, researchers make explicit their own views on the study and its findings. The researcher may take a position with respect to the *explanations*, *implications*, *limitations*, or *applications* of the findings.

Example: One possible explanation is that the maximum Mises stress exceeds the ultimate strength of the material. (*explanation*)

Example: We can no longer assume that it is satisfactory to seek explanations only in load factors. (*implication*)

Example: We acknowledge that other experiments may produce different results. (*restriction*)

Example: Clearly, this technique has promise as a tool in nondestructive monitoring. (*application*)

(2) Language Conventions

Now we examine the sentence structure used in the **discussion** section to present elements of information and to give a point of view about that information. We also look at the verb forms that commonly occur in this section and at some of the special expressions authors use to indicate their positions towards the information they present.

(a) **Complex Structure in Discussion Statements**

To accommodate the information requirements of the *discussion* section, writers often use statements that are complex in grammatical structure—that is, that contain a main clause and a *noun clause*. Typically, the researcher's position is carried by the main clause while the information being reported is contained in the noun clause.

Example: We can conclude with certainty that both theories are able to explain the phenomenon of damage evolution.

(b) **Verb Tense Used in Discussion Statements**

The verb tenses used in the *discussion* section depend on the type of information you want to present. Remember that the first information elements of the discussion refer specially to the study and its findings. The verb tense most commonly used in referring to the purpose, the hypothesis, and the findings is the *simple past*.

Example: This research *attempted* to assess two theories of behavior. (Referring to the purpose)

Example: We originally *assumed* that mean stress would not shorten the fatigue life of the component. (Referring to the hypothesis)

Example: Deformations of all the components analyzed *were* in elastic. (Restating the findings)

Note: In some fields the *present perfect tense* may be used in referring to the purpose.

In discussion statements that explain possible reasons for, or limitations to, the findings, the *past*, *present*, or *modal auxiliaries* may be used. The choice depends on whether the explanation for the specific findings is *restricted* to your study (past) or whether it refers to a *general condition* (present). Modal auxiliary may also be used to emphasize the *speculative nature* of these statements.

Example: It is possible that coaction of wind and rain excites large vibration of stayed-cable bridges. (Explaining the findings)

Example: Our sample was very small. (Limiting the findings)

When comparing your findings to those of other researchers, use the *present tense*.

Example: These results *are* in substantial agreement with those of Rice [7]. (Comparing findings)

As you move from the specific considerations of your study to broader, more general statements about the importance of the study as a whole, use *simple present tense* and *modal auxiliary/ tentative verbs*.

Example: It *appears* that stayed-cable bridges behave longer spans. (Implications)

Example: The approach outlined in this study *should be replicated* in other manufacturing plants. (Recommendations and applications)

(c) **Expressions Indicating the Researcher's Position**

The main clause of a complex sentence in the discussion section often contains special expressions that indicate the researcher's own point of view, or position, towards the information contained in the noun clauses. At the beginning of the discussion section, certain expressions make it clear that you are reconsidering the hypothesis of your study.

Example: It was *anticipated* (The theory led us to *infer* /In line with this hypothesis, we *assumed* /The results *seem inconsistent with* our hypothesis) that the stiffness of the structure would be increased after being strengthened with rebars.

Other expressions are typically used when you need to explain your findings.

Example: These results can be explained by assuming that skill increases with experience.

Still other expressions are used when you wish to suggest the implications of your findings.

Example: These findings *suggest*(*imply / lend support to the assumption / lead us to believe / provide evidence*) that the relationship between stress and strain is greatly affected by the raising rate of temperature.

◇◦◇◦◇◦◇◦◇◦◇◦◇◦◇◦◇◦◇◦◇◦◇◦

Reading Material(1): Basic Structural Elements[10]

All structural systems are composed of a number of basic structural elements—beams, columns, hangers, trusses, and so forth. In this section we describe the main characteristics of these basic elements so that you will understand how to use them most effectively.

Columns—Axially Loaded Members in Compression

Columns also carry load in direct stress very efficiently. The capacity of a compression member is a function of its slenderness ratio l/r. If l/r is large, the member is slender and will fail by buckling when stresses are low—often with little warning. If l/r is small, the member is stocky. Since stocky members fail by overstress—by crushing or yielding—their capacity for axial load is high. The capacity of a slender column also depends on the restraint supplied at its ends. For example, a slender cantilever column—fixed at one end and free at the other—will support a load that is one-fourth as large as that of an identical column with two pinned ends (Fig. 1 (b),(c)).

In fact, columns supporting pure axial load occur only in idealized situations. In actual practice, the initial slight crookedness of columns or an eccentricity of the applied load creates bending moments that must be taken into account by the designer. Also in reinforced concrete or welded building frames where beams and columns are connected by rigid joints, columns carry both axial load and bending moment. These members are called beam-columns (see Fig. 1(d)).

Beams—Shear and Bending Moment Created by Loads

Beams are slender members that are loaded perpendicular to their longitudinal axis

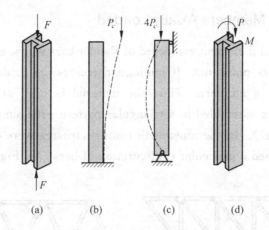

Figure 1 (a) Axially loaded column; (b) Cantilever column with bucking load P_c; (c) Pin-supported column with buckling load $4P_c$; (d) Beam-column.

(see Fig. 2(a)). As load is applied, a beam bends and deflects into a shallow curve. At a typical section of a beam, internal forces of shear V and moment M develop (Fig. 2(b)). Except in short, heavily loaded beams, the shear stresses produced by V are relatively small, but the longitudinal bending stresses produced by M are large. If the beam behaves elastically, the bending stresses on a cross section (compression on the top and tension on the bottom) vary linearly from a horizontal axis passing through the centroid of cross section. The bending stresses are directly proportional to the moment, and vary in magnitude along the axis of the beam.

Shallow beams are relatively inefficient in transmitting load because the arm between the force C and T that make up the internal couple is small. To increase the size of the arm, material is often removed from the center of the cross section and concentrated at the top and bottom surfaces, producing an I-shape section (see Fig. 2(c) and (d)).

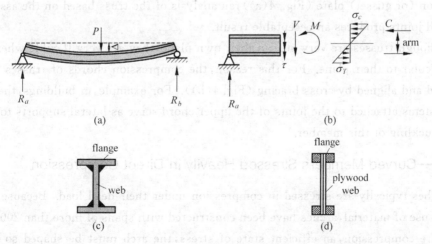

Figure 2 (a) Beam deflects into a shallow curve; (b) Internal forces (shear V and moment M); (c) I-shaped steel section; (d) Glue-laminated wood I-beam.

Planar Trusses—All Members Axially Loaded

A truss is a structural element composed of slender bars whose ends are assumed to be connected by frictionless pin joints. If pin-jointed trusses are loaded at the joints only, direct stress develops in all bars. Thus the material is used at optimum efficiency. Typically, truss bars are assembled in a triangular pattern—the simplest stable geometric configuration (Fig. 3(a)). In the nineteenth century, trusses were often named after the designers who established a particular configuration of bars (see Fig. 3(b)).

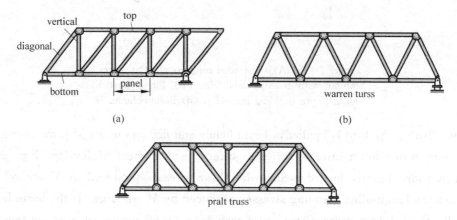

Figure 3 (a) Assembly of triangular elements to form a truss; (b) Two common types of trusses named after the original designer.

The behavior of a truss is similar to that of a beam in which the solid web (which transmits the shear) is replaced by a series of vertical and diagonal bars. By eliminating the solid web, the designer can reduce the dead weight of the truss significantly. Since trusses are much lighter than beams of the same capacity, trusses are easier to erect. Although most truss joints are formed by welding or bolting the ends of the bars to a connection (or gusset) plate (Fig. 4(a)), an analysis of the truss based on the assumption of pinned joints produces an acceptable result.

Although trusses are very stiff in their own plane, they are very flexible when loaded perpendicular to their plane. For this reason, the compression chords of trusses must be stabilized and aligned by cross-bracing (Fig. 4(b)). For example, in buildings, the roof or floor systems attached to the joints of the upper chord serve as lateral supports to prevent lateral buckling of this member.

Arches—Curved Members Stressed Heavily in Direct Compression

Arches typically are stressed in compression under their dead load. Because of their efficient use of material, arches have been constructed with spans of more than 2000 ft. To be in pure compression, an efficient state of stress, the arch must be shaped so that the resultant of the internal forces on each section passes through the centroid. For a given

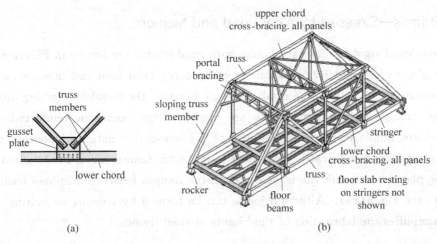

Figure 4 (a) Bolted joint detail; (b) Truss bridge showing cross-bracing needed to stabilize the two main trusses.

span and rise, only one shape of arch exists in which direct stress will occur for a particular force system. For other loading conditions, bending moments develop that can produce large deflections in slender arches. The selection of the appropriate arch shape by the early builders in the Roman and Gothic periods represented a rather sophisticated understanding of structural behavior. (Since historical records report many failures of masonry arches, obviously not all builders understood arch action.)

Because the base of the arch intersects the end supports (called abutments) at an acute angle, the internal force at that point exerts a horizontal as well as vertical thrust on the abutments. When spans are large, when loads are heavy, and when the slope of the arch is shallow, the horizontal component of the thrust is large. Unless natural rock walls exist to absorb the horizontal thrust (Fig. 5(a)), massive abutments must be constructed (Fig. 5(b)), the ends of the arch must be tied together by a tension member (Fig. 5(c)), or the abutment must be supported on piles (Fig. 5(d)).

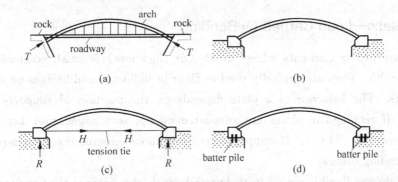

Figure 5 (a) Fixed-end arch carries roadway over a canyon where rock walls provide a natural support for arch thrust T; (b) Large abutments provided to carry arch thrust; (c) Tension tie added at base to carry horizontal thrust, foundations designed only for vertical reaction R; (d) Foundation placed on piles, batter piles used to transfer horizontal component of thrust into ground.

Rigid Frames—Stressed by Axial Load and Moment

Examples of rigid frames (structures with rigid joints) are shown in Figure 6(a) and (b). Members of a rigid frame, which typically carry axial load and moment, are called beam-columns. For a joint to be rigid, the angle between the members framing into a joint must not change when the members are loaded. Rigid joints in reinforced concrete structures are simple to construct because of the monolithic nature of poured concrete. However, rigid joints fabricated from steel beams with flanges (Fig. 2(c)) often require stiffening plates to transfer the large forces in the flanges between members framing into the joint (see Fig. 6(c)). Although joints can be formed by riveting or bolting, welding greatly simplifies the fabrication of rigid joints in steel frames.

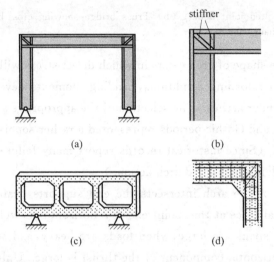

Figure 6 Rigid-jointed structure. (a) One-story rigid frame; (b) Vierendeel truss, loads transmitted both by direct stress and bending; (c) Details of a welded joint at the corner of a steel rigid frame; (d) Reinforcing detail for corner of concrete frame in (b).

Plates or Slabs—Load Carried by Bending

Plates are planar elements whose depth (or thickness) is small compared to their length and width. They are typically used as floor in buildings and bridges or as walls for storage tanks. The behavior of a plate depends on the position of supports along the boundaries. If rectangular plates are supported on opposite edges, they bend in single curvature (see Fig. 7(a)). If supports are continuous around the boundaries, double curvature bending occurs.

Since slabs are flexible owing to their small depth, the distance they can span without sagging excessively is relatively small. (For example, reinforced concrete slabs can span approximately 12 to 16 ft.) If spans are large, slabs are typically supported on beams or stiffened by adding ribs (Fig. 7(b)).

If the connection between a slab and the supporting beam is properly designed, the two elements act together (a condition called composite action) to form a T-beam (Fig. 7(c)). When the slab acts as the flange of a rectangular beam, the stiffness of the beam will increase by a factor of approximately 2.

By corrugating plates, the designer can create a series of deep beams (called folded plates) that can span long distance. At Logan Airport in Boston, a prestressed concrete folded plate of the type shown in Fig. 7(d) spans 270 ft to act as the roof of a hanger.

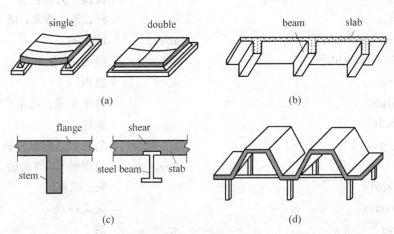

Figure 7 (a) Influence of boundaries on curvature; (b) Beam and slab system. (c) Slab and beams act as a unit. On left, concrete slab cast with stem to form a T-beam; right, shear connector joins concrete slab to steel beam, producing a composite beam; (d) A folded plate roof.

Words and Expressions

element ['elimənt]	n.	构件,要素,成分
hanger ['hæŋə]	n.	挂钩,悬挂物
truss [trʌs]	n.	桁架
slenderness ['slendənis]	n.	细长;细长度
member ['membə]	n.	构件,元件
stocky ['stɔki]	adj.	矮壮的;结实的
overstress ['əuvə'stres, ,əuvə'stres]	n.	过应力
crush [krʌʃ]	vt. & vi.	压碎;折皱
cantilever ['kæntili:və]	n.	悬臂;支架
pinned end		销轴支承
crookedness ['krukidnis]	n.	弯曲;不正
eccentricity [,eksen'trisiti]	n.	离心;偏心率
reinforced concrete		增强混泥土,钢筋混凝土
weld [weld]	vt. & vi.	焊接
	n.	焊接

deflect [di'flekt]	vt.&vi.	偏斜,转向
deflection [di'flekʃən]	n.	挠曲,挠度,偏斜
longitudinal [ˌlɔndʒi'tjuːdinəl]	adj.	纵向的,经度的
arm [ɑːm]	n.	臂
couple ['kʌpl]	n.	力偶
	vt.	偶合
I-shaped steel		工字钢
pin joint		铰接;关节接头
bar [bɑː]	n.	杆;条;横木;栅
optimum ['ɔptiməm]	adj.	最优的
assembly [ə'sembli]	n.	组集,集合
web [web]	n.	腹板
dead weight		静止重量;自重;净重
bolt [bəult]	n.	螺栓
gusset ['gʌsit]	n.	角板;三角形衬料
flexible ['fleksəbl]	adj.	柔度的,可弯曲的,柔韧的
chord [kɔːd]	n.	弦;弦杆
cross-bracing		交叉撑条
arch [ɑːtʃ]	n.	拱
masonry ['meisnri]	n.	石造建筑;石造工程
abutment [ə'bʌtmənt]	n.	桥墩;桥基;桥台
acute angle		锐角
thrust [θrʌst]	vt.&vi.	抛掷
pile [pail]	n.	柱,桩,堆
fixed-end		固定端
rigid frame		刚架
monolithic [ˌmɔnə'liθik]	adj.	独石的;单体的;整体的
flange [flændʒ]	n.	凸缘;边缘;轮缘
rivet ['rivit]	n.	铆钉;铆接
Vierendeel truss		空腹桁架;弗伦第尔桁架
slab [slæb]	n.	平板;厚板
curvature ['kəːvətʃə]	n.	弯曲;曲率
sag [sæg]	n.	弧垂;垂度
stiffen ['stifn]	vt.&vi.	刚化;使坚硬
rib [rib]	n.	肋
T-beam		T型梁
corrugate ['kɔrugeit]	vt.&vi.	起皱纹
folded plate		褶皱板

Reading Material(2): General Theory of Plane Trusses[11]

We return now to the general problem of assembling a system of bars in one plane so as to form a rigid truss. We have already seen that this can be done in two ways. In one case we begin with three bars pinned together at their ends in the form of a triangle and attach each joint thereafter by means of two additional bars. By this procedure we obtain a simple truss(Fig. 1(a)) for which there will always exist, between the number of members m and the number of joints j, the relationship

$$m = 2j - 3 \qquad (2.1a)$$

The rigidity of such a truss is, of course, entirely independent of any attachment to a foundation. In the other case, we begin directly with a foundation and establish each joint by means of two intersecting bars as shown in Fig. 1(b). In this way, we obtain a simple truss the rigidity of which depends on its interconnection with points of the foundation and for which, instead of Eq. (2.1a), we have

$$m = 2j \qquad (2.1b)$$

Any simple truss of the first kind requires, for the completion of its constraint in one plane, three additional bars or their equivalent, whereas for any simple truss of the second kind the constraint is already complete. Thus, in either case we come finally to the same conclusion: namely, for the complete constraint of j pins in one plane we must interconnect them between themselves and the foundation by $m=2j$ bars or equivalent constraints.

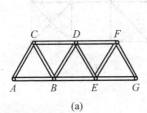

Figure 1

A great variety of plane trusses satisfying the foregoing general requirement of rigidity can be obtained by variously rearranging the bars of a simple truss in such a way that neither the total number of bars nor the total number of joints is changed. Consider, for example, the simple truss shown in Fig. 2(a). Regarding this as a system of two simple trusses that are interconnected by three bars that neither are parallel nor intersect in one point, we conclude that we can substitute for the bar CF with a bar BH and obtain the rigid truss shown in Fig. 2(b). By this substitution we change neither the number of bars nor the number of joints, but we now have a compound truss instead of a simple truss.

As a second example, consider the simple truss shown in Fig. 3(a). Replacing the bar CG by a bar AD, we obtain the truss shown in Fig. 3(b). This arrangement of bars and external constraints still satisfies the relationship $m=2j$ but otherwise fails to fulfill either the definition of a simple truss or that of a compound truss. Such a system is called *complex truss*.

It must not be concluded from the foregoing discussion that we can indiscriminately interconnect $2j$ bars with j joint and expect to obtain a rigid system. That is, the condition $m=2j$ is not alone a complete criterion of rigidity. Consider again, for example, the simple truss shown in Fig. 2(a). If we remove the diagonal FC from the middle panel, we destroy the rigidity of the system and introduce the possibility of relative translation between the two rigid shaded portions. A bar BH as shown in Fig. 2(b) prevents such distortion and is therefore a legitimate substitute for the bar FC. In fact, as already noted, we now have a compound truss. On the other hand, if we replace the bar FC by a second diagonal CH in the end panel, as shown in Fig. 2(c), we do not restore the rigidity of the truss; there is still the same freedom for relative translation between the two shaded portions. Thus, notwithstanding the fact that $m=2j$, the system in Fig. 2(c) is not a rigid one. Accordingly, we conclude that we must modify our criterion of rigidity and say that $2j$ bars are necessary and, *when properly arranged*, sufficient for the rigid interconnection between themselves and the foundation of j joints in one plane.

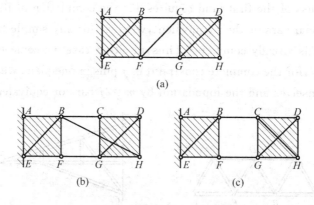

Figure 2

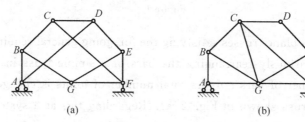

Figure 3

We shall now consider a further significance of the relationship $m=2j$. In Fig. 4, we take any completely constrained plane truss (simple, compound, or complex) comprised of m bars and j joints and load it in its own plane and at the joints only as shown. Then, to make a complete analysis of the truss, we must determine the axial force in each of the m

bars. Replacing each bar by the two equal but opposite reactions that it exerts on the pins at its ends, we obtain j systems of concurrent coplanar forces for each of which there exist two conditions of equilibrium. Hence, we have altogether $2j$ simultaneous equations involving m unknown axial forces; and we see that, if $m = 2j$, there are exactly as many unknowns as there are equations of statics. Thus, in all but exceptional cases, to be considered later, these equations give a definite solution to the problem. For this reason any completely constrained plane truss that satisfies the condition $m = 2j$ is said to be *statically determinate*. That is, the axial forces in the bars can be found from equations of statics alone; it is unnecessary to take account of the elastic deformations throughout the system. Consider, for example, the system shown in Fig. 5(a), for which $m = 2j$. Under the action of a load p applied as shown, we see that the bars AC and AD are inactive, while BC and BD carry, respectively, tension and compression, the magnitudes of which can be found from statical considerations of the hinge B. Owing to these internal forces, BC will be slightly elongated, while BD will be shortened; consequently, the joint B moves slightly downward and to the right, while the joint A remains stationary. Thus, the distance AB is greater after loading than before; but this small elastic distortion of the system does not affect the internal forces, and we need take no account of it.

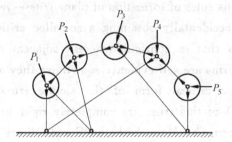

Figure 4

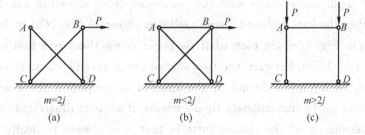

Figure 5

If $m > 2j$, there will, of course, be more unknown axial forces than there are independent equations of statics, and these equations fail to yield a unique solution. Accordingly, the truss is said to be statically indeterminate. Such a case is shown in Fig. 5(b), which is identical with Fig. 5(a) except for the extra bar AB. In this case, owing to the presence of the bar AB, the joint B cannot move relative to the joint A, as before, without stretching the bar AB and thus inducing some movement of A, also. Thus, part of the load P will be transmitted to the joint A, and the bars AC and AD also become active. The way in which P is divided between B and A in this case depends on the relative rigidities of the bars. For example if AB is very flexible in comparison with the other four bars, most of the load will be carried at B; in the extreme case where AB has no rigidity, all the load is carried at B as in Fig. 5(a). On the other hand, if AB is relatively very rigid, it will remain practically constant in length, and A and B will have to move about the same amount. Accordingly, the load will be about equally divided between these two joints. Thus, we see that when a truss is statically indeterminate ($m > 2j$), the distribution of internal forces depends on the elastic deformations throughout the system, and, to make an analysis, these deformations must be taken into account.

If $m < 2j$ (Fig. 5(c)), the system is not rigid and can be in equilibrium only under certain conditions of external loading. That is, since there are more equations of statics than unknown axial forces, it follows that these equations will determine the unknowns and, in addition, impose certain limitations on the system of external loads. In Fig. 5(c), for example, we can have equilibrium for vertical loads as shown, but any lateral loads will cause the frame to collapse.

In following the various rules of formation of plane trusses, already discussed, there is always the possibility of accidentally obtaining a so-called critical form, i. e., a certain configuration of the truss that is nonrigid, whereas adjacent configurations are rigid. Sometimes these critical forms are self-evident; sometimes they are not. We consider first the obvious example of a critical form of the simple truss shown in Fig. 6. The configurations (a) and (c) of this truss are completely rigid, but between them lies the possibility of the critical form (b). Here the bars CE and DE are collinear, and appreciable movement of the joint E relative to the other joints can result from the most minute changes in the lengths of the bars or from slight play in the hinges. In short, such a truss is not completely rigid. In the same way, the compound truss shown in Fig. 2. 7(a) has a critical form when the bars 1, 2, and 3 are parallel as shown in Fig. 7(b) or intersect in one point as shown in Fig. 7(c), in each of these latter cases, there is a limited freedom for relative lateral translation between the two shaded portions, and we must regard them as nonrigid forms. Such critical forms in the case of a compound truss are, of course, completely similar to the incompletely rigid systems of support illustrated in Fig. 8.

Another peculiarity of the critical form is that it is always statically indeterminate notwithstanding the fact that the condition $m = 2j$ is satisfied. Consider, for example, the critical form of simple truss shown in Fig. 6(b). Loaded as shown in Fig. 9(a), this system behaves as the truss in Fig. 5(b), and we conclude accordingly that it is statically indeterminate. That is, the portion of the load P that is transmitted to CD (which functions as one bar in this case) depends on the relative elastic deformations of the bars. When loaded as shown in Fig. 9(b), we see, by making a free body of the hinge E, that the bars

CE and DE must carry infinite tensions in order to balance the vertical component of the external force P; and this, of course, is physically impossible. Actually, upon application of the load P, all bars of the system will deform slightly, allowing the hinge E to assume an appreciably lower position whereby CE and DE become sufficiently inclined to balance the load P with finite tensions. However, these elongations and consequently the final configuration of equilibrium of the system depend on the elastic deformations of the bars, and these deformations must be taken into account in the analysis of the truss. Thus, again, the truss is statically indeterminate.

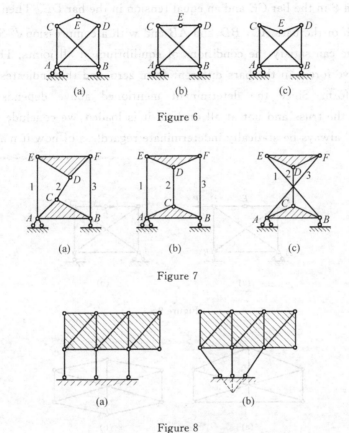

Figure 6

Figure 7

Figure 8

In the more general case of a complex truss, it is not always possible to detect a critical form by inspection. The complex truss in Fig. 10(b), for example, has a critical form, whereas the one in Fig. 10(a) has not. In such cases a general method of detecting a critical form of truss can be based on a consideration of the *determinant* of the system of $2j$ equations of equilibrium for its j joints. If this determinant is different from zero, the equations yield a unique solution: namely, there is one and only one set of values for the axial forces that can satisfy the conditions of equilibrium at each joint, and the truss is rigid and statically determinate. On the other hand, if the determinant happens to be zero, the equations of equilibrium fail to yield a unique solution, and this will always be an indication that the truss has a critical form. This suggests, then, a convenient method of testing for critical form, generally known as the zero-load test. With no loads on the truss, we see at once that one possible solution satisfying the conditions of equilibrium at each joint will be obtained by assuming all bars to be inactive, i. e. , with zero axial force. Hence, if under the same condition of loading we can find another set of values different from zero that also satisfy the conditions of equilibrium at each joint, we shall know that the truss has a critical form.

Consider, for example the truss in Fig. 6(b). With no external forces at the joints, we assume a tension S in the bar CE and an equal tension in the bar DE. Then, with the same tension S in each of the bars AC, BD, and AB and with a compression $\sqrt{2}S$ in each of the diagonal bars, we can satisfy the conditions of equilibrium at all joints. Thus, under zero load, we may have forces in the bars different form zero, and this indicates that the truss has a critical form. Since the determinant mentioned above depends only on the configuration of the truss and not at all on how it is loaded, we conclude that a truss of critical form will always be statically indeterminate regardless of how it may be loaded.

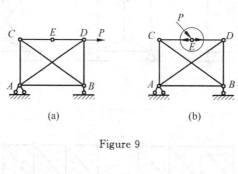

Figure 9

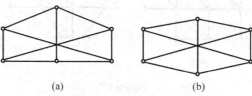

Figure 10

Words and Expressions

rigidity [ri'dʒiditi]	n.	刚度,刚性
complex truss		复式桁架
simple truss		简支桁架
indiscriminately [indi'skriminitli]	adv.	无差别地;任意地
criterion [krai'tiəriən]	n.	标准;准则
coplanar [kəu'pleinə]	adj.	共平面的

concurrent [kən'kʌrənt]	adj.	同时发生的
simultaneous [ˌsaiməl'teinjəs]	adj.	同时发生的；同步的
stationary ['steiʃənəri]	adj.	不动的；稳定的
configuration [kənˌfigju'reiʃən]	n.	构型，结构，形态
collinear [kɔ'linjə]	adj.	同线的；共轴的
notwithstand [ˌnɔtwiθ'stændiŋ]	prep.	尽管；虽然
critical form		危形

Unit Six

Free Vibrations: One Degree of Freedom[12]

There are many cases where the response of a structure to moving or pulsating loads or to suddenly applied loads must be investigated. Examples of such dynamic problems are illustrated by the behavior of buildings subjected to earthquakes, bridges subjected to moving loads, and structures subjected to wind gusts or bomb blasts.

Since any structure consists of distributed mass interconnected in some manner by elastic constraints, it will perform vibrations if disturbed from its configuration of equilibrium. In dealing with this problem of vibration of a given structure, it is sometimes possible to represent the structure by a single rigid-body mass supported by an elastic massless spring. Such an idealized representation of the structure is called a model. Consider, for example, the case of a simply supported prismatic beam that carries a heavy generator at mid-span as shown in Fig. 1.1(a). Treating the elastic beam as *a spring* which supports the mass of the generator, we obtain the model of the system as shown in Fig. 1.1(b). Assuming that motion of the mass is restricted to the vertical direction, we have a system with one degree of freedom; i. e., a single coordinate x defines the configuration of the system. As a second example, we consider the portal frame structure shown in Fig. 1.1(c), consisting of a very stiff heavy beam supported by flexible vertical columns. Assuming that the beam is completely rigid and that the columns are massless, we see that for horizontal motion of the beam, the structure behaves like the spring-supported mass shown in Fig. 1.1(d), and again we have a model with one degree of freedom.

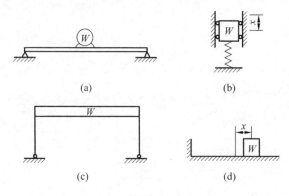

Fig. 1.1

Let us now consider, in detail, the dynamic behavior of a spring-suspended mass with one degree of freedom as shown in Fig. 1. 2. Under the action of the gravity force W, the spring will be extended by the amount

$$\delta_{st} = \frac{W}{k} \qquad (a)$$

where k, called the *spring constant*, denotes the load required to produce a unit extension of the spring. If the weight W is measured in pounds and extension of the spring in inches, the spring constant k will have the dimension of pounds per inch. The quantity δ_{st} determines the equilibrium position of the load as shown in the figure.

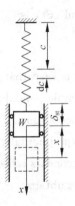

Fig. 1. 2

By means of an impulse or sudden application and removal of a vertical force, vibrations of the system can be produced. Such vibrations which are maintained by the elastic force in the spring alone are called free or natural vibrations. In studying these vibrations, we shall use Newton's second law of motion stating that the product of the mass of a particle and its acceleration is equal to the force acting in the direction of the acceleration. In this case, the mass of the vibrating body is W/g, where g is the acceleration due to gravity.

The acceleration of the body is given by the second derivative of the displacement x, from the equilibrium position, with respect to time and will be denoted by $\ddot{x}$. The forces acting on the vibrating body are the gravity force W, acting downward, and the force in the spring, which, for the position of the weight indicated in Fig. 1. 2, acts upward and is equal to $W+kx$. Thus, the differential equation of motion, in the case under consideration, becomes

$$\frac{W}{g}\ddot{x} = W - (W + kx) = -kx \qquad (b)$$

Introducing the notation

$$p^2 = \frac{kg}{W} = \frac{g}{\delta_{st}} \qquad (c)$$

Eq. (b) can be represented in the following form:

$$\ddot{x} + p^2 x = 0 \qquad (1.1)$$

This equation will be satisfied if we take either

$$x = C_1 \cos pt \quad \text{or} \quad x = C_2 \sin pt$$

where C_1 and C_2 are arbitrary constants. By adding these two solutions, we obtain the general solution of Eq. (1. 1). Thus,

$$x = C_1 \cos pt + C_2 \sin pt \qquad (1.2)$$

It is seen that the vertical motion of the weight W has a vibratory character since $\cos pt$ and $\sin pt$ repeat themselves after intervals of time τ such that

$$p(t+\tau) - pt = 2\pi \qquad (d)$$

This interval of time is called the *period of vibration*. Its magnitude, from Eqs. (d) and (c), is

$$\tau = \frac{2\pi}{p} = 2\pi\sqrt{\frac{W}{kg}} = 2\pi\sqrt{\frac{\delta_{st}}{g}} \qquad (1.3a)$$

It is seen that the period of oscillation of the suspended weight W is the same as that of a simple pendulum the length of which is equal to δ_{st} and is independent of the magnitude of oscillations. To determine the period τ, we have only to calculate, or to obtain experimentally, the static deflection δ_{st}. The number of oscillations per unit time, say per second, is called the *frequency of vibration* and will be denoted by f. Thus, from Eq. (1.3a), we obtain

$$f = \frac{1}{\tau} = \frac{1}{2\tau}\sqrt{\frac{g}{\delta_{st}}} \qquad (1.3b)$$

The vibratory motion represented by Eq. (1.2) is called *simple harmonic motion*. To determine the constants C_1 and C_2 in this equation, we must consider the initial conditions of motion. Assume, for instance, that at the initial moment ($t=0$) the weight W has *initial displacement* x_0 from the equilibrium position and *initial velocity* $\dot{x}_0$. Then, substituting $t=0$ and $x=x_0$ in Eq. (1.2), we obtain $C_1=x_0$. Likewise, substituting $t=0$ and $\dot{x}=\dot{x}_0$ in the first time derivative of Eq. (1.2), we find $C_2=\dot{x}_0/p$. With these values of the constants C_1 and C_2, Eq. (1.2) becomes

$$x = x_0 \cos pt + \frac{\dot{x}_0}{p}\sin pt \qquad (1.4a)$$

It is seen that this expression for vibrations consists of two parts; one, depending on initial displacement, is proportional to $\cos pt$, and the other, depending on initial velocity, is proportional to $\sin pt$.

Sometimes it is advantageous to represent the solution (1.4a) in another form by means of rotating vectors. Referring to Fig. 1.3, let $\overline{OB}$ be a vector of length x_0 which rotates in the counterclockwise direction about the origin O with constant angular velocity p. Counting time from the instant $t=0$ when this vector coincides with the x axis, we see that at any time t it will make with the x axis an angle pt, and its projection on the x axis is represents the first term in Eq. (1.4a). Now, at right angles to the vector $\overline{OB}$, let us construct a second vector $\overline{BC}$ of length $\dot{x}_0/p$. Then its projection on the x axis represents the second term in Eq. (1.4a), and we see that the projection on the x axis of the resultant vector $\overline{OC}$, of length A, represents the complete solution given by Eq. (1.4a). Denoting the angle between $\overline{OB}$ and $\overline{OC}$ by α, we may now write expression (1.4a) in the form

$$x = A\cos(pt - \alpha) \qquad (1.4b)$$

where, by reference to Fig. 1.3,

$$A = \sqrt{x_0^2 + \left(\frac{\dot{x}_0}{p}\right)^2} \qquad (e)$$

The quantity A, representing the maximum displacement of the vibrating weight, is called the *amplitude of vibration*; it is readily calculated from Eq. (e) when x_0 and $\dot{x}_0$ are given. The quantity α, defined by Eq. (f), is called the *phase angle*. We see from Fig. 1.3 that α/p represents the time that elapses after the initial moment $t=0$ until the vibrating weight reaches the first extreme position. This *time lag* is also shown in Fig. 1.4, which represents Eq. (1.4b) in graphic form.

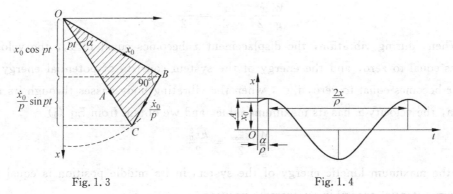

Fig. 1.3   Fig. 1.4

$$\alpha = \arctan \frac{\dot{x}_0}{px_0} \tag{f}$$

Natural frequencies of vibrating systems can often be calculated by using the law of conservation of energy, provided damping is negligible. Consider, for example, the system shown in Fig. 1.2. Neglecting the mass of the spring and considering only the mass of the suspended body, the kinetic energy of the system during vibration is

$$T = \frac{W}{g} \frac{\dot{x}^2}{2} \tag{g}$$

The potential energy of the system in this case consists of two parts: (1) the strain energy of deformation in the spring and (2) the potential energy of the weight W by virtue of its position. Considering the strain energy first, the tension in the spring for any displacement x from the equilibrium position is $k(\delta_{st}+x)$, and the corresponding strain energy is $k(\delta_{st}+x)^2/2$. For the position of equilibrium($x=0$), this energy becomes $k\delta_{st}^2/2$. Hence, the energy stored in the spring during the displacement x is

$$\frac{k(\delta_{st}+x)^2}{2} - \frac{k\delta_{st}^2}{2} = k\delta_{st}x + \frac{kx^2}{2} = Wx + \frac{kx^2}{2}$$

The potential energy due to position of the weight W diminishes during the displacement x by the amount Wx. Hence, the total change in the potential energy of the system during the displacement x is

$$V = Wx + \frac{kx^2}{2} - Wx = \frac{kx^2}{2} \tag{h}$$

It will be noted that this is simply the strain energy in the initially unstressed spring extended by the amount x.

Having expressions (g) and (h) and neglecting damping, we see that the equation of conservation of energy for the vibrating system becomes

$$\frac{W}{g}\frac{\dot{x}^2}{2} + \frac{kx^2}{2} = const \qquad (i)$$

The magnitude of the constant on the right-hand side of this equation is determined by the initial conditions of motion. Assuming that, for $t=0$, $x=x_0$ and $\dot{x}=0$, the initial total energy of the system is $kx_0^2/2$, and Eq. (i) becomes

$$\frac{W}{g}\frac{\dot{x}^2}{2} + \frac{kx^2}{2} = \frac{kx_0^2}{2} \qquad (j)$$

When, during vibration, the displacement x becomes equal to x_0, the velocity $\dot{x}$ becomes equal to zero, and the energy of the system consists of potential energy only. When x becomes equal to zero, i.e., when the vibrating body passes through its middle position, the velocity $\dot{x}$ has its maximum value, and we obtain from Eq. (j)

$$\frac{W}{g}\frac{\dot{x}_{max}^2}{2} = \frac{kx_0^2}{2} \qquad (1.5)$$

Thus, the maximum kinetic energy of the system in its middle position is equal to the maximum potential energy in an extreme position.

In all cases where it can be assumed that the vibration of a system is a simple harmonic motion, Eq. (1.5) can be used to calculate the frequency. We simply assume that the motion is represented by the equations

$$x = x_0 \cos pt, \quad \dot{x} = -x_0 \sin pt$$

Then we see that for such simple harmonic motion

$$\dot{x}_{max} = px_0 \qquad (k)$$

Substituting this relationship into Eq. (1.5), we find

$$p^2 = \frac{kg}{W}$$

which coincides with Eq. (c) obtained previously.

Words and Expressions

degree of freedom		自由度
response [ri'spɔns]	n.	响应,反应,回答
pulsating load		脉动载荷
gust [gʌst]	n.	阵风
bomb blast		炸弹爆炸
rigid-body		刚体
spring-supported		弹簧支撑
spring constant		弹簧常数
period of vibration		振动周期
frequency of vibration		振动频率
vibratory ['vaibrətəri]	adj.	振动的

harmonic motion		简谐振动
initial displacement		初始位移
initial velocity		初始速度
amplitude of vibration		振动幅值；振幅
phase angle		相位角
time lag		时间滞后
natural frequency		固有频率
damping ['dæmpiŋ]	adj.	阻尼
strain energy		应变能
extreme position		极端位置

Writing Skill of Experimental Research Report：ABSTRACT[32]

The last major section of the experimental research report we look at is the ***abstract***. As you know, the abstract is actually the first section of a report, coming after the title and before the introduction. The abstract provides the reader with a brief preview of your study based on information from the other sections of the report. We have reserved our examination of the abstract in the last because it is often the last part of the report to be written.

（1）**Information Conventions**

Many readers depend on the abstract to give them enough information about the study to decide if they will read the entire report or not.

（a）**Ordering Your Information**

Abstracts from almost all fields are written in a very similar way. The type of information included and their order are very conventional. The order of typical elements included in an abstract is as the following：

- some *background information*
- the ***principal activity*** (or purpose) of the study and its ***scope***
- some information about the ***methodology*** used in the study
- the most important ***results*** of the study
- a statement of ***conclusion*** or ***recommendation***

Note：On some publications this section is titled"**summary**". Check with your editor or professor to determine the appropriate title for you to use.

（b）**Reducing the Abstract**

Abstracts are usually written to be as brief and concise as possible. For journal articles the editor often establishes a word limit for the abstract that authors cannot exceed. In order to shorten an abstract to satisfy such limitations, you can eliminate or combine much of the information mentioned above.

The reduced abstract typically focuses on only two or three elements, with the emphasis placed on the *results* of the study. Information concerning the purpose and method is presented first (background information is not included). Then the most important results are summarized. Finally, conclusions and recommendations may be included in one or two sentences. The order of information elements in reduced abstract is as the following:

- purpose and method of the study
- results
- conclusions and recommendations (optional)

(2) **Language Conventions**

The verb tenses used in writing sentences in the *abstract* are directly related to those you used in the corresponding sections earlier in your report. For example, background sentences in the abstract are similar to background sentences in Stage I of the introduction: They both are written in the *present tense*.

Background information (present tense)

Example: The analysis of wave propagation phenomena in fluid-saturated porous media plays a very important role in many engineering practices such as transient consolidation, noise control, earthquake engineering and bioengineering.

Principal activity (past tense/ present perfect tense)

Example: Analyses for dynamic characteristics of the space shuttle have been carried out numerically and experimentally.

Methodology (past tense)

Example: The stress distribution of the bridge under dead load was analyzed by ABAQUS software.

Results (past tense)

Example: Residual compressive stress at surface of the bending component extended its fatigue life.

Conclusions (present tense/ tentative verbs/ modal auxiliaries)

Example: The final results show that the present techniques perform quite well in spite of the little structural information and measurement inaccuracies.

(3) **Samples**

There are two samples of Abstract adopted from papers published in international journals.

Abstract sample 1[34]:

System health monitoring of structures is important not only for conducting safe operation but also maitaining system performance. In this paper, two identification algorithms for assessing structural damages using the modal test data have been developed. An important characteristic in the present approaches is that the employment of the global numerical models (e. g. FEM model) and some important information (e. g. Young's modulus) of structures are avoided to a great extent. As the first step of the damage identification, two algorithms for the detection of damage location are proposed, which are similar in concept to the subspace rotation algoritm or best achievable eigenvector technique. Furthermore, a quadratic programming model is set up for the two approaches to predict the damage extent. To demonstrate the capability of the proposed approaches, an example of a 10-bay planar truss structure is employed for checking the present approaches numerically. Furthermore, the experimental data from the vibration test of a beam with two fixed ends are used directly in the present approaches. The final results show that the present techniques perform quite well in spite of the little structural information and measurement inaccuracies.

Abstract sample 2[35] (reduced abstract):
Numerical modeling of an overhead transmission line section and the digital simulation of stochastic wind field, to which the transmission line section is exposed, are presented. Time-domain analyses of typical transmission line sections in stochastic wind fields are carried out by ABAQUS software. It is discovered that the numerically determined dynamic swing angles of the suspension insulator strings in the transmission line sections are larger than those calculated with the formulas proposed in the technical code for designing overhead transmission lines. A dynamic wind load factor is suggested to be introduced into the formulas proposed in the design code.

◇◇◇◇◇◇◇◇◇◇◇◇◇◇◇◇◇◇◇◇◇◇◇◇

Reading Material(1): Forced Harmonic Vibration[12]

Harmonic excitation is often encountered in engineering systems. It is commonly produced by the unbalance in rotation machinery. Although pure harmonic excitation is less likely to occur than periodic or other types of excitation, understanding the behavior of a system undergoing harmonic excitation is essential in order to comprehend how the system will respond to more general types of excitation. Harmonic excitation may be in the form of a force or displacement of some point in the system.

We will first consider a single-DOF system with viscous damping, excited by a harmonic force $F_0 \sin \omega t$, as shown in Fig. 3.1.1. Its differential equation of motions is found from the free-body diagram to be

$$m\ddot{x} + c\dot{x} + kx = F_0 \sin \omega t \qquad (3.1.1)$$

The solution to this equation consists of two parts, the *complementary function*, which is the solution of the homogeneous equation, and the particular integral. The complementary function, in this case, is a damped free vibration.

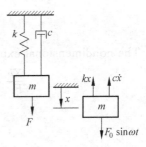

Figure 3.1.1 Viscously damped system with harmonic excitation

The particular solution to the preceding equation is a steady-state oscillation of the same frequency ω as that of the excitation. We can assume the particular solution to be of the form

$$x = X \sin (\omega t - \phi) \qquad (3.1.2)$$

where X is the amplitude of oscillation and ϕ is the phase of the displacement with respect to the exciting force.

The amplitude and phase in the previous equation are found by substituting Eq. (3.1.2) into the differential Eq. (3.1.1). Remembering that in harmonic motion the phases of the velocity and acceleration are ahead of the displacement by 90° and 180°, respectively, the terms of the differential equation can also be displayed graphically, as in Fig. 3.1.2. It is easily seen from this diagram the

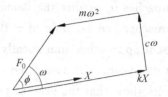

Figure 3.1.2 Vector relationship for forced vibration with damping

$$X = \frac{F_0}{\sqrt{(k-m\omega^2)^2 + (c\omega)^2}} \qquad (3.1.3)$$

and

$$\phi = \arctan \frac{c\omega}{k - m\omega^2} \qquad (3.1.4)$$

We now express Eqs. (3.1.3) and (3.1.4) in nondimensional form that enables a concise graphical presentation of these results. Dividing the numerator and denominator of Eqs. (3.1.3) and (3.1.4) by k, we obtain

$$X = \frac{F_0/k}{\sqrt{(1 - m\omega^2/k)^2 + (c\omega/k)^2}} \qquad (3.1.5)$$

and

$$\tan \phi = \frac{c\omega/k}{1 - m\omega^2/k} \qquad (3.1.6)$$

These equations can be further expressed in terms of the following quantities:

$\omega_n = \sqrt{k/m} =$ natural frequency of undamped oscillation
$c_c = 2m\omega_n =$ critical damping
$\zeta = c/c_c =$ damping factor

$$\frac{c\omega}{k} = \frac{c}{c_c} \frac{c_c}{k} \omega = 2\zeta \frac{\omega}{\omega_n}$$

The nondimensional expressions for the amplitude and phase then become

$$\frac{Xk}{F_0} = \frac{1}{\sqrt{[1-(\omega/\omega_n)^2]^2 + [2\zeta(\omega/\omega_n)]^2}} \qquad (3.1.7)$$

and

$$\tan \phi = \frac{2\zeta(\omega/\omega_n)}{1-(\omega/\omega_n)^2} \qquad (3.1.8)$$

These equations indicate that the nondimensional amplitude Xk/F_0 and the phase ϕ are functions only of the frequency ration ω/ω_n and the damping factor ζ and can be plotted as shown in Fig. 3.1.3. These curves show that the damping factor has large influence on the amplitude and phase angle in the frequency region near resonance. Further understanding of the behavior of the system can be obtained by studying the force diagram corresponding to Fig. 3.1.2 in the regions ω/ω_n small, $\omega/\omega_n = 1$, and ω/ω_n large.

For small values of $\omega/\omega_n \ll 1$, both the inertia and damping forces are small, which results in a small phase angle ϕ. The magnitude of the impressed force is then nearly equal to the spring force, as shown in Fig. 3.1.4(a).

For $\omega/\omega_n = 1.0$, the phase angle is 90° and the force diagram appears as in Fig. 3.1.4(b). The inertia force, which is now larger, is balanced by the spring force, whereas the impressed force overcomes the damping force. The amplitude at resonance can be found, either from Eqs. (3.1.5) or (3.1.7) or from Fig. 3.1.4(b), to be

$$X = \frac{F_0}{c\omega_n} = \frac{F_0}{2\zeta k} \tag{3.1.9}$$

At large values of $\omega/\omega_n \gg 1$, ϕ approaches 180°, and the impressed force is expended almost entirely in overcoming the large inertia force as shown in Fig. 3.1.4(c).

In summary, we can write the differential equation and its complete solution, including the transient term as

$$\ddot{x} + 2\zeta\omega_n \dot{x} + \omega_n^2 x = \frac{F_0}{m}\sin\omega t \tag{3.1.10}$$

$$x(t) = \frac{F_0}{k} \frac{\sin(\omega t - \phi)}{\sqrt{[1-(\omega/\omega_n)^2]^2 + [2\zeta(\omega/\omega_n)]^2}} + X_1 e^{-\zeta\omega_n t}\sin(\sqrt{1-\zeta^2}\,\omega_n t + \phi_1) \tag{3.1.11}$$

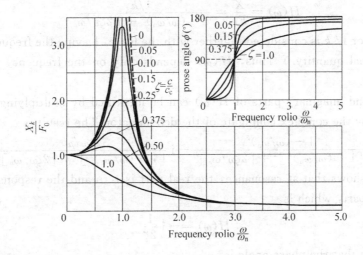

Figure 3.1.3   Plot of Eqs. (3.1.7) and (3.1.8)

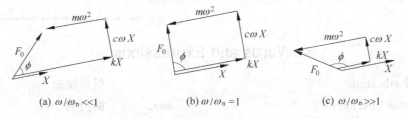

Figure 3.1.4   Vector relationship in forced vibration

Complex frequency response. From the vector force polygon of Fig. 3.1.2, it is easily seen that the terms of Eq. (3.1.1) are projections of the vectors on the vertical axis. If the force had been $F_0 \cos \omega t$ instead of $F_0 \sin \omega t$, the vector force polygon would be unchanged and the terms of the equation then would have been the projections of the vectors on the horizontal axis. Taking note of this, we could let the harmonic force be represented by

$$F_0(\cos \omega t + i \sin \omega t) = F_0 \, e^{i\omega t} \tag{3.1.12}$$

This would be equivalent to multiplying the quantities along the vertical axis by $i = \sqrt{-1}$ and using complex vectors. The displacement can then be written as

$$x = X \, e^{i(\omega t - \phi)} = (X \, e^{-i\phi}) \, e^{i\omega t} = \overline{X} \, e^{i\omega t} \tag{3.1.13}$$

where $\overline{X}$ is a complex displacement vector:

$$\overline{X} = X \, e^{-i\phi} \tag{3.1.14}$$

Substituting into the differential equation and canceling from each side of the equation gives the results

$$(-\omega^2 m + i\, c\omega + k)\overline{X} = F_0$$

and

$$\overline{X} = \frac{F_0}{(k - \omega^2 m) + i\,(c\omega)} = \frac{F_0/k}{1 - (\omega/\omega_n)^2 + i\,(2\zeta\omega/\omega_n)} \tag{3.1.15}$$

It is now convenient to introduce the complex frequency response $H(\omega)$ defined as the output divided by input:

$$H(\omega) = \frac{\overline{X}}{F_0} = \frac{1/k}{1 - (\omega/\omega_n)^2 + i\, 2\zeta\omega/\omega_n} \tag{3.1.16}$$

(Often the factor $1/k$ is considered together with the force, leaving the frequency response a nondimensional quantity.) Thus, $H(\omega)$ depends only on the frequency ratio and the damping factor.

The real and imaginary parts of $H(\omega)$ can be identified by multiplying and dividing Eq. (3.1.16) by the complex conjugate of the denominator. The result is

$$H(\omega) = \frac{1 - (\omega/\omega_n)^2}{[1 - (\omega/\omega_n)^2]^2 + [2\zeta\omega/\omega_n]^2} - i\,\frac{2\zeta\omega/\omega_n}{[1 - (\omega/\omega_n)^2]^2 + [2\zeta\omega/\omega_n]^2} \tag{3.1.17}$$

This equation shows that at resonance, the real part is zero and the response is given by the imaginary part, which is

$$H(\omega) = -i\,\frac{1}{2\zeta} \tag{3.1.18}$$

It is easily seen that the phase angle is

$$\tan \phi = \frac{2\zeta\omega/\omega_n}{1 - (\omega/\omega_n)^2}$$

✧✧✧✧✧✧✧✧✧✧✧✧✧✧✧

Words and Expressions

forced vibration		强迫振动
harmonic [hɑː'mɔnik]	*adj.*	简谐的
	n.	谐波

excitation [ek'saitətiv]	n.	激励
unbalance ['ʌn'bæləns]	n.	不平衡
single-DOF		单自由度
viscous damping		粘性阻尼
harmonic force		谐力
complementary function		余函数
homogeneous equation		齐次方程
particular integral		特积分；特解
free vibration		自由振动
nondimensional ['nɔndi'menʃənəl]	n.	无量纲
	adj.	无量纲(的)
numerator ['nu:mə,reitə]	n.	分子
denominator [di'nɔmə,neitə]	n.	分母
undamped [ʌn'dæmpt]	adj.	无阻尼的
critical damping		临界阻尼
damping factor		阻尼系数
resonant ['rezənənt]	adj.	共振的
inertia [in'ə:ʃiə, in'ə:ʃə]		惯性
impress [im'pres]	n.	印象；特征；传送
	vi.	印象；传送
transient term		暂时项；衰减项
complex frequency response		复频响应
imaginary part		虚部
conjugate ['kɔndʒə,geit]	adj.	共轭的

◇◆◇◆◇◆◇◆◇◆◇◆◇◆◇◆◇◆◇◆◇◆◇◆

Reading Material(2): Response to Arbitrarily Time-varying Forces[13]

A general procedure is developed to analyze the response of an SDF system subjected to force $p(t)$ varying arbitrarily with time. This result will enable analytical evaluation of response to forces described by simple functions of time.

We seek the solution of the differential equation of motion
$$m\ddot{u} + c\dot{u} + ku = p(t)$$
Subject to the initial conditions
$$u(0) = 0, \quad \dot{u}(0) = 0$$

In developing the general solution, $p(t)$ is interpreted as a sepuence of impulses of infinitesimal duration, and the response of the system to $p(t)$ is the sum of the responses to individual impulses. These individual responses can conveniently be written in terms of the response of the system to a unit impulse.

Reponse to Unit Impulse

A very large force that acts for a very short time but with a time integral that is finite is called an impulsive force. Shown in Fig. 4.1.1 is the force $p(t) = 1/\varepsilon$, with time duration ε starting at the time instant $t = \tau$. As ε approaches zero the force becomes infinite; however, the magnitude of the impulse, defined by the time integral of $p(t)$, remains equal to unity. Such a force in the limiting case $\varepsilon \to 0$ is called the unit impulse. The Dirac delta function $\delta(t-\tau)$ mathematically defines a unit impulse centered at $t = \tau$.

According to Newton's second law of motion, if a force P acts on a body of mass m, the rate of change of momentum of the body is equal to the applied force, that is,

$$\frac{d}{dt}(m\dot{u}) = P \qquad (4.1.1)$$

For constant mass, this equation becomes

$$P = m\ddot{u} \qquad (4.1.2)$$

Integrating both sides with respect to t gives

$$\int_{t_1}^{t_2} p\,dt = m(\dot{u}_2 - \dot{u}_1) = m\Delta\dot{u} \qquad (4.1.3)$$

The integral on the left side of this equation is the magnitude of the impulse. The product of mass and velocity is the momentum. Thus Eq. (4.1.3) states that the magnitude of the impulse is equal to the change in momentum.

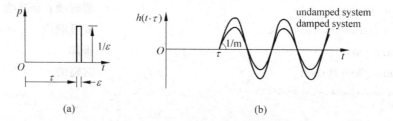

Fig. 4.1.1 (a) Unit impulse; (b) Response to unit impulse

This result is also applicable to an SDF mass-spring-damper system if the spring or damper has no effect. Such is the case if the force acts for an infinitesimally short duration so that the spring and damper have no time to respond. Thus a unit impulse at $t = \tau$ imparts to the mass, m, the velocity [from Eq. (4.1.3)]

$$\dot{u}(\tau) = \frac{1}{m} \qquad (4.1.4)$$

but the displacement is zero prior to and up to the impulse:

$$u(\tau) = 0 \qquad (4.1.5)$$

A unit impulse causes free vibration of the SDF system due to the initial velocity and displacement given by Eqs. (4.1.4) and (4.1.5). The response of undamped systems can be written as:

$$h(t-\tau) \equiv u(t) = \frac{1}{m\omega_n}\sin[\omega_n(t-\tau)], \quad t \geq \tau \qquad (4.1.6)$$

Similarly, the result for viscously damped systems is:

$$h(t-\tau) \equiv u(t) = \frac{1}{m\omega_D} e^{-\zeta\omega_n(t-\tau)}\sin[\omega_D(t-\tau)], \quad t \geq \tau \qquad (4.1.7)$$

These unit impulse-response functions, denoted by $h(t-\tau)$, are shown in Fig. 4.1.1(b).

Response to Arbitrary Force

A force $p(t)$ varying arbitrarily with time can be represented as a sequence of infinitesimally short impulses (Fig. 4.2.1). The response of a linear dynamic system to one of these impulses, the one at time τ of magnitude $p(\tau)d\tau$, is this magnitude times the unit impulse response function:

$$du(t) = [p(\tau)d\tau]h(t-\tau), \quad t > \tau \qquad (4.2.1)$$

The response of the system at time t is the sum of the responses to all impulses up to that time (Fig. 4.2.1). Thus

$$u(t) = \int_0^t p(\tau)h(t-\tau)d\tau \qquad (4.2.2)$$

This is known as the convolution integral, a general result that applies to any linear dynamic system.

Specializing Eq. (4.2.2) for the SDF system by substituting Eq. (4.1.7) for the unit impulse response function gives Duhamel's integral:

$$u(t) = \frac{1}{m\omega_D}\int_0^t p(\tau) e^{-\zeta\omega_n(t-\tau)}\sin[\omega_D(t-\tau)]d\tau \qquad (4.2.3)$$

For an undamped system this result simplifies to

$$u(t) = \frac{1}{m\omega_D}\int_0^t p(\tau)\sin[\omega_D(t-\tau)]d\tau \qquad (4.2.4)$$

Implicit in this result are "at rest" initial conditions, $u(0)=0$ and $\dot{u}(0)=0$. If the initial displacement and velocity are $u(0)$ and $\dot{u}(0)$, the resulting free vibration response should be added to Eqs. (4.2.3) and (4.2.4), respectively.

Duhamel's integral provides a general result for evaluating the response of a linear SDF system to arbitrary force. This result is restricted to linear systems because it is based on the principle of superposition. Thus it does not apply to structures deforming beyond their linearly elastic limit. If $p(\tau)$ is a simple function, closed-form evaluation of the integral is possible. Then the Duhamel's integral method is an alternative to the classical method for solving differential equations. If $p(\tau)$ is a complicated function that is described numerically, evaluation of the integral requires numerical methods.

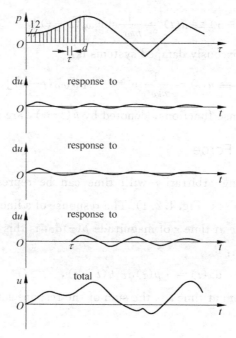

Fig. 4.2.1 Schematic explanation of convolution integral

Words and Expressions

step excitation	阶跃激励
pulse excitation	脉冲激励
Duhamel's integral	杜哈美积分
rise time	上升时间
shock spectrum	冲击谱
unit impulse	单位脉冲
Dirac delta function	狄拉克 δ 函数
mass-spring-damper system	质量-弹簧-阻尼系统
impulse-response function	脉冲响应函数
closed form	闭型

Unit Seven

Description of Elastoplastic Material Response under Uniaxial Case[14]

We begin our consideration in the elastoplastic regime with the case of a uniaxial rod specimen of metallic material under tension. This simple case encompasses all the essential features of elastoplastic material response which may be deduced directly from macroscopic experimental observations. Beyond the importance of the conventional tension test for obtaining material properties, the mathematical methodology of elastoplastic material description can be introduced herewith as a basis for the subsequent extension to multiaxial stress and strain states. For the tensile specimen with length l and cross-section A in Fig. 1.1, we define the uniaxial stress

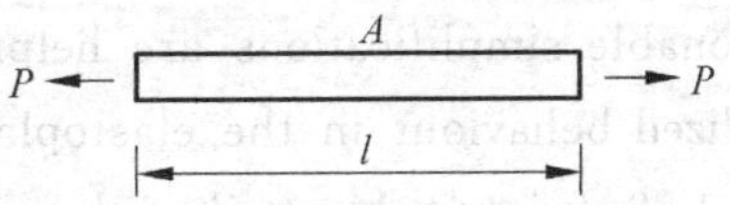

$$\sigma = \frac{P}{A} \qquad (1.1)$$

Fig. 1.1 Uniaxial specimen under tension (schematic)

where P denotes the axially applied force, and the longitudinal strain

$$\gamma = \frac{\delta}{l} \qquad (1.2)$$

where δ denotes the elongation of the specimen.

Stress strain diagram

The uniaxial specimen is considered originally undeformed. A monotonic increase of the tensile force from zero produces values of stress and strain lying along the solid line in the diagram of Fig. 1.2 (left). Inspection of the plot of the recorded stress and strain values indicates the deviation from the initial linear part—inherent to elastic response—at point L, the linearity limit. Beyond this point the stress—strain diagram is curvilinear with a decreasing slope.

The above refers to monotonic loading conditions. If, in a different test programme, the specimen is first stressed to a state well beyond point L and is then unloaded, the strain follows the dashed line in Fig. 1.2. It is thereby observed that the removal of the stress restores the strain only partially while part of it adheres permanently to the specimen. Careful examination of the test data reveals that permanent, or plastic, strains appear beyond point E, the elasticity limit.

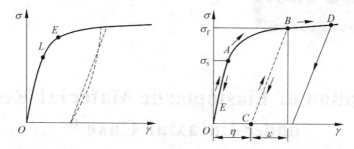

Fig. 1.2   Elastoplastic stress-strain diagram and idealization (right)

Reloading takes place along a slightly different path until the monotonic tensile characteristic is again reached. The latter is observed when the loading is increased further. The above behaviour is typical of any unloading and reloading operation in the elastoplastic regime of the test programme independently of the stress level. The path difference between unloading and reloading is known as the hysteresis loop.

The actual elastoplastic behaviour illustrated in Fig. 1.2 appears to be complex. Therefore, despite an increasing tendency to pay particular attention to secondary effects, reasonable simplifications are helpful to a suitable description of metal plasticity. The idealized behaviour in the elastoplastic regime depicted in the stress—strain diagram of Fig. 1.2 (right) is attributed to Ludwig Prandtl. Accordingly, the elasticity limit is assumed to coincide with the linearity limit at A, the yield point of the material under uniaxial tension. We denote the associated yield stress by σ_s. The material response to stresses below the yield limit is elastic, and in this region unloading completely restores the deformation of the specimen.

Continuous loading beyond A follows the same curvilinear path as in Fig. 1.2 (left), but unloading from point B, for instance, is assumed here along a straight line parallel to the initial elastic one. Thereby, the elastic part ε of the strain is restored, whilst the plastic part η remains after the removal of the stress. Reloading from point C takes place along the same elastic path as unloading, and the increase of the strain is purely elastic up to B, the state before unloading. Thus, the plastic strains at B and C are the same. For a further increase of the stress beyond σ_f, the stress at state B, the material follows the monotonic loading diagram as if unloading had not occurred. Stress removal from a further advanced state D on the diagram indicates that this transition from B has been accompanied by additional plastic strain.

The appearance of a permanent plastic strain η in addition to the reversible elastic strain ε is characteristic to the elastoplastic regime. The total strain γ may be presented as

$$\gamma = \varepsilon + \eta \tag{1.3}$$

The additive decomposition refers to the strain γ defined by Eq. (1.2). Partition of the total elongation of the specimen δ into elastic and plastic terms specifies the respective strains ε and η for $l=$ const.

The development of plastic strain along the tensile stress-strain diagram initially requires loading beyond the yield stress σ_s. The maximum stress, once imposed under plastic deformation, however, is recorded by the material and becomes the actual yield limit σ_f for additional plastic straining. Thus σ_f takes the place of the original σ_s when the specimen is unloaded and later reloaded. A functional dependence

$$\sigma_f = \sigma_f(\eta) \quad \text{with} \quad \sigma_f(0) = \sigma_s \tag{1.4}$$

can be deduced from the tension test after substraction of the elastic strain ε from the measured strain γ. Since the yield stress σ_f is increasing with plastic strain η, the material is said to strain-harden, and the function $\sigma_f(\eta)$ describes the hardening characteristic.

Nature of the stress-strain relations

The additive composition of the strain as by Eq. (1.3) suggests the description of elastoplastic material behaviour by means of an elastic and a plastic constituent. This is demonstrated in Fig. 1.3 where the uniaxial stress-strain characteristic is split into two distinct diagrams appertaining to the parts ε and η of the strain γ. At a given stress level σ, the elastic strain can be determined by Hooke's law as

$$\varepsilon = \frac{\sigma}{E} \tag{1.5}$$

where E denotes the modulus of elasticity of the material. Equation (1.5) between stress and elastic strain may be considered an equation of state, relating uniquely ε to σ regardless of the particular loading programme producing the actual stress. Any variation of the stress is accompanied by variations of the elastic strain along the straight path described by the law of elasticity.

Conversely, the stress may be considered a result of the elastic strain. Using Eq. (1.3), we obtain from Eq. (1.5)

$$\sigma = E\varepsilon = E(\gamma - \eta) \tag{1.6}$$

Determination of σ requires knowledge of the permanent strain η in addition to the measured strain γ. The stress-plastic strain diagram in Fig. 1.3 (right) represents the hardening characteristic $\sigma_f(\eta)$ of the material. It is obtained from the original tensile stress-strain curve by a reduction of the strain γ by the elastic strain ε from Eq. (1.5). Simple knowledge of the instantaneous stress proves to be insufficient for a unique determination of the plastic strain. While the hardening characteristic provides a value for η at the given stress level, the same stress can be reached by unloading from any higher point of the hardening curve, and may therefore be associated with different values of the plastic strain unless the preceding loading history is specified.

For the above reason, we shall pay attention instead to the relations between incremental variations of stress and plastic strain along a prescribed stress path. For changes in plastic strain

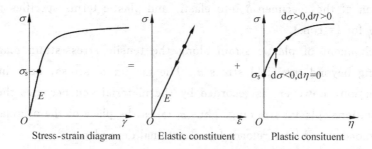

Fig. 1.3　Elastic and plastic constituents

(plastic flow), the applied tensile stress σ must be raised to the state $\sigma_f(\eta)$ ultimately attained in the past by the material. Then, an incremental increase of the stress by $d\sigma>0$ produces an increment $d\eta$ in plastic strain. Reduction of the stress by $d\sigma<0$ corresponds to elastic unloading and leaves the plastic strain unaffected, $d\eta=0$. In contrast to elasticity, an essential difference between loading and unloading becomes obvious in plasticity and introduces a nonlinear response even to incremental variations of the mechanical state.

◇◇◇◇◇◇◇◇◇◇◇◇◇◇◇◇◇◇◇◇◇◇◇◇◇◇◇◇◇◇◇◇◇◇

Words and Expressions

elastoplastic [i'læstəplæstik]	n.	弹塑性
	adj.	弹塑性（的）
longitudinal strain		纵向应变
monotonic [mɔnəu'tɔnik]	adj.	单调的
dash line		虚线
reloading [riː'ləudiŋ]	vt. & vi.	重复加载
hysteresis loop		迟滞环；滞后回线
elasticity [ˌelæs'tisəti]	n.	弹性
plasticity [plæs'tisiti]	n.	塑性
uniaxial tension		单轴拉伸
reversible [ri'vəːsəbl]	adj.	可逆的
constituent [kən'stitjuənt]	adj.	本质的，本构的
hardening characteristic		硬化特性

科技英语翻译技巧：科技文章的特点[31]

科技文章文体的特点是：清晰、准确、精炼、严密。在翻译过程中应根据科技英文文章的特点进行处理。现将科技英文的语言结构特色陈述如下。

1. 名词化结构

大量使用名词化结构是科技英语的特点之一。这是因为科技英语要求行文简洁、表达客观、内容确切、信息量大、强调存在的事实。比较下列各组句子：

Archimedes first discovered the principle that water is displaced by solid bodies.

Archimedes first discovered the principle *of displacement of water by solid bodies*.

阿基米德最先发现固体排水的原理。

句中 of displacement of water by solid bodies 系名词化结构，一方面简化了同位语从句，另一方面强调 displacement 这一事实。

The earth rotates on its own axis, which causes the change from day to night.

The rotation of the earth on its own axis causes the change from day to night.

地球绕轴自转，引起昼夜的变化。

名词化结构 The rotation of the earth on its own axis 使复合句简化成简单句，而且使表达的概念确切严密。

2. 被动句

广泛采用被动句是科技英语的又一个特点。科技文章侧重叙事推理，强调客观准确。第一、第二人称使用过多，会造成主观臆断的现象，因而应尽量使用第三人称叙述，采用被动语态。如：

A round sample *is placed* in the upper and lower jaws of the material testing system.

把一根圆形试样安装在材料试验机的上下夹具中。

The strain gage *is connected* into an electrical measurement circuit called the Wheatstone bridge.

将应变片接入惠斯通电桥中。

此外，科技英文常将主要信息前置，放在主语部分。这也是广泛使用被动态的主要原因之一。如：

Attention *must be paid* to the working temperature of the material.

必须注意材料的工作温度。

3. 非限定动词

科技文章要求行文简练，结构紧凑，为此，往往使用分词短语代替定语从句或状语从句；使用分词独立结构代替状语从句或并列分句；使用不定式短语代替各种从句；介词＋动名词短语代替定语从句或状语从句。这样可缩短句子，又比较醒目。比较下列各组句子：

Vibrating objects produce sound waves *and each vibration* produces one sound wave.

Vibrating objects produce sound waves, *each vibration producing one sound wave*.

振动着的物体产生声波，每一次振动产生一个声波。

Materials *which are used for structural purpose* are chosen *so that they behave elastically in the environmental conditions*.

Materials *to be used for structural purposes* are chosen *so as to behave elastically in the environmental conditions*.

结构材料的选择应使其在外界条件中保持其弹性。

4. 后置定语

大量使用后置定语也是科技文章的特点之一。常见的结构有以下几种：

（1）介词短语

The forces *due to friction* are called frictional forces.

由于摩擦而产生的力称为摩擦力。
（2）形容词及形容词短语
The only way *available* is to change its structural form.
改变其结构形式是唯一可行的途径。
（3）副词
The force *upward* equals to the force *downward* so that the balloon stays at the level.
向上的力与向下的力相等，所以气球就保持在这一高度。
（4）单个分词，但仍保持较强的动词意义
The stress distribution *obtained* must be analyzed.
获得的应力分布必须加以分析。
（5）定语从句
The derivation of the flexure formula is based on the principle of equilibrium, *which requires that the sum of the moments about any point must be zero*.
挠度公式的推导基于平衡原理，该平衡原理要求绕任意点的力矩之和为零。

5. 常用句型

科技英文中经常使用若干特定的句型，从而形成科技文体区别于其他文体的标志。例如 It…that 结构句型；被动态结构句型；as 结构句型；分词短语结构句型；省略句型等。举例如下：

It is evident that any structure must behave sufficient strength, stiffness and stability.
显然，任何结构都必须具有足够的强度、刚度和稳定性。
Materials may *be classified as* metal, polymer, ceramics and composite.
材料可分为金属、聚合物、陶瓷和复合材料。
An object, *once in motion*, will keep on moving because of its inertia.
物体一旦运动，就会因惯性而持续运动。

6. 长句

为了表达一个复杂概念，使之逻辑严密，结构紧凑，科技文章中往往出现许多长句。以下即是一例：

Advances in solid mechanics are central to assuring safety, reliability, and economy in design of devices, machines, structures and complete systems, and hence to the continued development of power generation technologies such as fusion, nuclear and gas turbine power, aerospace and surface transportation vehicle, earthquake resistant design, offshore structures, orthopedic devices, and materials processing and manufacturing technologies.

固体力学的进展是设备、机器、结构和完整系统设计中确保其安全性、可靠性和经济性的关键，因而是持续发展诸如核聚变、核动力燃气轮机发电技术、航空运载器和地面运输车辆、抗震设计、海上结构、整形设备、材料加工和制造技术的关键。

7. 复合词与缩略词

大量使用复合词与缩略词是科技文章的特点之一。复合词从过去的双词组合发展到多词组合；缩略词趋向于任意构词，例如某一篇论文的作者可以就仅在该文中使用的术语组成缩略词。例如：

work-harden	加工硬化（双词合成动词）
one-degree-of-freedom	单自由度（多词合成名词）
math (mathematics)	数学（裁减式缩略词）
FEM (finite element method)	有限单元法（用首字母组成的缩略词）
BEM (boundary element method)	边界元法
SIF (stress intensity factor)	应力强度因子
FRP (fiber reinforce polymer)	纤维增强聚合物

Reading Material(1): Yield Criteria of Metals[15]

The macroscopic theory of plasticity is based on certain experimental observations regarding the behavior of ductile metals. The theory rests on the assumption that the material is homogeneous and is valid only at temperatures for which thermal phenomena may be neglected. For the present purpose, it is also assumed that the material is isotropic and has identical yield stresses in tension and compression. A law governing the limit of elastic behavior, consistent with the basic assumptions, defines a possible criterion of yielding under any combination of the applied stresses.

The state of stress in any material element may be represented by a point in a nine-dimensional stress space. Around the origin of the stress space, there exists a domain of elastic range representing the totality of elastic states of stress. The external boundary of the elastic domain defines a surface, known as the initial yield surface, which may be expressed in terms of the components of the true stress σ_{ij}, as

$$f(\sigma_{ij}) = constant$$

Since the material is initially isotropic, plastic yielding depends only on the magnitudes of the three principal stresses, and not on their directions. This amounts to the fact that the yield criterion is expressible as a function of the three basic invariants of the stress tensor. The yield function is therefore a symmetric function of the principal stresses and is also independent of the hydrostatic stress, which is defined as the mean of the three principal stresses. Plastic yielding therefore depends on the principal components of the deviatoric stress tensor, which is defined as

$$s_{ij} = \sigma_{ij} - \sigma\delta_{ij} \qquad (1)$$

where σ denotes the hydrostatic stress, equal to $(\sigma_1 + \sigma_2 + \sigma_3)/3$. Since the sum of the principal deviatoric stresses is $s_{ii}=0$, the principal components cannot all be independent. It follows that the yield criterion may be expressed as a function of the invariants J_2 and J_3 of the deviatone stress tensor, which are given by

$$\left. \begin{array}{l} J_2 = -(s_1 s_2 + s_2 s_3 + s_2 s_1) = \dfrac{1}{2}(s_1^2 + s_2^2 + s_3^2) = \dfrac{1}{2} s_{ij} s_{ij} \\ J_3 = s_1 s_2 s_3 = \dfrac{1}{3}(s_1^3 + s_2^3 + s_3^3) = \dfrac{1}{3} s_{ij} s_{jk} s_{ki} \end{array} \right\} \qquad (2)$$

The absence of Bauschinger effect in the initial state implies that yielding is unaffected by the reversal of the sign of the stress components. Since J_3 changes sign with the stresses, an even function of this invariant should appear in the yield criterion.

In a three-dimensional principal stress space, the yield surface is represented by a right cylinder whose axis is equally inclined to the three axes of reference, Fig. 1. The generator of the cylinder is therefore perpendicular to the plane $\sigma_1 + \sigma_2 + \sigma_3 = 0$, known as the deviatoric plane. Since $\sigma_1 = \sigma_2 = \sigma_3$, along the geometrical axis of the cylinder, it represents purely hydrostatic states of stress. Points on the generator therefore represent stress states with varying hydrostatic part, which does not have any influence on the yielding. The yield surface is intersected by the deviatoric plane in a closed curve, known as the yield locus, which is assumed to be necessarily convex.

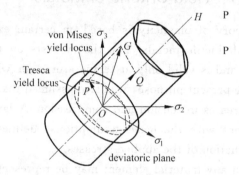

Figure 1 Geometrical representation of yield criteria in the principal stress space

Due to the assumed isotropy and the absence of the Bauschinger effect, the yield locus must possess a six-fold symmetry with respect to the projected stress axes and the lines perpendicular to them, as indicated in Fig. 2(b). In an experimental determination of the initial yield locus, it is therefore only necessary to apply stress systems covering a typical 30° segment of the yield locus. This may be achieved by introducing the Lode parameter μ, which is defined as

$$\mu = \frac{2\sigma_2 - \sigma_3 - \sigma_1}{\sigma_3 - \sigma_1} = -\sqrt{3}\tan\theta, \quad \sigma_1 > \sigma_2 > \sigma_3 \tag{3}$$

where θ is the counterclockwise angle made by the deviatoric stress vector with the direction representing pure shear. To obtain the shape of the yield locus, it is only necessary to apply stress systems varying between pure shear ($\mu = \pm 1$, $\theta = 0$) and uniaxial tension or compression ($\mu = \pm 1$, $\theta = \pm \pi/6$). The yield locus is called regular when it has a unique tangent at each point and singular when it has sharp corners.

The simplest yield criterion expressed in terms of the invariants of the deviatoric stress tensor is $J_2 = k^2$, suggested by von Mises, where k is a constant. The yield function does not therefore involve J_3 at all. In terms of the stress component referred to an arbitrary set of rectangular axes, the von Mises yield criterion may be written as

$$\left.\begin{array}{l} s_{ij}s_{ij} = s_x^2 + s_y^2 + s_z^2 + 2(\tau_{xy}^2 + \tau_{yz}^2 + \tau_{zx}^2) = 2k^2 \\ \text{or} \\ (\sigma_x - \sigma_y)^2 + (\sigma_y - \sigma_z)^2 + (\sigma_z - \sigma_x)^2 + 6(\tau_{xy}^2 + \tau_{yz}^2 + \tau_{zx}^2) = 6k^2 \end{array}\right\} \quad (4)$$

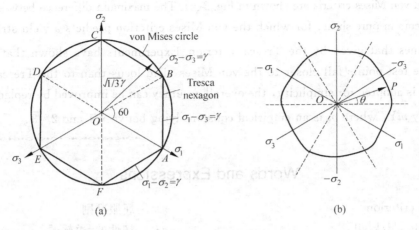

Figure 2　Deviatoric yield locus. (a) Tresca hexagon and von Mises circle and (b) general shape of the locus

　　The second expression in (4) follows from the first on subtracting the identically zero term $(s_x + s_y + s_z)^2/3$ and noting the fact that $s_x - s_y = \sigma_x - \sigma_y$, etc. The constant k is actually the yield stress in simple or pure shear, as may be seen by setting $\sigma_x = \sigma$ and $\sigma_y = -\sigma$ as the only nonzero stress components. According to (4), the uniaxial yield stress Y is equal to $\sqrt{3}k$, which is obtained by considering $\sigma_x = Y$ as the only nonzero stress. The von Mises yield surface is evidently a right circular cylinder having its geometrical axis perpendicular to the deviatoric plane. The principal deviatoric stresses according to the von Mises criterion may be expressed in terms of the deviatoric angle θ as

$$s_1 = \frac{2}{3}Y \cos\left(\frac{\pi}{6} + \theta\right), \quad s_2 = \frac{2}{3}Y \sin\theta, \quad s_3 = -\frac{2}{3}Y \cos\left(\frac{\pi}{6} - \theta\right) \quad (5)$$

　　In the case of plane stress, the actual principal stresses σ_1 and σ_2 may be expressed in terms of θ using the fact that the sum of these stresses is equal to $-3s_3$ which ensures that σ_3 is identically zero.

　　On the basis of a series of experiments involving the extrusion of metals through dies of various shapes, Tresca concluded that yielding occurred when the magnitude of the greatest shear stress attained a certain critical value. In terms of the principal stresses, the Tresca criterion may be written as

$$\sigma_1 - \sigma_3 = 2k, \quad \sigma_1 \geqslant \sigma_2 \geqslant \sigma_3 \quad (6)$$

where k is the yield stress in pure shear, the uniaxial yield stress being $Y = 2k$ according to this criterion. All possible values of the principal stresses are taken into account when the Tresca criterion is expressed by a single equation in terms of the invariants J_2 and J_3, but the result is too complicated to have any practical usefulness. For a given uniaxial yield stress Y, the Tresca yield surface is a regular hexagonal cylinder inscribed within the von

Mises cylinder.

The Tresca yield surface is not strictly convex, but each face of the surface may be regarded as the limit of a convex surface of vanishingly small curvature. The deviatoric yield loci for the Tresca and von Mises criteria are shown in Fig. 2(a). The maximum difference between the two criteria occurs in pure shear, for which the von Mises criterion predicts a yield stress which is $2/\sqrt{3}$ times that given by the Tresca criterion. Experiments have shown that for most metals the test points fall closer to the von Mises yield locus than to the Tresca locus. If the latter is adopted for simplicity, the overall accuracy can be improved by replacing $2k$ in Eq. (6) by mY, where m is an empirical constant lying between 1 and $2/\sqrt{3}$.

Words and Expressions

yield criterion		屈服准则
ductile ['dʌktail]	*adj.*	韧性的,柔软的
hydrostatic pressure		静水压力
initial yield surface		初始屈服面
principal stress		主应力
invariant [in'vɛəriənt]	*n.*	不变量；*adj.* 无变化的,不变的
yield function		屈服函数
deviatoric stress		偏应力
Bauschinger effect		包辛格效应
deviatoric plane		偏平面
isotropy [ai'sɔtrəpi]	*n.*	各向同性
Lode parameter		Lode 参数
pure shear		纯剪切
von Mises yield criterion		冯米赛斯屈服准则
Tresca yield criterion		特雷斯加屈服准则

Reading Material(2): Some Plasticity and Viscoplasticity Constitutive Theories[16]

The constitutive equation of the material is an essential ingredient of any structural calculation. It provides the indispensable relation between the strains and the stresses, which is a linear relation in the case of elastic analyses (Hooke's law) and a much more complex nonlinear relation in inelastic analyses, involving time and additional internal variables.

Here, we limit ourselves to considering the conventional "Continuum" approach, i.e. that the Representative Volume Element (RVE) of material is considered as subject to a near-uniform macroscopic stress. This Continuum assumption is equivalent to neglecting the local heterogeneity of the stresses and strains within the RVE, working with averaged quantities, as the effects of the heterogeneities act only indirectly through a certain number of "internal variables". Moreover, in the framework of the "local state" assumption of Continuum Thermomechanics, it is considered that the state of a material point (and of its immediate vicinity in the sense of the RVE) is independent of that of the neighboring material point. Therefore the stress strain gradients do not enter into the constitutive equations. This assumption is obviously questioned in recent theories of Generalized Continuum Mechanics, that are not addressed here.

The entire presentation will be limited to quasi-static movements considered to be slow enough, in the framework of small perturbations (small strains of less than 10%, for example). Also, the equations indicated will be formulated without explicitly stating the effect of temperature (although this may be very large in certain cases). In other words, in accordance with the common practice for determining the constitutive equations of solid materials, we will assume the temperature is constant (and uniform over the RVE). The effect of the temperature will come into play only by the change of the "material" parameters defining the constitutive equations. Moreover, the above mentioned Continuum Thermodynamic framework will not be considered in detail. Only a few remarks are made as consequences of such a theoretical framework for the temperature rate effect in the hardening rules.

The presentation is more directly oriented toward metallic type materials with elasto-plastic or elasto-viscoplastic properties even though, in a way, viscoelasticity, i.e. the effect of viscosity on elasticity, could be modeled from a viscoplastic model. Among the effects considered, we will thus have: irreversible strain, or plastic strain, the associated phenomena of strain hardening, the time effects, whether they enter by the effect of the loading velocity or through slow time variations of the various variables (static recovery, for example). Aging phenomena (associated with possible changes in the metallurgical structure) and damage effects will be mentioned only briefly. The anelasticity of the metals (very low viscous hysteresis in the "elastic" range), which corresponds to reversible motions of the dislocations, will not be discussed either. Only initially isotropic materials are considered, in which anisotropy is the result of plastic flow and associated hardening processes.

In the present paper, the presentation of constitutive equations is made by following an increasing order of complexity. It can essentially be considered in two parts:
- half the paper addresses to readers who are not too much informed about the plasticity/viscoplasticity framework. It is more or less an introduction to unified viscoplastic constitutive models, mainly based on the works made around the author;
- the second part considers more elaborated aspects, reviewing some other unified viscoplastic constitutive theories, pointing out some similarities and differences.

Other constitutive frameworks are also discussed. The present capabilities of the various kinematic hardening models are compared in the context of predicting ratchetting effects, including modified Armstrong-Frederick based rules as well as multi-surface and two-surface theories.

A special mention here about the Armstrong-Frederick Report that serves of common basis for many kinematic hardening rules. This work was never published, only available as a Technical Report from CEGB (Central Electricity Generating Board). By using this rule in the context of unified viscoplasticity and generalising it continuously, the author contributed to the knowledge and citation of this report. In 2007, it has been published in "Materials at High Temperature", accompanied with a Preface retracing this story.

Let us point out that the review of existing modelling methodologies in the context of cyclic plasticity and viscoplasticity cannot be at all exhaustive. We hope only to provide the indispensable general elements, as well as the main types of modelling. The interested reader should refer to more complete specialized works

The general context of modelling the inelastic behaviour in rate-independent plasticity or in viscoplasticity is supposed to be known, as being sufficiently standard. Many more details and interesting exercises on this current and standard framework can be found in textbooks, like in Khan and Huang (1995). Only the main assumptions and equations are indicated and briefly commented here, as they could be necessary for understanding further developments in the paper.

We assume the small strain framework. This is justified by the domain of application to cyclic loading conditions. The main equations are given below, considering also isothermal conditions. The first equation defines the partition of total strain tensor into an elastic strain and a plastic strain, though the second one gives corresponding Hooke's Law of linear elasticity.

$$\boldsymbol{\varepsilon} = \boldsymbol{\varepsilon}^e + \boldsymbol{\varepsilon}^p \tag{1}$$

$$\boldsymbol{\sigma} = \boldsymbol{L} : (\boldsymbol{\varepsilon} - \boldsymbol{\varepsilon}^p) \tag{2}$$

$$f = \| \boldsymbol{\sigma} - \boldsymbol{X} \|_H - k \leqslant 0 \tag{3}$$

$$\dot{\boldsymbol{\varepsilon}}^p = \dot{\lambda} \frac{\partial f}{\partial \boldsymbol{\sigma}} = \dot{\lambda} \boldsymbol{n} \tag{4}$$

An aside on the notations: the symbol " · " between two tensors designates the product contracted once ($\sigma_{ik}\sigma_{kj} = \sigma_{ij}^2$ with Einstein's summation, represents the square of the tensor $\boldsymbol{\sigma}$); the symbol " : " designates the product contracted twice (for example the scalar $\sigma_{ij}\sigma_{ji} = \text{Tr}\,\boldsymbol{\sigma}^2$).

In the framework of rate-independent plasticity, we need the use of an elasticity domain, $f \leqslant 0$, as given by (3). The yield surface $f = 0$ is defined in (3) with Hill's criterion, using a fourth rank tensor $\boldsymbol{H}$ within a quadratic norm definition as

$$\| \boldsymbol{\sigma} \|_H = \sqrt{\boldsymbol{\sigma} : \boldsymbol{H} : \boldsymbol{\sigma}} \tag{5}$$

More sophisticated yield surface or loading surface definitions could be used.

In Eq. (3) parameter k is the initial yield surface size. Moreover, hardening induced by plastic flow is assumed to be described by a combination of kinematic hardening and isotropic hardening. We use the back-stress $\boldsymbol{X}$ for kinematic hardening and the increase of yield surface size R for the isotropic hardening.

Figures 1 and 2 illustrate, in the deviatoric stress plane and in the uniaxial tension-compression particular case, the transformation of the elastic domain and yield surface by the two particular cases of pure isotropic hardening and pure linear kinematic hardening.

In what follows we also assume the associated plasticity framework (the flow potential is identical with the yield surface) and the normality law (4) expresses the consequence of the maximum dissipation principle. In the rate-independent framework, the plastic multiplier $\dot{\lambda}$ is determined by the consistency condition $f = \dot{f} = 0$.

In case of a viscoplastic behaviour (or rate dependency), the above plasticity framework is generalized by using a viscoplastic potential $\Omega(f)$. The stress state goes beyond the elasticity domain with a positive value of $\sigma_V = f > 0$, that can be called the viscous stress, or the overstress. In that case, normality rule reads:

$$\dot{\boldsymbol{\varepsilon}}^p = \frac{\partial \Omega(f)}{\partial \boldsymbol{\sigma}} = \frac{\partial \Omega}{\partial f} \frac{\partial f}{\partial \boldsymbol{\sigma}} = \dot{p} \frac{\partial f}{\partial \boldsymbol{\sigma}} = \dot{p} \boldsymbol{n} \tag{6}$$

$\dot{\lambda}$ is replaced by $\dot{p}$, the norm of the viscoplastic strain rate, as defined by

$$\dot{p} = \| \dot{\boldsymbol{\varepsilon}}^p \|_{H^{-1}} \tag{7}$$

Therefore, p is the length of the plastic strain path in the plastic strain space.

Let us conclude this brief introduction of the general framework by indicating the particular case where orthotropic Hill's criterion is restricted to von Mises one, with

$$\boldsymbol{H} = \frac{3}{2} \boldsymbol{I}^d = \frac{3}{2}\left(\boldsymbol{I} - \frac{1}{3}\boldsymbol{I} \otimes \boldsymbol{I}\right) \tag{8}$$

where $\boldsymbol{I}$ and $\boldsymbol{I}^d$ are respectively the fourth rank unit tensor and deviatoric projector. In such case, von Mises elastic domain is given by

$$f = \| \boldsymbol{\sigma} - \boldsymbol{X} \| - R - k = \sqrt{\frac{3}{2}(\boldsymbol{\sigma}' - \boldsymbol{X}') : (\boldsymbol{\sigma}' - \boldsymbol{X}')} - R - k \leqslant 0 \tag{9}$$

where $\boldsymbol{\sigma}'$ and $\boldsymbol{X}'$ are deviatoric parts, like $\boldsymbol{\sigma}' = \boldsymbol{\sigma} - \frac{1}{3} Tr\boldsymbol{\sigma} \boldsymbol{I}$. Correspondingly, the direction of the plastic strain rate is

$$\dot{\boldsymbol{\varepsilon}}^p = \frac{\partial \Omega}{\partial \boldsymbol{\sigma}} = \dot{p} \frac{3}{2} \frac{\boldsymbol{\sigma}' - \boldsymbol{X}'}{\| \boldsymbol{\sigma} - \boldsymbol{X} \|} = \dot{p} \boldsymbol{n} \tag{10}$$

The accumulated plastic strain rate then writes

$$\dot{p} = \sqrt{\frac{2}{3} \dot{\boldsymbol{\varepsilon}}^p : \dot{\boldsymbol{\varepsilon}}^p} \tag{11}$$

Let us note that, the yield surface being independent on the first stress invariant, plastic flow does not induce a volume change ($Tr\dot{\boldsymbol{\varepsilon}}^p = 0, \boldsymbol{n}:\boldsymbol{n} = 3/2$). Moreover, any stress state can be broken down into the following form, in which the function $\sigma_V(\dot{p})$ is deduced

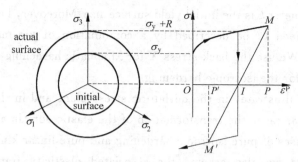

Figure 1　Schematics of the isotropic hardening. Left: in the deviatoric plane; right: the stress vs plastic strain response.

by inversion of the relation $\dot{p}=\partial\Omega/\partial f$.

$$\boldsymbol{\sigma} = \boldsymbol{X} + (R + k + \sigma_V(\dot{p}))\boldsymbol{n} \tag{12}$$

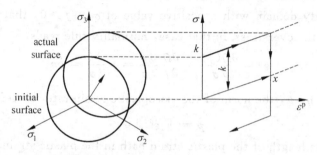

Figure 2　Schematics of the linear kinematic hardening. Left: in the deviatoric plane; right: the stress vs plastic strain response.

Words and Expressions

constitutive theory		本构理论
constitutive equation		本构方程
internal variable		内变量
Representative Volume Element (RVE)		代表性体积单元
heterogeneity [ˌhetərɔdʒi'ni:iti]	n.	非均匀性
thermomechanics [θə:məumi'kæniks]	n.	热力学
quasi-static		准静态,拟静态
hardening rule		强化准则,强化定律
elasto-viscoplastic		弹粘塑性的
viscoelasticity ['viskəuilæs'tisiti]	n.	粘弹性
variable ['vɛəriəbl]	n.	变量
	adj.	可变的
metallurgical [ˌmetə'lə:dʒikl]	adj.	冶金的
hysteresis [ˌhistə'ri:sis]	n.	滞后(现象),滞后作用

dislocation [ˌdɪsləˈkeɪʃən]	n.	位错
anisotropy [ænaɪˈsɒtrəpi]	n.	各向异性
isothermal [ˌaɪsəʊˈθɜːməl]	adj.	等温的
	n.	等温线
plastic flow		塑性流动
kinematic hardening		运动强化
isotropic hardening		各向同性强化
dissipation principle		耗散定理
multiplier [ˈmʌltɪplaɪə]	n.	乘数
viscoplastic potential		粘塑性势

Unit Eight

Experimental Stress Analysis[4]

The primary goal of experimental stress analysis is to help you develop skills to determine the magnitude of stresses analytically. But there are cases in which that is difficult or impossible. Examples include:

- Components that have a complex shape for which the calculation of areas and other geometrical factors needed for stress analysis is difficult.
- The loading patterns and the manner of support may be complex, leading to an inability to compute the appropriate loads at a point of interest.
- Combinations of complex shape and loading may make it difficult to determine where the maximum stress occurs.

Photoelastic Stress Analysis. When a component is basically a two-dimensional shape with a constant thickness, a model of the shape can be produced using a special material that permits the visualization of the stress distribution within the component. The material is typically a transparent plastic that is illuminated while being loaded.

Figure 1-1 shows an example in which a flat bar with a centrally located hole is subjected to an axial load. Variations in the stresses within the bar show as variations in black and white lines and areas in the loaded component. The stress in the main part of the bar away from the hole is nearly uniform and that part shows as a dark field. But in the vicinity of the hole, bands of dark and light areas, called fringes, appear, indicating that a gradient in stress levels occurs around the hole.

Figure 1-1 Photoelastic model of a flat bar with an axial load and a central hole.

Indeed the presence of hole causes higher stress to occur not only because material has been removed from the bar, but also because the change in cross-sectional shape or dimensions occur will produce stress concentrations. Knowing the optical characteristics of the photoelastic material allows the determination of the stress at any point.

Photoelastic Coatings. For more complex three-dimensional shapes it is impossible to model the geometry in the rigid photoelastic material. Also, it is often desired to measure the stress distribution on real solid components such as an engine block, a valve body, or the structure of a large machine. For such cases, a special photoelastic coating material can be applied to the surface of the part. It is molded to follow contours and adhered to the surface. See Figure 1-2(a).

(a) Photoelastic coating being applied to a complex casting

(b) Evaluating a stress pattern in a photoelastic material using polarized light.

Figure 1-2

When the component is loaded, the strains at the surface are transferred to the coating material. A polarized light is then directed at the material and fringes are evident that indicate the gradients in stresses in the actual part. See Figure 1-2 (b). From these observations, you can determine the areas where the maximum stresses occur and compute their approximate values. Then, knowing the general stress distribution and the locations of the highest stress levels, more precise testing can be done if greater accuracy is desired. Strain gaging, described next, is typically used at this time.

Strain Gaging. One of the most frequently used experimental stress analysis devices is the electrical resistance strain gage. It is a very thin metal foil grid made from a strain-sensitive material, such as constantan, with an insulating backing. One style is shown in Figure 1-3 (a). The gage is carefully applied with a special adhesive to the surface of the component where critical stresses are likely to occur. Figure 1-3 (b) shows a typical installation.

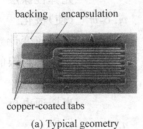

(a) Typical geometry

(b) Strain gage mounted on a flat bar

Figure 1-3 Strain gage-typical geometry and installation

When the component is loaded, the gage experiences the same strains as the surface. The resistance of the gage changes in proportion to the applied strain. The gage is then connected into an electrical measurement circuit called a Wheatstone bridge as illustrated in Figure 1-4. The bridge has four arms and the strain gage is connected as one arm. The other arms contain dummy resistors of the same nominal resistance. When the strain gage is subjected to stain, its resistance changes causing the voltage measured across the diagonal of the bridge to change. The voltage reading can be converted to strain when a calibration factor called the gage factor is applied. For one-directional strain, as due to direct axial tension, you can use Hooke's law to determine stress from,

$$\sigma = E\varepsilon$$

where ε is the strain; E is the tensile modulus of elasticity of the material for the part being tested; σ is the normal stress, either tension or compression.

Other styles of strain gages and other patterns of installation are used for cases that involve more complex stress conditions.

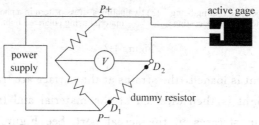

Two-wire circuit for single active gage (quarter bridge)

Figure 1-4 Wheatstone bridge with strain gage installed in one arm.

Words and Expressions

experimental stress analysis		实验应力分析
photoelastic [fəutəui'læstik]	adj.	光弹性的
photoelastic stress analysis		光弹性应力分析
fringe [frindʒ]	n.	条纹
stress concentration		应力集中
photoelastic coating		光弹性涂层
polarize ['pəulə,raiz]	vi.&vt.	(使)极化
electrical resistance strain gage		电阻应变计
constantan ['kɔnstəntæn]	n.	一种铜与镍的合金
insulating backing		绝缘基
Wheatstone bridge		惠斯通电桥
calibration [,kæli'breiʃən]	n.	标定
encapsulation [in,kæpsju'leiʃən]	n.	包装;封装
backing ['bækiŋ]	n.	衬底;基底
dummy resistor		假电阻;仿真电阻
gage factor		应变灵敏度系数
active gage		工作片

科技英语翻译技巧：词义引申和词量增减[31]

1. 词义引申

词义的引申，是指在一个词所具有的基本词义的基础上，进一步加以引申，选择比较恰当的汉语词来表达，使原文的思想表现得更加准确，译文更加通顺流畅。词义的引申主要有词义转译、词义具体化、词义抽象化和考虑词的搭配等四种手段。

(1) 词义转译

遇到一些无法直译或不宜直译的词或词组，应根据上下文和逻辑关系引申转译。

Solar energy seems *to offer more hope than* any other source of energy.

太阳能似乎比其他能源**更有前途**。（不译"提供更多希望"）

(2) 词义具体化

有时应根据汉语的表达习惯，把原文中某些词义较笼统的词引申为词义较具体的词。

The purpose of a driller is *to cut holes*.

钻床的功能是**钻孔**。

(3) 词义抽象化

把原文中词义较具体的词引申为词义较抽象的词，或把词义较形象的词引申为词义较一般的词。

The major contributors to enhance strength and stiffness of the structures are the stiffners.

在增强这些结构强度和刚度中**起主要作用的**是加强筋。（不译"主要贡献者"）

(4) 词的搭配

遇到动词、形容词与名词搭配时，应根据汉语的搭配习惯，而不应受原文字面意义的束缚。

High stress will occur if the cross-section of that cantilever beam is decreased.

如果减小那根悬臂梁的横截面将会出现**大的应力**。（不译"高的应力"）

2. 词量增减

英译汉时往往需要在译文中增加一些原文中无其形而有其意的词，或减去原文中某些在译文中属于多余的词。这种改变原文词量的译法就叫词量增减。

(1) 词量增加

(a) 增补英语中省略的词

Potential energy can be changed into dynamic energy, and dynamic into potential.

势能可以转化为动能，动能**也可以转化**为势能。

(b) 某些句子结构须增加关联词

If A is equal to D, A plus B equals D plus B.

若 A ＝ D，则 A ＋ B ＝ D ＋ B

(c) 增加表示复数的词

A gas exerts the same pressure in a mixture of gases as it would exert alone if it were in the container.

在混合的**几种**气体中，每一种气体所具有的压力与它单独在容器中的压力一样。

(d) 具有动作意义的抽象名词的增译

Oxidation will make iron and steel rusty.

氧化作用会使钢铁生锈。

(e) 逻辑加词，顺理成章

Both the air pressure and temperature decrease with altitude.

气压和温度两者均随海拔高度的增加而下降。

(f) 补充概括性的词

The resistance of the pipe to the flow of water through it depends upon the length of the pipe, the diameter of the pipe, and the feature of the inside walls (rough or smooth).

水管对通过的水流的阻力取决于下列三个因素：管道长度、管道直径、管道内壁的特性（粗糙或光滑）。

(g) 修辞加词，语气连贯

Heat from the sun stirs up the atmosphere, generating winds.

太阳发出的热能搅动大气，于是产生了风。

(2) 词量减少

(a) 冠词的省译

Any substance is made of atoms whether it is *a* solid, *a* liquid, or *a* gas.

任何物质，不论是固体、液体或气体，都是由原子组成。

(b) 介词省略

In the absence *of* force, a body will either remain *at* rest, or continue to move *with* constant speed *in* a straight line.

无外力作用，物体则保持静止状态，或作匀速直线运动。

(c) 人称代词、物主代词、反身代词的省译

A rod lengthens while *it* is pulled.

杆受拉则伸长。

(d) "it" 在某些句型中的省译

It requires 10kN force to speed up the body.（it 作形式主语）

需要 10kN 的力加速该物体。

(e) 连词的省译

Nearly all substances expand when heated *and* contract when cooled.

几乎所有的物质都是热胀冷缩的。

(f) 动词的省译

Some new types of ceramics *possess* good hardness and high strength.

一些新型陶瓷硬度大、强度高。

(g) 关系代词的省译

A force *which* is a vector quantity has three elements.

力是矢量，有三个要素。

(h) 名词的省译

The laws in science are frequently stated in words, but more often in the *form* of equations.

科学定律常用文字表达,但更多的是用公式表达。

◇◇◇◇◇◇◇◇◇◇◇◇◇◇◇◇◇◇◇◇◇◇◇◇◇◇◇◇◇◇◇◇◇◇◇◇◇

Reading Material(1): Strain Gage System[17,18]

Historical, the development of strain gages has followed many different paths and gages have been developed which are based on mechanical, optical, electrical, acoustical and pneumatic principles. No single gage system, regardless of the principle upon which it is based, has all the properties required of an optimum gage. Thus there is a need for a wide variety of gage systems to meet the requirements of a wide range of different engineering problems involving strain measurement.

Some of the characteristics commonly used to judge the adequacy of a strain-gage system for a particular application are the following:

1. The calibration constant for the gage should be stable; it should not vary with time, temperature or other environmental factors.

2. The gage should be able to measure strains with an accuracy of $\pm 1\mu\varepsilon$ over a strain range of $\pm 10\%$.

3. The gage size, i.e., the gage length L_0 and width W_0, should be small so that strain at a point is approximated with small error.

4. The response of the gage, largely controlled by its inertia, should be sufficient to permit recording of dynamic strains with frequency components exceeding 200 kHz.

5. The gage system should permit on-location or remote readout.

6. The output from the gage during the readout period should be independent of temperature and other environmental parameters.

7. The gage and the associated auxiliary equipment should both be inexpensive to enable wide usage.

8. The gage system should be easy to install and operate.

9. The gage should exhibit a linear response to strain over a wide range.

10. The gage should be suitable for use as the sensing element in other transducer systems where an unknown quantity such as pressure is measured in terms of strain.

No single strain-gage system satisfies all of these characteristics. However, a strain-gage system for a particular application can be selected after proper consideration is given to each of these characteristics in terms of the requirements of the measurement to be made. Over the last 60 years a large number of systems, with wide variations in design, have been conceived, developed and marketed. Each of these systems has four basic characteristics that deserve additional consideration; namely, the gage length L_0, gage sensitivity, range of strain measurement and accuracy.

Brief History

Although it was Lord Kelvin who, in 1856, first discovered that the resistance of an electrical conductor changed when it was stretched, it was not until the late 1930s that the principle of the use of a grid of fine resistance wire bonded to a test surface as a means of measuring strain was suggested by Edward Simmons at the California Institute of Technology, and Professor Arthur C. Ruge, quite independently, developed a wire strain gauge at Massachusetts Institute of Technology (MIT).

Interestingly enough, however, in early 1939, Professor Ruge was advised by the Chairman of the Patent Committee of MIT that "while this development [Resistance Strain Gauges, Wire Type] is interesting, the Committee does not feel that the commercial use is likely to be of major importance!"

The strain sensitivity of resistance wires had, however, first been developed and utilised some years prior to this by Roy Carlson in the unbonded wire strain gauge. This consisted of an arrangement of wire, wound around a series of pins actuated by linkages, any movement of which stretched the wire and changed its resistance. This was essentially an electrical extensometer, and the principle is still used today in some special types of transducers.

It is also important to acknowledge the first use of a bonded resistance strain gauge device in the early 1930s. This consisted of a carbon composition resistor on an insulating strip, used by Charles Kearns of Hamilton Standard to measure vibratory strains in high performance propeller blades for aircraft. The carbon gauge was, however, limited to the indication of dynamic strains, and could measure these to only a moderate degree of accuracy, owing to the lack of resistance stability with time and temperature.

During World War II, strain gauge measurements were being widely used for structural testing in the aircraft industry. A letter in November 1943 to Professor Ruge from the then American NACA Director of Aeronautical Research concluded "There should be no doubt that each of these apparently insignificant bundles of wire and scraps of paper is contributing much to the success of thousands of our military aeroplanes".

They continued to be used mainly in the aircraft industry for a number of years, and it was the requirements of this industry that led to the significantly important development of the foil type of strain gauge in 1952. The Saunders-Roe Company in the UK was seeking improvements in the bonded wire gauges, which were presenting problems in harsh testing environments on helicopters and flying boats. At that time, printed circuit techniques were appearing, and Peter Scott-Jackson of Saunders-Roe developed the idea of making a strain gauge by etching the grid from a thin foil of the appropriate resistance material. Foil gauge manufacture was commenced in co-operation with Technograph Printed Circuits Ltd, and they were found to have a number of distinct advantages, and were rapidly adopted, particularly by manufacturers and users in the USA. It opened the way for much more extensive industrial use of strain gauge techniques, and today the foil gauge is by far the most widely used type.

Variations of the foil strain gauge are produced by die cutting, as opposed to etching, and by vacuum deposition techniques. The majority of development effort since the introduction of the foil gauge has, however, been toward improved control and understanding of strain gauge materials, characteristics and design.

Wire Strain Gauges

The original "paper-backed" wire strain gauge consisted typically of a grid of resistance wire wound on a special jig, to which the paper backing, coated with nitrocellulose cement, was attached (Fig. 1(a)). The grid was normally covered with another layer of paper, and the assembly completely impregnated with the nitrocellulose to give it strength and flexibility. The bottom layer of paper also serves the very important purpose of electrically insulating the grid from the bonding surface, and in some cases the top layer of paper is replaced by a thin felt pad. General purpose wire gauges usually employ measuring grids of approximately 0.02mm diameter copper-nickel wire, and an overall thickness approximately 0.1mm in the grid area.

Because it would be difficult to attach instrumentation wires in the field to the fine diameter wire used in the grid, heavier wires of about 0.2mm diameter are soldered to the grid for connection to the signal wires after gauge installation.

Many other types of wire gauges exist, involving different features to better meet special performance requirements. Replacing the paper-nitrocellulose backing with glass fibre and thermosetting resins, such as the epoxies or phenolics already discussed, extends the useful temperature range of the gauge. The grid may be of alloys other than copper-nickel for improved performance at very high or very low temperatures, or to exhibit better fatigue life under cyclic strain at high strain levels.

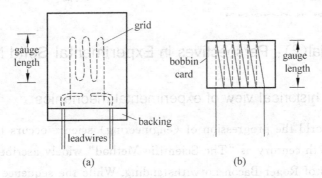

Fig. 1 Wire strain gauge outline. (a) flat-grid type; (b) wraparound grid type

An alternative form of one of the early types of strain gauge construction is the "wraparound" or bobbin type, in which the grid is wound on a porous bobbin card about 0.05mm thick, covered with layers of paper adhered to both sides of the bobbin. Wraparound gauges are easier and cheaper to make, especially in smaller sizes, but performance of this type is inferior to the flat-grid construction, because the gauge is much thicker, and strain transmission poorer. Wraparound grid construction is illustrated in Fig. 1(b).

Words and Expressions

strain gage		应变计
pneumatic [njuː'mætik]	adj.	气动的；充气的
calibration constant		标定常数
transducer [træns'djuːsə]	n.	传感器
extensometer [ˌeksten'sɔmitə]	n.	伸长计；引伸计
printed circuit technique		印刷电路技术
etch [etʃ]	vt.	蚀刻
foil strain gauge		箔氏应变计
vacuum deposition technique		真空淀积技术
wire strain gauge		金属丝应变计
impregnate [im'pregneit]	vt.	注入，使充满；adj. 充满的
nitrocellulose ['naitrəu'seljuləus]	n.	硝化纤维素
felt pad		毛毡坐垫
solder ['sɔldə]	n.	焊接剂；接合剂
thermosetting resin		热固性树脂
epoxy [ep'ɔksi]	n.	环氧树脂
	adj.	环氧(化物)的
phenolics [fi'nɔliks]	n.	酚醛树脂
wraparound ['ræpə,raund]	adj.	围绕的；围绕物
bobbin ['bɔbin]	n.	线轴

Reading Material(2): Perspectives in Experimental Solid Mechanics[19]

An abbreviated historical view of experimental mechanics

In an ideal world the progression of (engineering) science occurs through a process identified in the 17th century as "The Scientific Method" widely ascribed to Galileo, the 13th century ideas of Roger Bacon notwithstanding. While the sequence of experimental/theoretical activity is not necessarily always clear a priori, the essence of the "method" consists in observing physical fact(s) and formulating an analytical framework for them to produce a scheme or theory by which other physical results can be predicted.

Important in the qualification for "theory" under this concept is that "predicted" facts must arise under circumstances separate from those which produced the original data and parameters; they must thus be in addition to those used to formulate the theory. Stated in a more graphic manner, a model first requires data to determine the physical parameters derived from a sufficiently broadly construed experiment or measurements, but does not become a theory until its predictive power is tested on data which are not part of the measurements that determined the original parameters of the proposed theory. The theory gains in respect and (quantitative) applicability as the number of situations, on which it is successfully tested, increases. Without this additional experimental examination an analytical framework does not become a theory but represents merely a data-fit. In this sense experimental data do not verify a theory, they simply add more credence to a reasonable construct of an analytical framework, if they transcend the establishment of the necessary parameters characterizing the model.

James Bell has made the observation that advances in the sciences move in spurts, and that the interaction between theory and experiment is not always in phase. Following the highly successful though largely empirical (trial and error) evolution of magnificent edifice construction from the Egyptian through the Gothic and Renaissance periods, attempts at an analytical formulation of failure (stress) analysis were initiated, as illustrated, for example, by Galileo, even if this first attempt was ultimately not correct in detail. To deal with the emerging problem formulations, roughly, the next phase comprised the evolution of describing the constitutive behavior for (isotropic) solids under the "guidance" of the one-constant theory during the early 19th century. This phase was simultaneously and consecutively enlarged by studies of nonlinear and inelastic material responses. However, it was not until the linearly elastic stress-strain behavior (approximation) was firmed up that the analytical development of the (mathematical) theory of elasticity could develop and burgeon, a process which has then dominated roughly half of the first of the 20th century. Although the time scale of such phases shortens in the same exponential manner as developments in science and engineering do in general, experimentation and analytical developments have interacted more closely for various reasons during the middle of this century in mechanics, being driven largely by the new developments in fracture, in structural instability and in high rate deformation response of solids.

Discussions on the mutually interactive roles of experiment and theory in modern mechanics have been offered repeatedly during the last decades. Because the holy grail(s) of mechanics seems to be the proclamation of a new theory, these writers also uniformly sense the low esteem often accorded the experimentalist's contribution to mechanics and misconceptions regarding the proper interaction between experiment and theory. For example, in identifying the primary aim of mechanics (stress analysis) as the improved understanding and determination of strength, Hetenyi states in the preface to his volume on Experimental Stress Analysis that:

"Experimental stress analysis strives to achieve these aims by experimental means. In doing so, it does not remain, however, a mere counterpart of theoretical methods of stress analysis but encompasses those, utilizing all the conclusions reached by theoretical considerations, and goes far beyond them in maintaining direct contact with the true physical characteristics of the problem under consideration."

In a similar vein, Drucker reminds us in the 1960's of the basic function of experiment in that:

"...all too often, experimental work in applied mechanics is thought of only as a check on existing theory or as a convenient substitute for analysis. This is a valid but rather inferior function of experiment. The greater and essential contribution is to guide the development of theory, by providing the fundamental basis for an understanding of the real world."

This is followed in 1973 by Bell's even more differentiating remarks, presented in the context of an enlightening review of the role of experimental mechanics since the beginning of the 19th century, that:

"It is essential to view the role of the experimentist as somewhat different from the currently accepted image... Since within some degree of precision several theories based upon different assumptions, may square with the same experiment; and, since in any given situation only one such theory may be currently available, with adjacent theory or theories yet to be produced; it is obvious that an experimentist does not "verify" theories. Moreover, in as much as adjacent theories are based upon different sets of initial assumptions, it is fallacious to presume that a correlation between data and prediction implies the validity of any one set of such assumptions."

It is thus surprising how attitudes have remained constant over the past quarter century. The issues seem to have remained the same in spite of the tremendous changes that have occurred in the details which mechanics has developed for addressing experimental and analytical problems in engineering.

Experimental methods and opportunities

The evolution of experimental tools has been a fundamentally enabling aspect for mechanics. Although we tend to think today that modern technology provides the mainstay for refined experimental procedures, it is quite enlightening that our forebears were able to make highly accurate measurements more than a century and a half ago. Thus interferometry allowed strains of 10^{-6} to be measured in the first half of the 19th century, and Gruneisen was able to improve those measurements to strains as small as 10^{-8} around the end of that century. Nevertheless, the advances in technology have made measurement methods much more convenient, and have fostered a tremendous proliferation of tools offering a large range of precision. Although it is beyond the scope of this presentation to address and analyze even the major methods in use today, it is appropriate to at least list them and refer the reader to more detailed documentation in the open literature.

One can separate methods roughly into two types, namely those that generate primarily information at a point on a solid, and those which produce field information. Amongst the former we find principally the (wire, foil and semiconductor) strain gages in unidirectional and rosette form; accelerometers as used in structural vibration (modal analysis) problems; and acoustic emitters/sensors which can also be arranged to function in a scanning mode to render field information. A particularly refined form of these is the acoustic microscope, which allows field examination inside a solid, but only in domains the depth of which are measured in millimeters or microns from the surface, depending on the frequency used: the high sound wave attenuation in virtually all materials at the high frequencies used (gigahertz) forces a trade-off between resolution and depth of observation. Finally, the optical shadow method or method of caustics also falls into this category, although it samples field information but delivers a single value (possibly as a function of time).

Most of the methods producing field information are optical in nature and are thus, practically speaking, limited in resolution by the wavelength of the light used, although many of them cannot approach that limit for other reasons. They comprise photoelasticity, moire and shadow moire, holography and speckle interferometry, heterodyning, gradient sensing, [Twyman-Green] interferometry, moire interferometry, and thermography. The information is obtained typically in the form of fringe fields that have yielded historically spatial resolutions on the order of a millimeter(s). This spatial resolution can be improved with the aid of computer processing, once improved reliable codes for representing fringes numerically have been established.

Perhaps the interferometric and moire interferometric methods deserve special attention because of their power to resolve displacements measured in terms of the wavelength of light ($\sim$ one micron) and because of their potential (when used carefully) for high spatial resolution of the displacement field. These two methods also illustrate the evolution of experimental methods over the last 100 years and thus demonstrate how the need in a certain science field (solid mechanics) culls a new method (moire interferometry) from a well established physical principle for a special application. As long as the surface normal remains so within 2° a spatial resolution of 5-10 microns is readily achievable by moire interferometry for in-plane displacements. Out-of-plane deformations of a micron or two are standard with interferometry. Because of this high resolution power of moire interferometry, it has been an important addition to the repertoire of tools for experiments and became thus a favorite tool for refined deformation measurements on electronic micro chips; in this connection this method has served virtually the same purpose for these small devices as photoelasticity has for the larger engineering structures during the middle of this century; the major difference being that photoelasticity addresses the stress state more directly than moire interferometry, which renders displacements.

Thermography is feasible for point as well as field measurements. In the first mode it is often used for high speed events because full field representation is too slow or too expensive with available technology. However, at 30 to 50 frames per second, full field thermal images can be captured today with commercially available "Thermal Camera" equipment.

A relatively new method for determining displacements and strains has evolved through the significant power of (desk) computers, the Digital Image Correlation method. First considered in the context of fluid mechanics investigations, this non-contact method records images of (shadows of) surface irregularities or painted-on spots before and after deformation. By postulating a (large deformation) continuum transformation for image points between these two states, which contain rigid body motions and local strains as parameters, the latter are determined such that a correlation function, connecting the deformed and undeformed states, is minimized. The capability of this method depends somewhat on the gradients of the strain field because a large field of view containing a (nearly) constantstrain field provides a larger "gage length" than a strain field that changes over a short distance. Improvements in the resolution capability are desired, since, typically, current values are limited (with some difficulty) to strains larger than 0.0005.

This new DIC imaging method is a potential boon to investigations at extremely small size scales, namely micro- and nano-mechanics. Along with the means of the Scanning Electron and the Transmission Electron Microscopes (SEMs and TEMs) the more recent arrival of probe microscopy (Scanning Tunneling and Atomic Force Microscopes) spatial resolution down to the atomic level is becoming available. These are the size domains that need to be addressed in order to resolve issues in what is often called meso-mechanics which ostensibly covers problem areas where the distinctions between classical continuum mechanics and atomic or discrete molecular formulations are essential. While these tools have a standing history in terms of providing images (rendition of topography), the major means of translating these images into displacement fields was offered through stereoscopic recording, with strain determinations limited to subsequent numerical differentiation. In contrast, the DIC method allows the simultaneous determination of displacements and their gradients. Inasmuch as SEMs, TEMs, STMs and AFMs yield pixelated images, the DIC method is a natural tool to evaluate such data. Attempts at extending that method in combination with the SEM are currently underway at Yale University.

Words and Expressions

formulate [ˈfɔːmjuleit]	vt.	公式化，用公式描述
trial and error		试错
holy grail		圣杯；圣盘
fallacious [fəˈleiʃəs]	adj.	谬误的；不合理的
interferometry [ˌɪntəfəˈrɒmitə]	n.	干涉测量法
rosette [rəuˈzet]	n.	玫瑰花形物
accelerometer [ækˌseləˈrɒmitə]	n.	加速度计
modal analysis		模态分析
acoustic emitter		声发射器
scanning mode		扫描方式

gigahertz [ˈgigəhəːts]	n.	十亿赫兹，千兆赫
trade-off	n.	权衡；取舍
holography [həuˈlɔgrəfi]	n.	全息照相技术
speckle interferometry		散斑干涉法
heterodyning [ˈhetərəuˌdainiŋ]	n.	外差作用
thermography [θəːˈmɔgrəfi]	n.	温度记录法；热熔印刷
cull [kʌl]	vt.	剔除
	n.	剔除
out-of-plane	n.	面外
repertoire [ˈrepətwaː]	n.	全部节目；全部技能
thermal camera		热感照相机
digital image correlation		数字图像相关
imaging method		成像法
nano-mechanics		纳米力学
micro-mechanics		微观力学
meso-mechanics		细观力学
macro-mechanics		宏观力学
Scanning Electron Microscope (SEM)		扫描电子显微镜
Transmission Electron Microscope (TEM)		透射电子显微镜
Atomic Force Microscope		原子力显微镜
Scanning Tunneling Microscope		扫描隧道电子显微镜
ostensibly [ɔsˈtensəbli]	adv.	表面上地；外表上地
rendition [renˈdiʃən]	n.	解释；演奏；投降
topography [təˈpɔgrəfi]	n.	地质，地形学
stereoscopic [ˌsteriəsˈkɔpik]	adj.	有立体感的
inasmuch [inəzˈmʌtʃ]	adv.	由于；因为
moire [mwaː]	n.	云纹
shadow moire		影栅云纹
moire interferometry		云纹干涉法
pixelate	vt.	使……像素化；将……分解成像素

Unit Nine

Direct Formulation of Finite Element Characteristics[20]

The "prescriptions" for deriving the characteristics of a "finite element" of a continuum, which were outlined in general terms, will now be presented in more detailed mathematical form.

It is desirable to obtain results in a general form applicable to any situation, but to avoid introducing conceptual difficulties the general relations will be illustrated with a very simple example of plane stress analysis of a thin slice. In this a division of the region into triangular-shaped elements may be used as shown in Fig. 1.1. Alternatively, regions may be divided into rectangles or, indeed using a combination of triangles and rectangles.

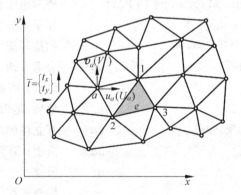

Fig. 1.1 A plane stress region divided into finite element

Displacement function

A typical finite element, e, with a triangular shape is defined by local nodes 1, 2 and 3, and straight line boundaries between the nodes as shown in Fig. 1.2(a). Similarly, a rectangular element could be defined by local nodes 1, 2, 3 and 4 as shown in Fig. 1.2(b). The choice of displacement functions for each element is of paramount importance and later we will show how they may be developed for a wide range of types; however, here we will consider only the 3-node triangular and 4-node rectangular element shapes.

Let the displacements u at any point within the element be approximated as a column vector, $\hat{\boldsymbol{u}}$:

$$\boldsymbol{u} \approx \hat{\boldsymbol{u}} = \sum_a \boldsymbol{N}_a \tilde{\boldsymbol{u}}_a^e = [\boldsymbol{N}_1, \boldsymbol{N}_2, \cdots] \begin{Bmatrix} \tilde{\boldsymbol{u}}_1 \\ \tilde{\boldsymbol{u}}_2 \\ \vdots \end{Bmatrix}^e = \boldsymbol{N} \tilde{\boldsymbol{u}} \qquad (1.1)$$

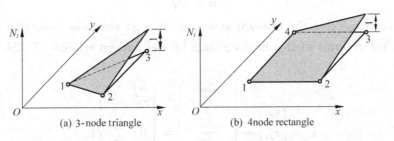

(a) 3-node triangle (b) 4node rectangle

Fig. 1.2 Shape function N_3 for one element

In the case of plane stress, for instance,

$$\boldsymbol{u} = \begin{Bmatrix} u(x, y) \\ v(x, y) \end{Bmatrix}$$

represents horizontal and vertical movements (see Fig. 1.1) of a typical point within the element and

$$\tilde{\boldsymbol{u}}_a = \begin{Bmatrix} \tilde{u}_a \\ \tilde{v}_a \end{Bmatrix}$$

the corresponding displacements of a node a.

The functions N_a, $a = 1, 2, \cdots$ are called shape functions (or basis functions, and, occasionally interpolation functions) and must be chosen to give appropriate nodal displacements when coordinates of the corresponding nodes are inserted in Eq. (1.1). Clearly in general we have

$$\boldsymbol{u}_a(x_a, y_a) = \boldsymbol{I} \quad \text{(identity matrix)}$$

while

$$\boldsymbol{u}_a(x_b, y_b) = 0, \quad a \neq b$$

If both components of displacement are specified in an identical manner then we can write

$$\boldsymbol{u}_a = N_a \boldsymbol{I} \qquad (1.2)$$

and obtain N_a from Eq. (1.1) by noting that $N_a(x_a, y_a) = 1$ but is zero at other vertices. The shape functions N will be seen later to play a paramount role in finite element analysis.

Strains

With displacements known at all points within the element the "strains" at any point can be determined. These will always result in a relationship that can be written in matrix notation as

$$\boldsymbol{\varepsilon} = \boldsymbol{S} \boldsymbol{u} \qquad (1.3)$$

where S is a suitable linear differential operator. Using Eq. (1.1), the above equation can be approximated by

$$\varepsilon \approx \hat{\varepsilon} = B \tilde{u}^e \qquad (1.4)$$

with

$$B = SN \qquad (1.5)$$

For the plane stress case the relevant strains of interest are those occurring in the plane and are defined in terms of the displacements by well-known relations 6 which define the operator S

$$\varepsilon = \left\{ \begin{array}{c} \varepsilon_x \\ \varepsilon_y \\ \gamma_{xy} \end{array} \right\} = \left\{ \begin{array}{c} \dfrac{\partial u}{\partial x} \\ \dfrac{\partial v}{\partial y} \\ \dfrac{\partial u}{\partial y} + \dfrac{\partial v}{\partial x} \end{array} \right\} = \left[\begin{array}{cc} \dfrac{\partial}{\partial x} & 0 \\ 0 & \dfrac{\partial}{\partial y} \\ \dfrac{\partial}{\partial y} & \dfrac{\partial}{\partial x} \end{array} \right] \left\{ \begin{array}{c} u \\ v \end{array} \right\}$$

With the shape functions N_1, N_2 and N_3 already determined for a triangular element, the matrix B can easily be obtained using (1.5). If the linear form of the shape functions is adopted then, in fact, the strains are constant throughout the element (i.e., the B matrix is constant).

A similar result may be obtained for the rectangular element by adding the results for N_4; however, in this case the strains are not constant but have linear terms in x and y.

Stresses

In general, the material within the element boundaries may be subjected to initial strains such as those due to temperature changes, shrinkage, crystal growth, and so on. If such strains are denoted by ε_0 then the stresses will be caused by the difference between the actual and initial strains.

In addition it is convenient to assume that at the outset of the analysis the body is stressed by some known system of initial residual stresses σ_0 which, for instance, could be measured, but the prediction of which is impossible without the full knowledge of the material's history. These stresses can simply be added on to the general definition. Thus, assuming linear elastic behaviour, the relationship between stresses and strains will be linear and of the form

$$\sigma = D(\varepsilon - \varepsilon_0) + \sigma_0 \qquad (1.6)$$

where D is an elasticity matrix containing the appropriate material properties.

Again for the particular case of plane stress three components of stress corresponding to the strains already defined have to be considered. These are, in familiar notation,

$$\sigma = \left\{ \begin{array}{c} \sigma_x \\ \sigma_y \\ \tau_{xy} \end{array} \right\}$$

and for an isotropic material the D matrix may be simply obtained from the usual stress-strain relationship

$$\varepsilon_x - \varepsilon_{x0} = \frac{1}{E}(\sigma_x - \sigma_{x0}) - \frac{\nu}{E}(\sigma_y - \sigma_{y0})$$

$$\varepsilon_y - \varepsilon_{y0} = -\frac{\nu}{E}(\sigma_x - \sigma_{x0}) + \frac{1}{E}(\sigma_y - \sigma_{y0})$$

$$\gamma_{xy} - \gamma_{xy0} = \frac{2(1+\nu)}{E}(\tau_{xy} - \tau_{xy0})$$

i. e. on solving,

$$\boldsymbol{D} = \frac{E}{1-\nu^2}\begin{bmatrix} 1 & \nu & 0 \\ \nu & 1 & 0 \\ 0 & 0 & (1-\nu)/2 \end{bmatrix}$$

Equivalent nodal forces

Let

$$\boldsymbol{q}^e = \begin{Bmatrix} \boldsymbol{q}_1^e \\ \boldsymbol{q}_2^e \\ \vdots \end{Bmatrix}$$

define the nodal forces which are statically equivalent to the boundary stresses and distributed body forces acting on the element. Each of the forces $\boldsymbol{q}_a^e$ must contain the same number of components as the corresponding nodal displacement $\tilde{\boldsymbol{u}}_a$ and be ordered in the appropriate, corresponding directions.

The distributed body forces $\boldsymbol{b}$ are defined as those acting on a unit volume of material within the element with directions corresponding to those of the displacements $\boldsymbol{u}$ at that point.

In the particular case of plane stress the nodal forces are, for instance,

$$\boldsymbol{q}_a^e = \begin{Bmatrix} U_a^e \\ V_a^e \end{Bmatrix}$$

with components U and V corresponding to the directions of u and v, respectively (viz. Fig. 1.1), and the distributed body forces are

$$\boldsymbol{b} = \begin{Bmatrix} b_x \\ b_y \end{Bmatrix}$$

in which b_x and b_y are the "body force" components per unit of volume.

In the absence of body forces equivalent nodal forces for the 3-node triangular element can be computed directly from equilibrium considerations. In Fig. 1.3(a) we show a triangular element together with the geometric properties which are obtained by the linear interpolation of the displacements. In particular we note from the figure that

$$b_1 + b_2 + b_3 = 0 \quad \text{and} \quad c_1 + c_2 + c_3 = 0$$

The stresses in the element are given by (1.6) in which we assume that ε_0 and σ_0 are constant in each element and strains are computed from (1.4) and, for the 3-node triangular element, are also constant in each element. To determine the nodal forces resulting from the stresses, the boundary tractions are first computed from

$$t = \begin{Bmatrix} t_x \\ t_y \end{Bmatrix} = t \begin{bmatrix} n_x & 0 & n_y \\ 0 & n_y & n_x \end{bmatrix} \begin{Bmatrix} \sigma_x \\ \sigma_y \\ \tau_{xy} \end{Bmatrix} \quad (1.7)$$

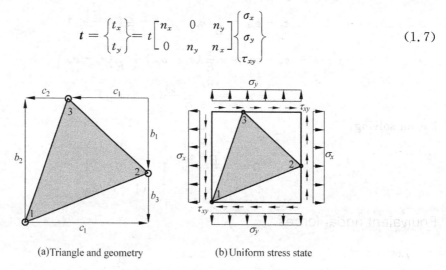

(a) Triangle and geometry (b) Uniform stress state

Fig. 1.3 3-node triangle, geometry and constant stress state

where t is a constant thickness of the plane strain slice and n_x, n_y are the direction cosines of the outward normal to the element boundary. For the triangular element the tractions are constant. The resultant for each side of the triangle is the product of the triangle side length (l_a) times the traction. Here l_a is the length of the side opposite the triangle node a and we note from Fig. 1.3(a) that

$$l_a n_x = -b_a \quad \text{and} \quad l_a n_y = -c_a \quad (1.8)$$

Therefore,

$$l_a t = \begin{Bmatrix} l_a t_x \\ l_a t_y \end{Bmatrix} = t \begin{bmatrix} -b_a & 0 & -c_a \\ 0 & -c_a & -b_a \end{bmatrix} \begin{Bmatrix} \sigma_x \\ \sigma_y \\ \tau_{xy} \end{Bmatrix}$$

The resultant acts at the middle of each side of the triangle and, thus, by sum of forces and moments is equivalent to placing half at each end node. Thus, by static equivalence the nodal forces at node 1 are given by

$$q_1 = \frac{t}{2} \left\{ \begin{bmatrix} -b_2 & 0 & -c_2 \\ 0 & -c_2 & -b_2 \end{bmatrix} + \begin{bmatrix} -b_3 & 0 & -c_3 \\ 0 & -c_3 & -b_3 \end{bmatrix} \right\} \sigma$$

$$= \frac{t}{2} \begin{bmatrix} -b_1 & 0 & -c_1 \\ 0 & -c_1 & -b_1 \end{bmatrix} \sigma = \boldsymbol{B}_1^T \sigma \Delta t \quad (1.9a)$$

Similarly, the forces at nodes 2 and 3 are given by

$$q_2 = \boldsymbol{B}_2^T \sigma \Delta t$$
$$q_2 = \boldsymbol{B}_3^T \sigma \Delta t \quad (1.9b)$$

Combining with the expression for stress and strain for each element we obtain

$$q = \boldsymbol{B}^T [\boldsymbol{D}(|\boldsymbol{B}\tilde{\boldsymbol{u}}^e - \varepsilon_0|) + \sigma_0] \Delta t$$
$$= \boldsymbol{K}^e \tilde{\boldsymbol{u}}^e + \boldsymbol{f}^e \quad (1.10a)$$

where

$$\boldsymbol{K}^e = \boldsymbol{B}^{\mathrm{T}} \boldsymbol{D} \boldsymbol{B} \Delta t \quad \text{and} \quad \boldsymbol{f}^e = \boldsymbol{B}^{\mathrm{T}} (\sigma_0 - \boldsymbol{D} \varepsilon_0) \Delta t \qquad (1.10b)$$

The above gives a result which is now in the form of the standard discrete problem. However, when body forces are present or we consider other element forms the above procedure fails and we need a more general approach. To make the nodal forces statically equivalent to the actual boundary stresses and distributed body forces, the simplest general procedure is to impose an arbitrary (virtual) nodal displacement and to equate the external and internal work done by the various forces and stresses during that displacement.

Words and Expressions

finite element		有限单元
displacement function		位移函数
shape function		形状函数
basis function		基函数
interpolation function		插值函数
nodal displacement		节点位移
identity matrix		单位矩阵
differential operator		微分算符
shrinkage ['ʃriŋkidʒ]	n.	收缩;减少;损耗
initial residual stress		初始残余应力
elasticity matrix		弹性矩阵
equivalent nodal force		等效节点力
linear interpolation		线性插值
direction cosine		方向余弦
product ['prɔdəkt]	n.	乘积
discrete [di'skri:t]	adj.	离散的

科技英语翻译技巧:词性的转换和句子成分转换[31]

1. 词性的转换

由于英汉两种语言属于不同的语系,在语言结构与表达形式方面各有其特点,因而要使译文既忠实于原意又顺畅可读,就不能局限于逐词对等,必须采用适当的词性转换。

(1) 转换成汉语动词

(a) 英语名词化结构及动名词一般均可译成汉语的动词。

Transformation of chemical energy into mechanical energy moves vechile.

化学能**转化**为机械能驱动汽车运行。

(b) 英语的介词在很多情况下,尤其是构成状语时,往往译成动词。

Response of a bridge under any dynamic load can be simulated *by* the finite element method.

桥梁在任何动载荷作用下的响应都可**利用**有限元方法模拟。

(c) 作表语的形容词可转译成动词。

A rigid body is not *deformable*.

刚体不能**变形**。

(d) 副词作表语时可转译为动词。

The thermal stress increases while temperature is *up*.

温度**升高**,热应力就增大。

(2) 转换成汉语名词

(a) 某些英语动词的概念难以直接用汉语的动词表达,翻译时可转换成名词。

This rubber is *characterized* by good insulation and high resistance to wear.

这种橡胶的**特点**是：绝缘性好,耐磨性强。

(b) 某些表示事物特征的形容词作表语时可将其转译成名词,其后往往加上"性"、"度"、"体"等,带有定冠词的某些形容词用作名词,应译成名词。

The cutting tool must be *strong*, *hard*, *tough*, and *wear resistant*.

刀具必须具有足够的**强度**、**硬度**、**韧性**和**耐磨性**。

(c) 英语中大量使用代词,汉语则不然,为了使概念清楚,符合汉语表达习惯,可将代词译成所代替的名词。

The accuracy of this new method is much better than *those* of previous ones.

这种新方法的精度比以往那些方法的**精度**高得多。

(d) 将某些副词转译成汉语的名词使译文更加顺畅。

Low carbon steel behaves *plastically* above their elastic range.

超过弹性极限时,低碳钢会表现出**塑性**。

(3) 转换成汉语形容词

(a) 修饰动词的副词,由于动词转换成名词,因而可相应地转译成形容词。

This sturcture is *chiefly characterized* by its light weight and good stability.

这种结构的**主要特点**是重量轻,稳定性好。

(b) 修饰形容词的副词,由于形容词转换成名词,因而可相应地转译成形容词。

It is demonstrated that gases are *perfectly* elastic.

已经证实,气体具有**理想的**弹性。

(c) 副词作定语修饰名词,译成形容词。

The equations *below* are derived from those *above*.

下面的方程式是由**上面的**那些方程式推导出来的。

(d) 有时把名词译成形容词更符合汉语的表达习惯。

This experiment was a *success*.

这个试验是**成功的**。

(4) 转换成汉语副词

(a) 修饰名词的形容词,由于名词转换成动词,因而相应地转译成副词。

The application of rebars in concretes makes for a *tremendous* rise in strength.

在混凝土中加入钢筋可以**大大地**提高强度。

(b) 为了使译文符合汉语习惯,有时形容词、动词应转译为副词。
The spring is *free* to vibrate after releasing external force.
释放外力后,弹簧可以**自由地**振动。
Damping in a dynamic system *tends* to make the vibration amplitude attenuate with time.
动力系统中的阻尼,**往往**使振动幅值随时间衰减。

2. 句子成分转换

句子成分转换是指词类不变而成分改变的译法。通过改变原文中某些句子成分,以达到译文逻辑正确,通顺流畅,重点突出等目的。

(1) 转译成主语

(a) 宾语转译成主语(动词宾语和介词宾语)

Water has a *density* of 1000 kilogram per cubic meter.
水的**密度**是 $1000 kg/m^3$。
Aluminum is very light in *weight*, being only one third as heavy as iron.
铝的**重量**很轻,只有铁的三分之一。

(b) 表语转译成主语

Rubber is a better *dielectric* but a poorer *insulator* than air.
橡胶的**介电性**比空气好,但**绝缘性**比空气差。

(c) 谓语转译成主语

Gases *differ* from solids in that the former have greater compressibility than the latter.
气体和固体的**区别**,在于前者比后者有更大的可压缩性。

(d) 状语转译成主语

Sodium is very active *chemically*.
钠的**化学反应性**很强。

(2) 转译成谓语

(a) 主语转译成谓语(以 case, need, attention, emphasis, improvement 等名词及名词化结构作主语时,常这样处理)

The *prevention* of certain types of damage in structures is possible.
结构中某些损伤可以**预防**。

(b) 表语转译成谓语

Also *present* in solids are numbers of free electrons.
固体中也**存在**着大量的自由电子。

(c) 定语转译成谓语(进行这种转换往往是为了突出定语所表达的内容)

This material has a *poor* elasticity at high temperature, but they may become a good elastor at room temperature.
这种材料在高温下弹性**差**,但在室温下,它可能成为好的弹性体。

(d) 状语转译成谓语

Advance in solid mechanics affects *tremendously* the development of other engineering disciplines.

固体力学的进展对其他工程学科的发展影响**极大**。

（3）转译成定语

(a) 主语转译成定语

Electronic circuits work a thousand times more rapidly than nerve cells in the human brain.

电子电路的工作速度比人类大脑中的神经细胞要快一千倍。

(b) 状语转译成定语

In Britain the first stand-by gas-turbine electricity generator was in operation in Manchester in 1952.

英国的第一台辅助燃气轮发电机于1952年在曼彻斯特开始运转。

(c) 宾语转译成定语

By 1914 Einstein had gained *world fame*.

1914年爱因斯坦已成了**著名的**科学家。

（4）转译成状语

(a) 定语转译成状语

It was an amazing piece of *scientific* clairvoyance, comparable perhaps to Charles Babbage's anticipation of the principle of the computer.

这个理论在**科学上**充满了远见卓识，也许可以跟巴贝奇的计算机原理相提并论。

(b) 谓语转译成状语

After some experiments, Rice *succeeded* in explaining the mechanism of crack nucleation.

做了一些实验之后，奈斯**成功地**解释了成裂机理。

(c) 主语转译成状语

The result of his revolutionary design is that the engine is much smaller, works more smoothly, and has fewer moving parts.

由于他在设计上的革新，发动机变得小多了，工作得更平稳了，活动部件也少了。

(d) 宾语转译成状语

He spent *the first three months of this year* in Chongqing University.

今年的前三个月期间，他在重庆大学度过。

（5）转译成宾语

(a) 主语转译成宾语（常用于翻译被动句）

The mechanical energy can be changed back into electrical energy by means of a generator.

利用发电机可以把**机械能**重新转变成电能。

(b) 状语转译成宾语

Computer aided design (CAD) has been *successfully* employed in the development of products.

计算机辅助设计在产品开发中已经获得了**成功**。

(c) 谓语转译成宾语

The volume fraction of fiber in a composite *affects* greatly both the strength and stiffness of the material.

复合材料中纤维的体积含量对其强度和刚度都有很大的**影响**。

(6) 转译成表语

(a) 主语转译成表语

A *great contribution of Edison* was the carbon microphone.

炭精传声器是**爱迪生的一大贡献**。

(b) 宾语转译成表语

It is *considerable difficulty* getting the analytical solution of this differential equation.

要获得该微分方程的解析解是**相当困难的**。

由此看来,句子成分的转译显得变化万千,异彩纷呈,难于穷究,几乎所有的句子成分都可互相转译,进行成分转译的目的是为了使译文通顺,合乎汉语习惯和更好地跟上下文响应。

◇◇◇◇◇◇◇◇◇◇◇◇◇◇◇◇◇◇◇◇◇◇◇◇

Reading Material(1): Variational Principle[20]

What are variational principles and how can they be useful in the approximation to continuum problems? It is to these questions that the following sections are addressed.

First a definition: a "variational principle" specifies a scalar quantity (functional) Π, which is defined by an integral form

$$\Pi = \int_\Omega F\left(u, \frac{\partial u}{\partial x}, \cdots\right) d\Omega + \int_\Gamma E\left(u, \frac{\partial u}{\partial x}, \cdots\right) d\Gamma \tag{9.1}$$

in which u is the unknown function and F and E are specified operators. The solution to the continuum problem is a function u which makes Π stationary with respect to small changes δu. Thus, for a solution to the continuum problem, the "variation" is

$$\delta \Pi = 0 \tag{9.2}$$

If a "variational principle" can be found, then immediately means are established for obtaining approximate solutions in the standard, integral form suitable for finite element analysis.

Assuming a trial function expansion in the usual form

$$u \approx \hat{u} = \sum_1^n N_i a_i$$

we can insert this into Eq. (9.1) and write

$$\delta \Pi = \frac{\partial \Pi}{\partial a_1} \delta a_1 + \frac{\partial \Pi}{\partial a_2} \delta a_2 + \cdots = \frac{\partial \Pi}{\partial a_n} \delta a_n = 0 \tag{9.3}$$

This being true for any variations δa yields a set of equations

$$\frac{\partial \Pi}{\partial \boldsymbol{a}} = \begin{Bmatrix} \frac{\partial \Pi}{\partial \boldsymbol{a}_1} \\ \vdots \\ \frac{\partial \Pi}{\partial \boldsymbol{a}_n} \end{Bmatrix} = 0 \qquad (9.4)$$

from which parameters $\boldsymbol{a}_i$ are found. The equations are of an integral form necessary for the finite element approximation as the original specification of Π was given in terms of domain and boundary integrals.

The process of finding stationarity with respect to trial function parameters $\boldsymbol{a}$ is an old one and is associated with the names of Rayleigh and Ritz. It has become extremely important in finite element analysis which, to many investigators, is typified as a "variational process".

If the functional Π is "quadratic", i.e., if the function u and its derivatives occur in powers not exceeding 2, then Eq. (9.4) reduces to a standard linear form, i.e.,

$$\frac{\partial \Pi}{\partial \boldsymbol{a}} \equiv \boldsymbol{K}\boldsymbol{a} + \boldsymbol{f} = 0 \qquad (9.5)$$

It is easy to show that the matrix $\boldsymbol{K}$ will now always be symmetric. To do this let us consider a variation of the vector $\partial \Pi / \partial \boldsymbol{a}$ generally. This we can write as

$$\delta\left(\frac{\partial \Pi}{\partial \boldsymbol{a}}\right) = \left[\frac{\partial}{\partial \boldsymbol{a}_1}\left(\frac{\partial \Pi}{\partial \boldsymbol{a}_1}\right)\delta \boldsymbol{a}_1, \frac{\partial}{\partial \boldsymbol{a}_2}\left(\frac{\partial \Pi}{\partial \boldsymbol{a}_1}\right)\delta \boldsymbol{a}_2, \cdots\right] \equiv \boldsymbol{K}_T \delta \boldsymbol{a} \qquad (9.6)$$

in which $\boldsymbol{K}_T$ is generally known as the tangent matrix of significance in non-linear analysis. Now it is easy to see that

$$\boldsymbol{K}_{Tij} = \frac{\partial^2 \Pi}{\partial \boldsymbol{a}_i \partial \boldsymbol{a}_j} = \boldsymbol{K}_{Tij}^T \qquad (9.7)$$

Hence $\boldsymbol{K}_T$ is symmetric.

For a quadratic functional we have, from Eq. (9.5),

$$\delta\left(\frac{\partial \Pi}{\partial \boldsymbol{a}}\right) = \boldsymbol{K}\delta \boldsymbol{a} \quad \text{or} \quad \boldsymbol{K} = \boldsymbol{K}^T \qquad (9.8)$$

and hence symmetry must exist.

The fact that symmetric matrices will arise whenever a variational principle exists is one of the most important merits of variational approaches for discretization. However, symmetric forms will frequently arise directly from the Galerkin process. In such cases we simply conclude that the variational principle exists but we shall not need to use it directly.

How then do "variational principles" arise and is it always possible to construct these for continuous problems?

To answer the first part of the question we note that frequently the physical aspects of the problem can be stated directly in a variational principle form. Such theorems as minimization of total potential energy to achieve equilibrium in mechanical systems, least energy dissipation principles in viscous flow, etc, may be known to the reader and are considered by many as the basis of formulation.

Variational principles of this kind are "natural" ones but unfortunately they do not exist for all continuum problems for which well-defined differential equations may be formulated.

However, there is another category of variational principles, which we may call "contrived". Such contrived principles can always be constructed for any differentially specified problems either by extending the number of unknown functions **u** by additional variables known as Lagrange multipliers, or by procedures imposing a higher degree of continuity requirements such as least square problems.

Before proceeding further it is worth noting that, in addition to symmetry arising in equations derived by variational means, sometimes further motivation arises. When "natural" variational principles exist the quantity Π may be of specific interest itself. If this arises a variational approach possesses the merit of easy evaluation of this functional.

The reader will observe that if the functional is "quadratic" and yields Eq. (9.5), then we can write the approximate "functional" Π simply as

$$\Pi = \frac{1}{2}\boldsymbol{a}^\mathrm{T}\boldsymbol{K}\boldsymbol{a} + \boldsymbol{a}^\mathrm{T}\boldsymbol{f} \qquad (9.9)$$

That this is true the reader can observe by simple differentiation.

Words and Expressions

variational principle		变分原理
scalar ['skeilə]	n.	标量
functional ['fʌŋkʃənəl]	n.	泛函
operator ['ɔpə,reitə]	n.	算符
stationary ['steiʃənəri]	adj.	稳定的;不动的
trial function		试函数
boundary integral		边界积分
stationarity [steiʃə'næriti]	n.	稳定性;稳态
quadratic [kwə'drætik]	adj.	二次的
tangent matrix		切线矩阵
quadratic functional		二次泛函
least energy dissipation principle		最小能量耗散原理
natural variational principle		自然变分原理
contrived variational principle		约束变分原理
Lagrange multiplier		拉格朗日乘子

Reading Material(2): Generalization of the Finite Element Concepts[20]

We have so far dealt with one possible approach to the approximate solution of the particular problem of linear elasticity. Many other continuum problems arise in engineering and physics and usually these problems are posed by appropriate differential equations and boundary conditions to be imposed on the unknown function or functions. It is the object of this chapter to show that all such problems can be dealt with by the finite element method.

Posing the problem to be solved in its most general terms we find that we seek an unknown function u such that it satisfies a certain differential equation set

$$A(u) = \begin{Bmatrix} A_1(u) \\ A_2(u) \\ \vdots \end{Bmatrix} \tag{3.1}$$

in a "domain" (volume, area, etc.), Ω, together with certain boundary conditions

$$B(u) = \begin{Bmatrix} B_1(u) \\ B_2(u) \\ \vdots \end{Bmatrix} \tag{3.2}$$

on the boundaries, Γ, of the domain as shown in Fig. 3.1.

The function sought may be a scalar quantity or may represent a vector of several variables.

Similarly, the differential equation may be a single one or a set of simultaneous equations and does not need to be linear. It is for this reason that we have resorted to matrix notation in the above.

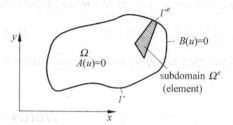

Fig. 3.1 Problem domain and boundary

The finite element process, being one of approximation, will seek the solution in the approximate form

$$u \approx \hat{u} = \sum_{a=1}^{n} N_a \tilde{u}_a = N\tilde{u} \tag{3.3}$$

where N_a are shape functions prescribed in terms of independent variables (such as the coordinates x, y, etc.) and all or most of the parameters $\tilde{u}_a$ are unknown.

In the previous chapter we have seen that precisely the same form of approximation was used in the displacement approach to elasticity problems. We also noted there that (a) the shape functions were usually defined locally for elements or subdomains and (b) the properties of discrete systems were recovered if the approximating equations were cast in an integral form. With this object in mind we shall seek to cast the equation from which the unknown parameters $\tilde{u}_a$ are to be obtained in the integral form

$$\int_\Omega G_b(\hat{u}) d\Omega + \int_\Gamma g_b(\hat{u}) d\Gamma = 0, \quad b = 1 \text{ to } n \tag{3.4}$$

in which G_b and g_b prescribe known functions or operators.

These integral forms will permit the approximation to be obtained element by element and an assembly to be achieved by the use of the procedures developed for standard discrete systems, since, providing the functions G_b and g_b are integrable, we have

$$\int_\Omega G_b \, d\Omega + \int_\Gamma g_b \, d\Gamma = \sum_{e=1}^m (\int_{\Omega_e} G_b \, d\Omega + \int_{\Gamma^e} g_b \, d\Gamma) = 0 \qquad (3.5)$$

where Ω_e is the domain of each element and Γ_e is part of the boundary.

Two distinct procedures are available for obtaining the approximation in such integral forms. The first is the method of weighted residuals (known alternatively as the Galerkin procedure); the second is the determination of variational functionals for which stationarity is sought. We shall deal with both approaches in turn.

If the differential equations are linear, i.e., if we can write Eq. (3.1) and (3.2) as

$$A(u) \equiv Lu + b = 0 \quad \text{in} \quad \Omega$$
$$B(u) \equiv Mu + t = 0 \quad \text{on} \quad \Gamma \qquad (3.6)$$

then the approximating equation system (3.4) will yield a set of linear equations of the form

$$K\tilde{u} + f = 0 \qquad (3.7)$$

with

$$K_{ab} = \sum_{e=1}^m K_{ab}^e, \quad f_a = \sum_{e=1}^m f_a^e$$

The reader not used to abstraction may well now be confused about the meaning of the various terms. We shall introduce here some typical sets of differential equations for which we will seek solutions (and which will make the problems a little more definite).

Example 3.1: Steady-state heat conduction equation in a two-dimensional domain.

Here the equations are written as

$$A(\phi) = -\frac{\partial}{\partial x}\left(k\frac{\partial \phi}{\partial x}\right) - \frac{\partial}{\partial y}\left(k\frac{\partial \phi}{\partial y}\right) + Q = 0 \quad \text{in } \Omega$$

$$B(\phi) = \begin{cases} \phi - \bar{\phi} = 0 & \text{on } \Gamma_\phi \\ k\frac{\partial \phi}{\partial n} + \bar{q} = 0 & \text{on } \Gamma_q \end{cases} \qquad (3.8)$$

where $u \equiv \phi$ indicates temperature, k is the conductivity, Q is a heat source, $\bar{\phi}$ and $\bar{q}$ are the prescribed values of temperature and heat flow on the boundaries and n is the direction normal to Γ. In the context of this equation the boundary condition for Γ_ϕ is called a Dirichlet condition and the one on Γ_q a Neumann one.

In the above problem k and Q can be functions of position and, if the problem is nonlinear, of ϕ or its derivatives.

Example 3.2: Steady-state heat conduction-convection equation in two dimensions.

When convection effects are added the differential equation becomes

$$A(\phi) = -\frac{\partial}{\partial x}\left(k\frac{\partial \phi}{\partial x}\right) - \frac{\partial}{\partial y}\left(k\frac{\partial \phi}{\partial y}\right) + u_x\frac{\partial \phi}{\partial x} + u_y\frac{\partial \phi}{\partial y} + Q = 0 \quad \text{in } \Omega \qquad (3.9)$$

with boundary conditions as in the first example. Here u_x and u_y are known functions of position and represent velocities of an incompressible fluid in which heat transfer occurs.

Example 3.3: A system of three first-order equations equivalent to Example 3.1.

The steady-state heat equation in two dimensions may also be split into the three equations

$$A(u) = \left\{ \begin{array}{c} \dfrac{\partial q_x}{\partial x} + \dfrac{\partial q_y}{\partial y} + Q \\ q_x + k\dfrac{\partial \phi}{\partial x} \\ q_y + k\dfrac{\partial \phi}{\partial y} \end{array} \right\} = 0 \quad \text{in } \Omega \tag{3.10}$$

and

$$B(u) = \left\{ \begin{array}{ll} \phi - \bar{\phi} = 0 & \text{on } \Gamma_\phi \\ q_n + \bar{q} = 0 & \text{on } \Gamma_q \end{array} \right.$$

where q_n is the flux normal to the boundary.

Here the unknown function vector u corresponds to the set

$$u = \left\{ \begin{array}{c} \phi \\ q_x \\ q_y \end{array} \right\}$$

This last example is typical of a so-called mixed formulation. In such problems the number of dependent unknowns can always be reduced in the governing equations by suitable algebraic operation, still leaving a solvable problem [e. g., obtaining Eq. (3.8) from (3.10) by eliminating q_x and q_y].

◈◈◈◈◈◈◈◈◈◈◈◈◈◈◈◈◈◈◈◈◈◈◈◈◈◈

Words and Expressions

simultaneous equation		联立方程
shape function		形状函数
subdomain	n.	子域
method of weigted residual		加权残值法
steady-state		稳态
heat conduction equation		热传导方程
Dirichlet condition		狄利克莱条件
Neumann condition		纽曼条件
flux [flʌks]	n.	流量；熔化
mixed formulation		混合型公式
irreducible formulation		不可约型公式

Unit Ten

Fatigue of Materials[22]

In a narrow sense, the term fatigue of materials and structural components means damage and fracture due to cyclic, repeatedly applied stresses. In a wide sense, it includes a large number of phenomena of delayed damage and fracture under loads and environmental conditions. The systematic study of fatigue was initiated by Wohler, who in the period 1858—1860 performed the first systematic experimentation on damage of materials under cyclic loading. In particular, Wohler introduced the concept of the fatigue curve, i. e., the diagram where a characteristic magnitude of cyclic stress is plotted against the cycle number until fatigue failure. Up to now, the Wohler curve has been used widely in the applied structural analysis. At the same time, fatigue and related phenomena are considered as a subject of mechanics of solids, material science, as well as that of basic engineering.

It is expedient to distinguish between high-cycle (classic) and low-cycle fatigue. If plastic deformations are small and localized in the vicinity of the crack tip while the main part of the body is deformed elastically, then one has high-cycle fatigue. If the cyclic loading is accompanied by elasto-plastic deformations in the bulk of the body, then one has low-cycle fatigue. Usually we say low-cycle fatigue if the cycle number up to the initiation of a visible crack or until final fracture is below 10^4 or 5×10^4 cycles.

The mode of damage and final fracture depends on environmental conditions. At elevated temperatures plasticity of most materials increases, metals display creep, and polymers thermo-plastic behavior. At lower temperatures plasticity of metals decreases, and brittle fracture becomes more probable. If a structural component is subjected both to cyclic loading and variable thermal actions, mixed phenomena take place, such as creep fatigue, creep accelerated by vibration, and thermo-fatigue. The combination of fatigue and corrosion is called corrosion fatigue. It is a type of damage typical for metals interacting with active media, humid air, etc. Hydrogen and irradiation embrittlement, as well as various wear and ageing processes, interact with fatigue, too. The delayed fracture occurs not only under cyclic, but also under constant or slowly varying loading. Typical examples are the delayed fracture of polymers and crack initiation and propagation in metals under the combination of active environment and non-cyclic loads. The latter kind of damage, opposite of corrosion fatigue, is called stress corrosion cracking. All these phenomena taken together form a class of damage frequently called static fatigue. Later on, when no special comment is given, we consider cyclic fatigue, calling it just fatigue.

Fatigue is a gradual process of damage accumulation that proceeds on various levels beginning from the scale of the crystal lattice, dislocations and other objects of solid state physics up to the scales of structural components. Three or four stages of fatigue damage are usually distinguishable. In the first stage, the damage accumulation occurs on the level of microstructure. Where a polycrystalline alloy is concerned, it is the level of grains and intergranular layers. The damage is dispersed over the volume of a specimen or structural component or, at least, over the most stressed parts. At the end of this stage, nuclei of macroscopic cracks originate, i. e., such aggregates of microcracks that are strong stress concentrators and, under the following loading, have a tendency to grow. Surface nuclei usually can be observed visually (at least with proper magnification). The second stage is the growth of cracks whose depth is small compared with the size of the cross section. At the same time, the sizes of these cracks are equal to a few characteristic scales of microstructure, say, to several grain sizes. Such cracks are called small cracks (in the literature the term short crack is also used). The number of small cracks in a body may be large. The pattern of their propagation is different from that of completely developed macroscopic cracks. Small cracks find their way through the nonhomogeneous material. Most of them stop growing upon meeting some obstacles, but one or several cracks transform into macroscopic, "long" fatigue cracks that propagate in a direct way as strong stress concentrators. This process forms the third stage of fatigue damage. The fourth stage is rapid final fracture due to the sharp stress concentration at the crack front and/or the expenditure of the material's resistance to fracture.

The initiation and following growth of a macroscopic crack are schematically shown in Figure 1.1(a) for the case of a polycrystalline material under uniaxial cyclic tension. Nuclei appear near the surface of the specimen, in particular, in the local stress concentration domains as well as near the damaged or weakest grains. The initial slip planes and microcracks in grains are oriented mostly

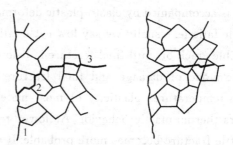

(a) near the regular surface (b) near a strong stress concentrator

Figure 1.1 Fatigue crack initiation in polycrystalline material

along the planes with maximal shear stresses. Small cracks are inclined, at least approximately, in the same directions. These cracks go through the grains, intergranular boundaries or in a mixed way. When one of the small cracks becomes sufficiently long, the direction of its growth changes: the crack propagates into the cross section of the specimen, in the so-called opening mode. Such a "long," macroscopic crack intersects in its growth a large number of grains. Therefore, this growth is determined mainly with averaged properties. The border between small and "long" cracks is rather conditional. In particular, it depends on the ratio of the current crack size a and the characteristic size of grains. If the grain size is of the order of 0.1mm, a crack may be considered as "long" when it reaches the magnitude $a_0 = 0.5$mm or 1mm.

The ratio of durations of these stages varies to a large extent depending on material properties, type of loading and environmental conditions. The first two stages are absent if a crack propagates from an initial macroscopic crack, sharp crack-like defect or another strong stress concentrator (Figure 1.1). In this case the position of the macroscopic crack is conditioned beforehand, and the crack begins to propagate after a comparatively small number of cycles. On the other hand, for very brittle materials the final fracture may occur suddenly, without the formation of any stable macroscopic cracks. For example, it may be a result that microcrack density attains a certain critical level.

A typical cyclic loading process is presented in Figure 1.2. The notation $s(t)$ is used here for any stress-related variable characterizing the loading process. It may be interpreted, for example, as a remotely applied normal stress relating to the whole cross section of a specimen subjected to cyclic tension/compression. If $s(t)$ is varying as a sinusoidal function, the duration of a cycle coincides with the period of the function $s(t)$. Each cycle contains maximal S_{max} and minimal S_{min} magnitudes of the applied stresses. A cycle is usually considered as a segment of the loading process limited with two neighboring up crossings of the average stress $S_m = (S_{max} + S_{min})/2$. The cyclic loading is usually described by the amplitude stress $S_a = (S_{max} - S_{min})/2$ or the stress range $\Delta S = S_{max} - S_{min}$. Stress ratio $R = S_{min}/S_{max}$ is also a significant characteristic of the cyclic loading. For symmetrical cycles $R = -1$; when a cycle contains non-negative stresses only, then $R > 0$. The cycle number N is an integer number, although it is usually treated as a continuous variable. Actually, the cycle number corresponding to significant damage, or moreover to final failure, as a rule is very large compared with unity. Time t is useful as an independent variable when the interactions between fatigue and other time-dependent damage phenomena are considered.

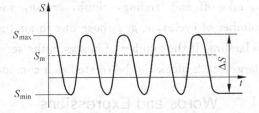

Figure 1.2 Cyclic loading and its characterictic stresses

Some types of cyclic loading are shown schematically in Figure 1.3. Among them are biharmonic (a), chaotic (pseudo-stochastic) (b), and piece-wise constant (c) processes. In

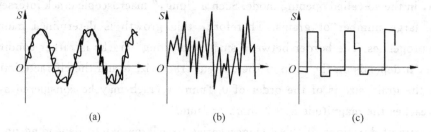

Figure 1.3　Cyclic loading processes: (a) biharmonic; (b) chaotic; (c) piecewise constant

practice stochastic processes are often met. These processes can be narrow-band or broadband, stationary or nonstationary. In the general case the concept of loading cycle becomes ambiguous. For example, a cycle may be determined as a segment of loading process that contains one maximum and one minimum; but often a cycle is treated as a segment limited with two neighboring up-crossings of a certain, generally nonstationary level. Relative freedom in choosing this level makes the concept of cycle even less determinate. For example, in Figure 1.4 a so-called compound cycle is shown limited with two time moments t_{N-1} and t_N. This cycle contains interior cycles that correspond to the high-frequency components of the loading process. The situation becomes more complicated when we deal with multiple-parameter loading, in particular in the case when the components of the stress tensor vary in time in a different way. In all such cases the questions of how to divide a process into cycles and how to identify cycle parameters are to be considered separately.

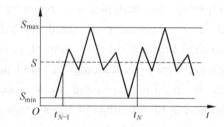

Figure 1.4　Compound cycle containing interior cycles

A generalization of cycle loading is block loading. Each block is also called a duty cycle, a mission, etc. The block corresponds to one of multiply repeated stages in the service of a structure or machine. A block of loading corresponding to one standard (specified) flight of an aircraft can be mentioned as an example. This block includes loads during ground motions, take-off and landing, climb, cruise, and descent flights. Each block contains a large number of cycles, e.g., those due to air turbulence, impacts, and vibration at take-off and landing. If the number of blocks in the service life of a structure or machine is sufficiently large, each block can be treated as a compound cycle.

Words and Expressions

fatigue [fə'tiːg]		n.	疲劳
		vi. & vt.	(使)疲劳
damage ['dæmidʒ]		n.	损伤

	vt.	损坏
cyclic stress		循环应力
fracture ['fræktʃə]	*n.*	断裂
	vi. & vt.	(使)断裂
cyclic loading		循环载荷
fatigue curve		疲劳曲线
cycle number		循环次数
fatigue failure		疲劳破坏
high-cycle fatigue		高周疲劳
low-cycle fatigue		低周疲劳
crack [kræk]	*n.*	裂纹
crack tip		裂尖
brittle fracture		脆性断裂
creep fatigue		蠕变疲劳
thermo-fatigue		热疲劳
corrosion fatigue		腐蚀疲劳
crack initiation		裂纹起始；起裂
crack propagation		裂纹扩展
non-cyclic load		非循环载荷
stress corrosion cracking		应力腐蚀起裂
static fatigue		静态疲劳
crystal lattice		晶格
dislocation [,dislə'keiʃən]	*n.*	位错
polycrystalline [pɔli'kristəlain]	*n.*	多晶体
	adj.	多晶的
macroscopic crack		宏观裂纹
aggregate ['ægrigit]	*n.*	偏析，聚合体
microcrack ['maikrəukræk, 'maikrəu,kræk]	*n.*	微裂纹
nonhomogeneous ['nɔnhɔmə'dʒi:njəs]	*adj.*	非均匀的
crack front		裂纹前沿
slip [slip]	*n.*	滑移
slip plane		滑移面
grain [grein]	*n.*	晶粒
defect [di'fekt]	*n.*	缺陷
stress concentrator		应力集中点
average stress		平均应力
amplitude stress		幅值应力
stress ratio		应力比
biharmonic [baihɑ:'mɔnik]	*adj.*	双调和的

chaotic [kei'ɔtik]	adj.	混乱的；混沌的
pseudo-stochastic		伪随机的
nonstationary ['nɔn'steiʃənəri]	adj.	不稳定的；非定常的
interior cycle		内循环
high-frequency component		高频分量
duty cycle		负载循环；工作周期

科技英语翻译技巧：常见多功能词的译法[31]

多功能词 as，it，that，what 在科技文章中广泛使用，下面讨论这些词的翻译技巧。

1. as 的译法

（1）as 作为介词

as 作为介词可引出主语补足语、宾语补足语、状语、同位语等，可译为"作为"、"为"、"以"、"是"、"当作"等。

Yield stresses of materials are usually taken *as* allowable stresses in the design of engineering strctures.

工程结构设计中常常将材料的屈服应力**作为**允许应力。

（2）as 作为关系代词

as 作为关系代词可以单独使用，也可以与 such，the same 等词搭配使用，引导定语从句。

（a）as 单独使用，引导定语从句或省略定语从句时，可译为"正如"、"如"或"这"、"这样"等，有时 as 可略去不译。

As is known to us, inertia is an absolute quality possessed by all bodies.

正如我们所知，惯性是所有物体都具有的一种绝对属性。

As have been found there are only two independent material parameters for isotropic elastic materials.

已经发现，各向同性弹性体仅有两个独立的材料常数。（略去不译）

（b）such …as，such as 引出的定语从句，可译为"像……这（那）样的"、"那样（种）的"、"像……之类的"等。

Mechanics deals with *such* ideas *as* inertia, motion, force and energy.

力学研究**诸如**惯性、运动、力和能量之类的概念。

（c）the same …as，the same as 引出的定语从句，可译为"和……一样"、"与……相同"、"和……相等"。

The weight of an object on the moon is *not the same as* its weight on the earth.

物体在月球上的重量**与**其在地球上的重量**不一样**。

（3）as 作为关系副词

as 作为关系副词引导定语从句的译法，与作为关系代词引导定语从句的译法基本相同。

A vector multiplied by a scalar quantity is a vector in the same direction *as* the original vector.

乘以标量的矢量是一个**与**原矢量同向的矢量。

(4) as 作为连词

as 作为连词,可引导时间、原因、比较、让步、方式等状语从句。不同的状语从句中的 as 有不同的译法,分述于后。

(a) as 引导时间状语从句,可译为"(当)……时"、"随着……"等。

The gravitational attraction between two bodies decreases *as* the distance between them increases.

两物体之间的引力**随着**两物体之间的距离增大而减小。

(b) as 引导原因状语从句,可译为"由于……"、"因为…… 所以……"等。

As liquids and gases flow, they are called fluids.

由于液体和气体能流动,因此称为流体。

(c) as 引导比较状语从句时,as+形容词或副词+as 可译为:"与……一样(同样)……";not so +形容词或副词+ as:"不如(没有)……(那样)……";as+形容词或副词+as 可译为:"又…… 又……"; as long as 可译为:"多久……多久"。

The wheel turns *as* fast *as* stable.

这只轮子旋转得**又快又稳**。

The development stage lasts *as long as* it needs to.

研制阶段需要持续**多久**,就持续**多久**。

(d) as 引导让步状语从句,可译为:"虽然……"、"尽管……"。

Complicated *as* the problem is, it can be worked out in a few minutes by a computer.

尽管那个问题很复杂,计算机能在几分钟内将它解出。

(e) as 引导方式状语从句,可译为:"像……那样"、"正如……"、"正如……一样"等。

Friction, *as* the term is understood in mechanics, is the resistance to relative motion between two bodies in contact.

正如大家在力学中所知,磨擦就是两个相接触的物体产生相对运动的阻力。

2. it 的译法

(1) it 在下列句型结构中,略去不译

(a) it 用作无人称主语,表示天气、时间、距离等。

It is just nine o'clock.

现在正好九点钟。

(b) it 用作先行主语

It is easier to roll something over a surface than to slide it.

在任一表面上滚动一个物体比滑动它更容易。

(c) it 用作先行宾语

We found *it* necessary using modern artificial materials for tall buildings.

我们认为,采用现代人造材料建造高层建筑是必要的。

(2) it 引导强调句型的译法

在这种句型中,it 本身无词汇意义,应在被强调部分的前面加译"是"、"正是"、"只有"等字。

It is to reduce friction that roller bearings are used.

正是为了减少磨擦,才使用滚珠轴承。

(3) it 用作人称代词的译法

(a) it 代替上文所提及之事物,一般可译成"它"。

A new branch of mechanics, nanomechanics, has emerged, and *it* is attracting more and more mechanicians.

出现了一新的力学分支——纳米力学,**它**正在吸引越来越多的力学工作者。

(b) 英语中的多数状语从句可位于主句之前或之后,因此指代同一事物在主句中可用名词也可用代词,但汉语中的状语从句一般位于主句之前,而指代同一事物总是先出现名词后使用代词。基于上述情况,it 往往译成所代替的名词。

The car is slowed down as *it* goes through the tunnel.

当**小车**通过隧道时,速度就减慢下来。

(c) it 代替上文所提及的某件事或上面的整个句子时,可译成"这"、"这一点"。

Does a structure deform when loaded? *It* is a problem to be studied.

结构受载会变形吗?**这**是一个需要研究的问题。

3. that 的译法

(1) that 作为限定词,可译成:"那"、"该"等。

Up to *that* time wood and stone were still the main building materials.

直到**那**时,木材和石头仍是主要建筑材料。

(2) that 作为指示代词

(a) that 代表前面的句子时,可译成"这"。

Plastics are light and strong and do not rust at all. *That* is why they find such wide uses in industry.

塑料既轻又牢,毫不生锈。**这**就是塑料在工业上如此广泛应用的原因。

(b) that 代替前面的某一名词时,翻译时往往重复所代替的名词。

Mild steel has a high tensile strength, this being 200 times *that* of concrete.

低碳钢具有很高的抗拉强度,大约是混凝土的**抗拉强度**的 200 倍。

(3) that 作为关系代词

that 作为关系代词,引出定语从句;定语从句可以合译也可分译,that 的处理方法也随之而异。

(a) 合译时 that 不译,在定语从句之末添"的"字。

Power is the rate *that* mechanical move is performed at.

功率是作机械运动**的**速率。

(b) 分译时,that 有两种译法:重复所代替的名词或译成"它"。

Matter is composed of molecules *that* are composed of atoms.

物质由分子组成,而**分子**由原子组成。

An element is a simple substance *that* cannot be broken up into anything simpler.

元素是一种单质,**它**不能再分成任何更简单的物质。

(4) that 作为连词引出同位语从句

(a) 同位语从句与主句分译,that 译成"即"。

Energy takes many forms, but all these forms can be reduced to the statement *that* energy is the capacity to do work.

能量具有很多形式，但所有这些形式都可以归纳为这样一句话，即能量是做功的能力。

(b) 同位语从句与主句合译，that 译成"这一"。

The idea *that* energy is conserved is the first law of thermodynamics.

能量守恒**这一**概念是热力学第一定律。

(c) 在主句与同位语从句之间加冒号，that 略去不译。

In 1905 Einstein worked out a theory *that* matter and energy were not completely different things.

1905 年，爱因斯坦提出了一个理论：物质和能量并非完全不同的东西。

(5) that 引出表语从句时，一般略去不译，如表语从句较长，可在主句之间增加冒号，或增加"在于"。

One of the advantages of concrete is *that* it can be easily shaped into any desired form.

混凝土的优点之一是它易于制成所需的任何形状。（略去不译）

The Newton's second law is *that* the net force on a particle of constant mass is proportional to the time rate of change of its linear momentum.

牛顿第二定律就是：作用于具有定常质量的质点上的力正比于其动量的变化率。

(6) that 引出主语从句、宾语从句；在强调句型时，一律略去不译；有时在宾语从句前加上逗号。

It is generally believed *that* oil is derived from marine plant and animal life.

通常认为石油来源于海生动植物。（引出主语从句）

(7) that 作为连词引出结果状语从句和目的状语从句；前者译成"因而"、"以致"、"从而"等，后者可译成"才"、"以便"等。

The climate is very hot and dry *that* much evaporation takes place.

气候既很炎热又很干燥，**因而**产生大量的蒸发。

The parts must be very strong *that* they may not break in use.

零件必须十分坚固，**才**不会在使用中破损。

4. what 的译法

(1) what 作为连接代词可译为："所谓"、"什么……"或可根据上下文译成名词。

What is large and *what* is small is only relative.

所谓大和小只是相对的。

Hydrogen and oxygen are *what* make up water.

氢和氧是组成水的**元素**。

(2) what 作为关系代词，可译为"所……的东西"、"所……的"，还可根据上下文译成"……的+名词"、"那种+名词"等。

What is worrying the world greatly now is a possible shortage of coal, oil, natural gas, or other sources of fuel in the not too distant future.

现在令全世界**所**担心**的**是，在不久的将来可能会出现煤、石油、天然气或其他能源的短缺。

(3) what 作为限定词，此时 what 在从句中作定语，可译成："什么"、"什么样的"、"哪"等。

One of the important problems to be solved is *what* material is most suitable for this particular part.

需要解决的重要问题之一是，对于这个特定的零件用**什么**材料最合适。

◇•◇•◇•◇•◇•◇•◇•◇•◇•◇•◇•◇•◇•◇•◇•◇•◇•

Reading Material(1): Linear Fracture Mechanics[22]

Consider the simplest problem of linear fracture mechanics, i. e., Griffith's problem of a plane opening mode crack in an unbounded medium. The crack with length $2a$ is considered as a mathematical cut, and the uniformly applied stresses σ_∞ are normal to the plane of the crack (Figure 1.1). The body is in the plane-strain state, and we refer all variables to unity size in the z-direction. Material is linear elastic with Young's modulus E and Poisson's ratio v.

The work required to advance the crack tip from a to $a + da$ is proportional to da. Griffith (1920) attributed this work to the energy of surface forces. In real structural materials the main part of this work is spent in plastic deformation and other irreversible phenomena. All these factors may be included in the specific fracture work γ. We relate this work to the unit area of the newborn crack (opposite to the tradition that this work is related to the unit area of the newborn free surface). Assume that the crack does not propagate if the increment of the potential energy of the system Π related to the crack tip advancement is less than the required fracture work, i. e., $-d\Pi < \gamma da$. When $-d\Pi > \gamma da$ the released energy exceeds the required fracture work. Then due to the energy surplus, dynamic crack growth becomes possible. For half of the body $x \geqslant 0$ the potential energy is

$$\Pi = const - \frac{\pi \sigma_\infty^2 a^2 (1-v^2)}{2E} \tag{1.1}$$

The constant in the right-hand side of (1.1) is equal to the total potential energy in the absence of the crack. Substituting (1.1) in the condition $-d\Pi = \gamma da$ we obtain the equation for the critical stress σ_c:

$$\sigma_c = \left[\frac{\gamma E}{\pi a (1-v^2)}\right]^{1/2} \tag{1.2}$$

The approach by Irwin (1954) is based on the analysis of singularities of the stress field in the vicinity of the crack tip. In a linear elastic body there is a square root singularity. If the fracture is a local phenomenon, it depends on the stress distribution close to the tip. The singular term in formulas for the stresses looks as follows:

$$\sigma_{jk}(r,\theta) = \frac{K_I}{(2\pi r)^{1/2}} f_{jk}(r,\theta) \tag{1.3}$$

Here r is the polar radius, θ is the polar angle; subscripts j and k run for the coordinate notations x, y, z (see Figure 1.1).

Parameter

$$K_I = \sigma_\infty (\pi a)^{1/2} \tag{1.4}$$

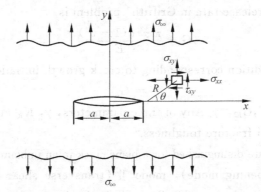

Figure 1.1 Griffith's problem of plane crack under uniform tension.

is called the stress intensity factor. Index I shows that the stress intensity factor relates to the opening mode of cracking (mode I). Equation (1.3) remains valid in the case of more general loading and geometry under the condition that the stress intensity factor K_I is properly calculated. A typical relation has the form

$$K_I = Y s_\infty (\pi a)^{1/2} \tag{1.5}$$

where s_∞ is the stress applied in the remote cross section. The correction, factor Y is usually of the order of unity. This factor depends on geometry and sometimes on the normalized elasticity parameters (e.g., on Poisson's ratio). For example, for a plate of width $2b$ with a central crack of length $2a$: approximate equations may be used, such as

$$K_I \approx \sigma_\infty (\pi a)^{1/2} [\sec(\pi a/2b)]^{1/2}$$

This equation yields satisfactory results for $b > 0.8 a$.

Other reference stresses may be used in Eq. (1.5) instead of the remotely applied stress; for example, the average stress in the cracked cross section. Sometimes it is convenient to take the reference stress equal to the maximal stress in the cracked section estimated by an elementary beam formula.

In terms of stress intensity factors, a crack does not grow at $K_I < K_{IC}$. The condition of the crack growth initiation takes the form

$$K_I = K_{IC} \tag{1.6}$$

where K_{IC} is the critical stress intensity factor. The latter is frequently also called the fracture toughness. Equations (1.2) and (1.6) become equivalent, if we put

$$K_{IC} = \left(\frac{\gamma E}{1-v^2}\right)^{1/2} \tag{1.7}$$

The fundamental relationship takes place between approaches based on the stress intensity factors and the energy conservation law. The amount of potential energy released when a crack advances in a unit of length is defined as follows:

$$G = -\frac{\partial \Pi}{\partial a} \tag{1.8}$$

This value, called energy release rate, has the dimension of force. Another name for G is the force driving the crack tip or, briefly, the driving force. Taking into account Eqs. (1.1) and (1.8), the energy release rate in Griffith' problem is

$$G = \frac{\pi \sigma_\infty^2 a(1-v^2)}{E} \quad (1.9)$$

The energy balance condition corresponding to crack growth initiation is

$$G = G_{IC} \quad (1.10)$$

where $G = K_I^2(1-v^2)/E$, $G_{IC} \equiv \gamma$. Any of three parameters, γ, K_{IC} and G_{IC}, may be used to characterize the material fracture toughness.

Three special cases are distinguished for a plane crack in an unbounded body (Figure 1.2). They are: mode Ⅰ (opening mode), mode Ⅱ (transverse shear mode), and mode Ⅲ (longitudinal shear or antiplane mode). Stress intensity factors for these modes are

$$K_I = \sigma_\infty (\pi a)^{1/2}, \quad K_{II} = K_{III} = \tau_\infty (\pi a)^{1/2}$$

Here σ_∞ and τ_∞ are applied (remote) stresses in tension and shear tress, respectively. Singular terms in equation (1.9) for stresses in the vicinity of crack tips can be found in any handbook or textbook on fracture mechanics.

Equations (1.1), (1.2), (1.7), and (1.9) correspond to the plane-strain state. In the case of the plane-stress state (for example, for an infinite thin plate), one has to replace $1-v^2$ with unity. The critical stress intensity factor K_{IC} corresponding to the plane-stress state depends on the plate thickness because of rather complicated patterns of crack propagation, including the shear fracture with significant plastic deformations. This is the reason that K_{IC} is used in applications as the measure of fracture toughness.

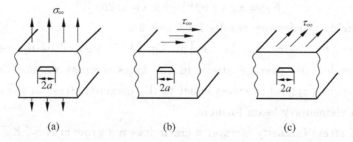

Figure 1.2 Three principal modes of cracking. (a) Opening (tearing); (b) Transverse shear mode; (c) Longitudinal shear (antiplane) mode.

When the condition given in Eq. (1.6) or Eq. (1.10) is attained, the crack becomes unstable. It begins to propagate dynamically with the velocity limited by the Rayleigh wave velocity. Generally, the attainment of equalities in Eq. (1.6) and Eq. (1.10) does not necessarily signify instability. A typical example is an infinite plate loaded with two normal forces that are applied to the crack faces. The crack size in this problem increases with the applied forces when the equality condition takes place between the energy release rate and its critical magnitude. When $G_C = \text{const}$, the criterion of stability is

$$\frac{\partial G}{\partial a} < 0$$

Words and Expressions

Griffith's problem	Griffith 问题
plane-strain	平面应变
dynamic crack growth	动态裂纹扩展
singularity [ˌsiŋgju'læriti] n.	奇异性
stress intensity factor	应力强度因子
opening mode of cracking	裂纹张开模式
central crack	中心裂纹
fracture toughness	断裂韧性
energy release rate	能量释放率
transverse shear mode of cracking	裂纹横向剪切模式
longitudinal shear (or antiplane) mode of cracking	裂纹纵向剪切(反对称)模式
fracture mechanics	断裂力学
Rayleigh wave	瑞利波

Reading Material(2): Fracture Mechanics[23]

Abstract

Fracture mechanics is an active research field that is currently advancing on many fronts. This appraisal of research trends and opportunities notes the promising developments of nonlinear fracture mechanics in recent years and cites some of the challenges in dealing with topics such as ductile-brittle transitions, failure under substantial plasticity or creep, crack tip processes under fatigue loading, and the need for new methodologies for effective fracture analysis of composite materials. Continued focus on microscale fracture processes by work at the interface of solid mechanics and materials science holds promise for understanding the atomistics of brittle vs ductile response and the mechanisms of microvoid nucleation and growth in various materials? Critical experiments to characterize crack tip processes and separation mechanisms are a pervasive need. Fracture phenomena in the contexts of geotechnology and earthquake fault dynamics also provide important research challenges.

Introduction

Fracture mechanics began as a means of understanding the tensile failure of brittle materials; it has grown into a field of great breadth and applicability. The subject is concerned with failure by cracking or cavitation of materials (structural, geological, biological, etc.) under a wide variety of loadings and environments. Applications range from the microscale of materials where cavity sizes may be a fraction of a micron to engineering structures with cracks in the millimeter to centimeter scale to earthquake rupture where faults are many kilometers in extent. Fracture mechanics is now being developed and applied around the world. Hardly a week goes by without some fracture-related problem reaching the nation's newspapers. Such problems have involved, for example, cracking in artificial heart valves, reactor piping, welding affected zones of bridges and offshore structure, aircraft landing gear, tail and engine attachments, ship structures, undercarriages of transit buses, turbine discs and blades, gas transmission pipelines, and train rails and railwheels.

The stage was set for the modern development of fracture mechanics in all its aspects by Irwin and Orowan, who in the 1950s and early 1960s reinterpreted and extended Griffith's classical work of the 1920s on brittle materials. Irwin's approach in particular brought progress in theoretical solid mechanics, especially on elastic stress analysis of cracked bodies, to bear on the practical problems of crack growth testing and structural integrity. The field has continued in this synergistic mode. It is characterized by remarkably close contact between advanced theoretical mechanics focused on nonlinear and often time-dependent material response, the examination and characterization of materials on the microscale, laboratory study of crack growth and fracture phenomena, and applications to structural integrity assurance that themselves drive new advances in materials testing and stress analysis methodology.

Irwin's approach to fracture, sometimes called linear elastic fracture mechanics, permitted engineers to analyze cracking in the more brittle structural materials such as high strength metal alloys. A precise measure of fracture toughness was one of the early successes of the new approach. The growing fracture mechanics community quickly extended the new approach to deal with fatigue cracking, a problem which had their begun to plague the aircraft industry and which still today presents many challenges, especially in circumstances of hostile environments and elevated temperatures.

Nonlinear Fracture Mechanics

Ductile structural metals

The early methods and concepts of fracture mechanics, being based on the theory of linear elasticity, were limited to applications in which plastic (nonlinear) deformations were confined to the immediate neighborhood of the crack tip itself. The theory could not be applied to a number of important cracking problems involving some of the tougher, more ductile structural materials, such as many steels for example, which often experience fracture only after extensive plastic deformation. Indeed, for many of these materials the linear approach did not even permit a practical means of assessing fracture toughness for overload failure. This posed a severe limitation on the applicability of fracture mechanics in such areas as nuclear reactor technology, sea and ground transport systems, pipelines, storage tanks, bridge safety, and the like. Crude ways for extending the linear theory were devised, but these have now been supplanted by nonlinear fracture mechanics developed by theoretical and experimental mechanics researchers over the last 15 years.

The new methods were based on parameters such as the crack tip opening displacement and J integral that characterize the intensity of near tip elastic-plastic deformation fields. In their range of validity, these are geometrically invariant parameters, the same for laboratory test specimen and cracked structural components. The parameters suffice for describing the onset of crack growth and limited stable growth when the fracture process zone is sufficiently localized to the crack tip and when there is adequate constraint to maintain high stress triaxiality at the tip. These conditions are met closely enough in many applications that the resulting methodology has been adopted widely in recent years. It is being used, for example, as a basis for fracture control of nuclear reactor coolant piping and of vessels under thermal shock. Significant problems remain in effectively performing the stress analysis necessary to relate the elastic-plastic crack tip parameters to remote loading conditions. This is expecially the case for cracks in complex structural geometries such as nozzle intersections, or in areas of mechanical heterogeneity such as welds where, also, large residual stresses may be present.

In addition, there are significant and fundamental research challenges in dealing with fracture in circumstances that involve transition from initially ductile failure to brittle low-energy cleavage and also with cases for which substantial initially stable crack growth occurs on the route to overload fracture. The analysis of such stable ductile crack growth requires contention with the full nonlinear strain path dependence of plastic response and poses difficult problems for mechanics analysis. Further, there is a critical need for improved experimental techniques to more directly characterize crack tip processes and separation mechanisms in the ductile regime. These should guide the use of advanced computational mechanics techniques for elastic-plastic response to predict crack growth.

Fracture with substantial plasticity is important for all aspects of metal forming. Significant progress has been made on evaluation of limits to sheet metal forming processes based on plastic flow concentrations into thin necking zones. The satisfactory explanation of forming ductility in common circumstances, e. g. punching, for which there are positive extensions in all directions in the plane of the sheet, is a recent development in this area. At present, ductile fracture mechanics is relatively well developed for cases dominated by a crack that is long compared to its fracture process zone, and for cases of plastic instability that are uninfluenced by macroscopic cracks. Very little progress has yet been made on understanding fracture nucleation, e. g. , from a localized shear zone, and growth as a crack in a region undergoing substantial plastic flow.

Creep fracture

A rapidly developing area involves high temperature cracking problems where nonlinear creep deformation must be taken into account. Such is important for components operating in the vicinity of half or more of the material melting temperature, as in gas turbine engines. There are then significant transients in the crack tip stress field associated even with the application of a simple step loading. Although the zone of significant nonlinear creep strain after loading is initially confined to the vicinity of the crack tip, like the plastic zone confined by essentially elastic surroundings in classical brittle fracture mechanics, ultimately the entire cracked component undergoes substantial creep and responds as a non-linear purely viscous body. Transitions of this type occur not only from nominally elastic to steady (secondary) creep but also involve primary creep and short-time plasticity effects. In these circumstances the problems are considerable in understanding how laboratory crack growth data at elevated temperature can be interpreted in terms of crack tip fields and used for rational prediction of growth rates in components in service. Such components typically experience complicated temperature and stress histories, as in turbine engine operating cycles. Fortunately, major steps have been made in recent years towards identifying the types of time-dependent singular crack tip stress/deformation fields that can exist and the transition times between them for step or other variable loading. Results have the strong dependence on load level and temperature expected for response in the creep regime, and the resulting basis for rationalizing creep crack growth data is impressive. Many challenges remain in dealing with general load histories, as in creep fatigue, and in properly accounting for oxidizing or corrosive environmental effects in high temperature crack growth.

As in lower temperature ductile failure, there are some cases where fracture is best modeled by the growth of a single dominant crack, autocatalytic in concentrating deformation at its tip, whereas in other cases creep flow and gradual material degradation by microcavitation occurs over a relatively extensive zone of a component. Older continuum damage theories have long been applied to describe such degradation, and it seems important to bring those approach into better correspondence with the microscopic mechanisms of failure and to understand the conditions leading to macroscale cracking vs. distributed damage.

Fatigue; Lifetime Prediction

Advances in nonlinear and time-dependent fracture mechanics of the type described set the stage for attaining a sounder basis for lifetime prediction in engineering systems. Typical failure routes involve crack nucleation and growth towards critically under variable loads, i.e., fatigue. At present the basis for using representative test data for fatigue crack growth under cyclic loading in prediction for more general variable load histories is largely empirical and little influenced by basic mechanics modeling. The fatigue process is often strongly affected by the chemical environment which, if sufficiently aggressive, may cause crack growth referred to as stress corrosion cracking even under fixed load. Further depending on material and application, time-dependent in-elastic response such as elevated temperature creep may interact with the fatigue crack growth process and cause additional effects of load hold time, frequency and the like under variable loading.

For a more fundamental understanding of fatigue crack growth, it would seem to be necessary to more fully identify how successive crack tip opening and closing relates to the load history and material constitutive response properties, how the process is affected by the inevitable mechanical contact between protruding features on the crack surfaces (i.e., crack closure), and how local environmental effects control the geometry and relative kinematic reversibility of opening and closing processes at the tip. The nonlinear solid mechanics analysis problems implied are formidable, but possibly they are within range of what can be attacked with modern numerical methods implemented on supercomputers. Concomitant advances in observational techniques and in instrumentation to detect crack closure and to determine how crack advance occurs within a loading cycle are also needed.

A major problem which has emerged in fatigue analysis involves the treatment of very short cracks, e.g., with lengths on the order of one to a few grain diameters or with lengths on the scale of local plasticity. Here the classical approach based on prediction from long crack laboratory data based on the stress intensity factor seems to be inadequate. Difficulties may arise from unusual surface closure, large scale nonlinearity, local environment effects, or other as yet unidentified sources. This is an important topic because large tractions of structural lifetime often involve crack sizes in this range. Further, it is essential to deal with the small crack range to develop rational life prediction methodologies inclusive of both fatigue crack nucleation and growth, which are classically treated separatedly.

Modeling of fatigue in composites, both fibrous and particulate is still in its infancy. Experimental results point to possibly large stiffness reductions and to strength degradation caused by distributed cracking prior to failure. Analysis of distributed cracking phenomena, as well as of fatigue-assisted growth of large cracks, poses many challenging problems of practical importance in both material and structural design.

Continuing advances in nondestructive evaluation so as to detect and size defects are essential in making advances in life prediction methodology useful in engineering practice. Also, it is important to develop a sounder probabilistic basis for lifetime prediction in design based on uncertainties of the inspection process, on flaw size statistics, and stochastic aspects of flaw growth. Such a development should have significant impact on understanding system reliability, setting inspection intervals and managing availability of replacement parts for critical engineering systems.

Words and Expressions

composite material		复合材料
microvoid [,maikrəu'vɔid]	n.	微孔
cavitation [,kævi'teiʃən]	n.	气穴；成洞

reactor piping		反应堆管道
offshore structure		离岸结构
linear elastic fracture mechanics		线性弹性断裂力学
hostile environment		恶劣环境
J integral		J 积分
triaxiality [traiæksi'æliti]	n.	三轴；三维
coolant ['ku:lənt]	n.	冷冻剂
cleavage ['kli:vidʒ]	n.	分裂；裂隙
metal forming		金属成型
necking zone		紧缩区域
creep fracture		蠕变断裂
gas turbine engine		汽轮机
brittle fracture mechanics		脆性断裂力学
oxidize ['ɔksi,daiz]	vt. & vi.	(使)氧化
autocatalytic [,ɔ:təukætə'litik]	adj.	自动催化的
microcavitation	n.	微空隙
lifetime ['laiftaim]	n.	寿命
crack nucleation		裂纹成核
concomitant [kən'kɔmitənt]	adj.	伴随的；共存的
fibrous ['faibrəs]	adj.	纤维的
particulate [pə'tikjulit]	adj.	微粒的
	n.	微粒状物质
nondestructive evaluation		无损评价

Basic Terminology of Laminated Fiber-Reinforced Composite Materials[24]

The fibers are long and continuous as opposed to whiskers. The concepts developed herein are applicable mainly to fiber-reinforced composite laminates, but are also valid for other laminates and whisker composites with some fairly obvious modifications. That is, fiber-reinforced composite laminates are used as a uniform example throughout this chapter, but concepts used to analyze their behavior are often applicable to other forms of composite materials. In many instances, the applicability will be made clear as an example complementary to the principal example of fiber-reinforced composite laminates.

The basic terminology of fiber-reinforced composite laminates will be introduced in the following paragraphs. For a lamina, the configurations and functions of the constituent materials, fibers and matrix, will be described. The characteristics of the fibers and matrix are then discussed. Finally, a laminate is defined to round out this introduction to the characteristics of fiber-reinforced composite laminates.

Laminae

The basic building block of a laminate is a lamina which is a flat (sometimes curved as in a shell) arrangement of unidirectional fibers or woven fibers in a matrix. Two typical flat laminae along with their principal material axes that are parallel and perpendicular to the fiber direction are shown in Figure 1. The fibers are the principal reinforcing or load-carrying agent and are typically strong and stiff. The matrix can be organic, metallic, ceramic, or carbon. The function of the matrix is to support and protect the fibers and to provide a means of distributing load among, and transmitting load between, the fibers. The latter function is especially important if a fiber breaks as in Figure 2. There, load from one portion of a broken fiber is transferred to the matrix and, subsequently, to the other portion of the broken fiber as well as to adjacent fibers. The mechanism for load transfer is the shearing stress developed in the matrix; the shearing stress resists the pulling out of the broken fiber. This load-transfer mechanism is the means by which whisker reinforced composite materials carry any load at all above the inherent matrix strength.

The properties of the lamina constituents, the fibers and the matrix, have been only briefly discussed so far. Their stress-strain behavior is typified as one of the four classes depicted in Figure 3. Fibers generally exhibit linear elastic behavior, although reinforcing steel bars in concrete are more nearly elastic-perfectly plastic. Aluminum, as well as many polymers, and some composite materials exhibit elastic-plastic behavior that is really nonlinear elastic behavior if there is no unloading. Commonly, resinous matrix materials are viscoelastic if not viscoplastic, i. e., have strain-rate dependence and linear or nonlinear stress-strain behavior. The various stress-strain relations are sometimes referred to as constitutive relations because they describe the mechanical constitution of the material.

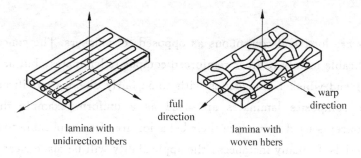

Figure 1 Two principal types of laminae

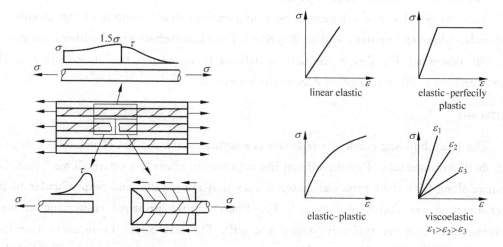

Figure 2 Effect of broken fiber on matrix and fiber stress

Figure 3 Various stress-strain behavior

Fiber-reinforced composite materials such as boron-epoxy and graphite-epoxy are usually treated as linear elastic materials because the essentially linear elastic fibers provide the majority of the strength and stiffness. Refinement of that approximation requires consideration of some form of plasticity, viscoelasticity, or both (viscoplasticity). Very little work has been done to implement those models or idealizations of composite material behavior in structural applications.

Laminates

A laminate is a bonded stack of laminae with various orientations of principal material directions in the laminae as in Figure 4. Note that the fiber orientation of the layers in Figure 4 is not symmetric about the middle surface of the laminate. The layers of a laminate are usually bonded together by the same matrix material that is used in the individual laminae. That is, some of the matrix material in a lamina coats the surfaces of a lamina and is used to bond the lamina to its adjacent laminae without the addition of more matrix material. Laminates can be composed of plates of different materials or, in the present context, layers of fiber-reinforced laminae. A laminated circular cylindrical shell can be constructed by winding resin-coated fibers on a removable core structure called a mandrel first with one orientation to the shell axis, then another, and so on until the desired thickness is achieved.

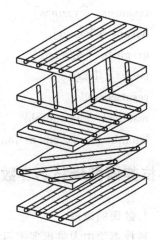

Figure 4 Unbonded view of laminate construction

A major purpose of lamination is to tailor the directional dependence of strength and stiffness of a composite material to match the loading environment of the structural element. Laminates are uniquely suited to this objective because the principal material directions of each layer can be oriented according to need. For example, six layers of a ten-layer laminate could be oriented in one direction and the other four at 90° to that direction; the resulting laminate then has a strength and extensional stiffness roughly 50% higher in one direction than the other. The ratio of the extensional stiffnesses in the two directions is approximately 6∶4, but the ratio of bending stiffnesses is unclear because the order of lamination is not specified in the example. Moreover, if the laminae are not arranged symmetrically about the middle surface of the laminate, the result is stiffnesses that represent coupling between bending and extension.

Words and Expressions

laminate ['læmineit]	n.	薄板；层压板；层板
fiber-reinforced		纤维增强
composite material		复合材料
whisker ['hwiskə]	n.	金须
lamina ['læmənə]	n.	薄板；薄片
matrix ['meitriks]	n.	基体(材料)
woven fiber		编织纤维

principal material axis		材料主轴
organic　[ɔ:'gænik]	adj.	有机的；有机物质
elastic-perfectly plastic		理想弹塑性
resinous　['rezinəs]	adj.	树脂的
boron　['bɔ:rɔn]	n.	硼
graphite　['græfait]	n.	石墨
layer　['leiə]	n.	层
resin-coated	adj.	树脂涂层的
mandrel　['mændrəl]	n.	心轴；拉延
lamination　[,læmi'neiʃn]	n.	制成薄板；薄板；层状体

科技英语翻译技巧：数词的译法和被动语态的译法[31]

1. 数词的译法

科技英语中大量出现表示数量、倍数增减的词语，在翻译时要特别注意英汉两种语言表达方式的异同。

(1) as ＋形容词＋ as ＋ 数词 ＋……；动词 ＋ as ＋ 副词 ＋ 数词 ＋……

as large as ＋数词……　　可译成"大到(至)……"
as many as ＋数词……　　可译成"多达……"
as high as ＋数词……　　可译成"高达……"
as heavy as ＋数词……　　可译成"重达……"
as low as ＋数词……　　可译成"低到(至)……"

The tensile strength of the cables used in this stayed-cable bridge is *as high as* 1400MPa.
这座斜拉桥中使用的拉索的拉伸强度**高达** 1400MPa。

(2) 倍数的比较

A is N times as large (long, heavy...) as B
A is N times larger (longer, heavier...) than B
A is larger (longer, heavier...) than B by N times

上述三种句型，虽其结构各异，但所表达的概念完全一样。因此在译成汉语时彼此之间不应有所区别。均可译成：A 的大小(长度、重量、……)是 B 的 N 倍。或 A 比 B 大(长、重、……) N－1 倍。

This substance reacts *three times as fast as* the other one.
这一物质的反应速度比另一物质**快两倍**。

In case of electronic scanning the beam width is broader *by a factor of two*.
电子扫描时，波束宽度扩大**一倍**。

(3) 倍数的增加

(a) 主语＋谓语　　double (treble; quadruple)＋ ……
double 可译成"增加一倍"或"翻一番"
treble 可译成"增加二倍"或"增加到三倍"

quadruple 可译成"增加三倍"或"翻两番"

Whenever we *double* the force on a given object, we *double* the acceleration.

每当作用在某一给定物体上的力**增加一倍**，加速度也**增加一倍**。

(b) Increase N times; increase to N times; increase by N times; increase N-fold; increase by a factor of N

上述五种结构表达的意思完全一致。均表示"乘以 N"、"成 N 倍"这一概念，因此应译成"增加到 N 倍"或"增加了 N－1 倍"。

A temperature rise of 200℃ *increases* the viscosity of this kind of material *by 2 times*.

温度上升 200℃，这种材料的粘性就**增加到两倍**。

(c) as much (many …) again as; again as much (many …) as 可译为"是……的两倍"或"比……多一倍"。

Half as much (many…) again as; half again as much (many …) as 可译成"是……的一倍半"；"比……多半倍"或"比……多一半"

The resistance of aluminum is approximately *half again as great as* that of copper for the same dimensions.

尺寸相同时，铝的电阻约为铜的**一倍半**。

(4) 倍数的减少

(a) Reduce by N times; reduce N times; reduce to N times; reduce N times as much (many…) as; N-fold reduction; N times less than

上述所有结构均表达"减少了 $\frac{N-1}{N}$"或"减少到 $\frac{1}{N}$"，所列结构中，除 reduce 外，尚有若干表示"减少"的同义词和近义词，如：decrease, shorten, drop, step-down, cut down 等。在 N times less than 结构中，less 可换成其他弱比较级的词，如：lighter, weaker, shorter 等。

The new equipment *will reduce* the error probability by *seven times*.

新设备的误差概率将**降低七分之六**。

The frictional resistebce *has dropped five times*.

摩擦阻力**降低了五分之四**。

(b) half as much as; twice less than

该两种结构均可译为"比……少一半"或"比……少二分之一"。

The power output of the machine is *twice less than* its input.

该机器的输出功率比输入功率**小二分之一**。

(5) 分数和百分数增减的译法

(a) 分数和百分数的增减，一般表示净增减的部分，不包括底数在内，因此可直译成"增加(减少)几分之几"，"增加(减少)百分之几"。

The pressure *will be reduced to one-fourth* of its original value.

压力**将减少到原来数值的四分之一**。

(b) X% + n.; v. + to + X%

上述两种结构表示增减后的结果，包括底数在内。可直接译出或按倍数的译法处理。

This year the factory has produced 250 % *the number of color TV sets* in 1985.

该厂今年生产的**彩电**是 1985 年**的 250 %**。或：该厂今年生产的**彩电**是 1985 年**的 2.5 倍**。或：该厂今年生产的**彩电比** 1985 年**增加了一倍半**。

2. 被动语态的译法

英语和汉语都有被动语态，但两种文字对被动语态的运用却不尽相同。语态的使用不同，语气和情调也随之而异。在英译汉时，必须注意被动语态的译出，不要过分拘泥于原文的被动结构。科技英语主要是叙述事理，往往不需要说出主动者，或对被动者比主动者更为关心。此外，科技工作者为了表示客观和谦虚的态度，往往避免使用第一人称，因而尽可能使用被动语态。因此，在翻译英语被动语态时，大量的应译成主动句，少数的仍可译成被动句。

(1) 译成汉语的主动句

(a) 原主语仍译为主语

当英语被动句中的主语为无生命的名词，又不出现由介词 by 引导的行为主体时，往往可译成汉语的主动句，原句的主语在译文中仍为主语。这种把被动语态直接译成主动语态的句子，实际是省略了"被"字的被动句。如

If a machine part *is* not well *protected*, it will become rusty after a period of time.

如果机器部件不好好**防护**，过一段时间后就会生锈。

(b) 把原主语译成宾语，而把行为主体或相当于行为主体的介词宾语译成主语。

Friction can be reduced and the life of the machine prolonged by *lubrication*.

润滑能减少摩擦，延长机器寿命。

(c) 在翻译某些被动语态时，增译适当的主语使译文通顺流畅。

增译逻辑主语：原句未包含动作的发出者，译成主动句时可以从逻辑出发，适当增加不确定的主语，如"人们"、"有人"、"大家"、"我们"等，并把原句的主语译成宾语。

To explore the moon's surface, rockets *were launched* again and again.

为了探测月球的表面，**人们**一次又一次地发射火箭。

某些要求复合宾语的动词，如 believe, consider, find, know, see, think 等，用于被动语态时，翻译时往往可加上不确定主语。

Salt *is known* to have a very strong corroding effect on metals.

大家知道，盐对金属有很强的腐蚀作用。

由 it 作形式主语的被动句型。这种句型在科技英语中比比皆是，十分普遍，汉译时一般均按主动结构译出。即将原文中的主语从句译在宾语的位置上，而把 it 作形式主语的主句译成一个独立语或分句。

It is believed to be natural that more and more engineers have come to prefer synthetic material to natural material.

愈来愈多的工程人员宁愿用合成材料而不用天然材料，**人们相信**这是很自然的。

(2) 译成汉语的其他句型

(a) 译成汉语的无主句：英语的许多被动句不需或无法讲出动作的发出者，往往可译成汉语的无主句，而把原句中的主语译成宾语。英语中有些固定的动词短语，如：make use of, pay attention to, take care of, put an end to 等用于被动句时，常译成被动句。

Attention has been paid to the new measures to prevent corrosion.

已经注意到采取防腐新措施。

（b）译成汉语的判断句。凡着重描述事物的过程、性质和状态的英语被动句,实际上与系表结构很相近,往往可译成"是……的"结构。

The oscillation *is not attenuated* in that way.

振动不是用那样的方法**减小的**。

（c）译成汉语的被动句:英语的有些着重被动动作的被动句,要译成被动句,以突出其被动意义。被动含义可用"被"、"由"、"给"、"受"、"加以"、"为……所"、"使"、"把"、"让"、"叫"、"为"、"挨"、"遭"等表达。

The metric system *is* now *used* by almost all countries in the world.

米制现在**被**全世界几乎所有的国家**采用**。

◇◇◇◇◇◇◇◇◇◇◇◇◇◇◇◇◇◇◇◇

Reading Material(1): Macromechanical Behavior of a Lamina[24]

Introduction

The basic questions of lamina macromechanics are: (1) what are the characteristics of a lamina? And (2) how does a lamina respond to applied stresses as in Figure 2-1? A lamina is a flat (or curved as in a shell) arrangement of unidirectional or woven fibers in a supporting matrix. The concepts developed here apply equally to both types of lamina, but we will explicitly address only unidirectional laminae. A lamina is the basic building block in laminated fiber-reinforced composite materials. Thus, knowledge of the mechanical behavior of a lamina is essential to the understanding of laminated fiber-reinforced structures.

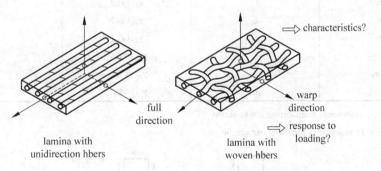

Figure 2-1　Basic questions of lamina macromechanics

Stress-Strain Relations for Anisotropic Materials

The generalized Hooke's law relating stresses to strains can be written in contracted notation as

$$\sigma_i = C_{ij}\varepsilon_j, \quad i,j = 1,\cdots,6 \tag{2.1}$$

where σ_i are the stress components shown on a three-dimensional cube in x, y, and z

coordinates in Figure 2-2, C_{ij} is the stiffness matrix, and ε_j are the strain components. The contracted notation for three dimensional stresses and stains is defined in comparison to the usual tensor notation in Table 2-1 for situations in which the stress and strain tensors are symmetric (the usual case when body forces are absent). Note that, by virtue of Table 2-1, the strains are therefore defined as

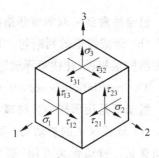

Figure 2-2　Stress on an element

$$\varepsilon_1 = \frac{\partial u}{\partial x}, \quad \varepsilon_2 = \frac{\partial v}{\partial y}, \quad \varepsilon_3 = \frac{\partial w}{\partial z}$$

$$\gamma_{23} = \frac{\partial v}{\partial z} + \frac{\partial w}{\partial y}, \quad \gamma_{31} = \frac{\partial w}{\partial x} + \frac{\partial u}{\partial z}, \quad \gamma_{12} = \frac{\partial u}{\partial y} + \frac{\partial v}{\partial x} \tag{2.2}$$

where u, v, and w are displacements in the x, y, and z directions (or the 1, 2, and 3 directions).

Note that the engineering shear strain, γ_{ij}, in Table 2-1 is the total angle of shearing under a state of simple shear in Figure 2-3. Also, the tensor shear strain, ε_{ij}, is half of the angle of shearing under pure shear stress in Figure 2-3. Engineering shear strain implies a rotation of the originally square element, whereas tensor shear strain does not have an accompanying rotation. These distinctions have little significance for the usual engineering calculations, but have crucial significance in what follows.

Table 2-1　Tensor versus contracted notation for stresses and strains

Stresses		Strains	
Tensor Notation	Contracted Notation	Tensor Notation	Contracted Notation
$\sigma_{11}(\sigma_1)$	σ_1	$\varepsilon_{11}(\varepsilon_1)$	ε_1
$\sigma_{22}(\sigma_2)$	σ_2	$\varepsilon_{22}(\varepsilon_2)$	ε_2
$\sigma_{33}(\sigma_3)$	σ_3	$\varepsilon_{33}(\varepsilon_3)$	ε_3
$\tau_{23}=\sigma_{32}$	σ_4	$\gamma_{23}=2\varepsilon_{11}^*$	ε_4
$\tau_{31}=\sigma_{31}$	σ_5	$\gamma_{31}=2\varepsilon_{11}$	ε_5
$\tau_{12}=\sigma_{12}$	σ_6	$\gamma_{12}=2\varepsilon_{11}$	ε_6

* Note that γ_{ij} represents engineering shear strain whereas $\varepsilon_{ij} (i \neq j)$ represents tensor shear strain

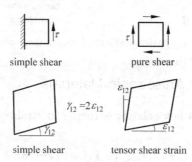

Figure 2-3　Engineering shear strain versus tensor shear strain

The stiffness matrix, C_{ij}, has 36 constants in Equation (2.1). However, less than 36 of the constants can be shown to actually be independent for elastic materials when important characteristics of the strain energy are considered. Elastic materials for which an elastic potential or strain energy density function exists have incremental work per unit volume of

$$dW = \sigma_i d\varepsilon_i \tag{2.3}$$

when the stresses σ_i act through strains $d\varepsilon_i$. However, because of the stress-strain relations, Equation (2.1), the incremental work becomes

$$dW = C_{ij}\varepsilon_j d\varepsilon_i \tag{2.4}$$

Upon integration for all strains, the work per nit of volume is

$$W = \frac{1}{2}C_{ij}\varepsilon_i\varepsilon_j \tag{2.5}$$

However, Hooke's law, Equation (2.1), can be derived from Equation (2.5):

$$\frac{\partial W}{\partial \varepsilon_i} = C_{ij}\varepsilon_j \tag{2.6}$$

whereupon

$$\frac{\partial^2 W}{\partial \varepsilon_i \partial \varepsilon_j} = C_{ij} \tag{2.7}$$

Similarly,

$$\frac{\partial^2 W}{\partial \varepsilon_j \partial \varepsilon_i} = C_{ji} \tag{2.8}$$

But the order of differentiation of W is immaterial, so

$$C_{ij} = C_{ji} \tag{2.9}$$

Thus, the stiffness matrix is symmetric, so only 21 of the constants are independent.

In a similar manner, we can show that

$$W = \frac{1}{2}S_{ij}\sigma_i\sigma_j \tag{2.10}$$

where S_{ij} is the compliance matrix defined by the inverse of the stress-strain relations, namely the strain-stress relations:

$$\varepsilon_i = S_{ij}\sigma_j, \quad i,j = 1,2,\cdots,6 \tag{2.11}$$

Reasoning similar to that in the preceding paragraph leads to

$$S_{ij} = S_{ji} \tag{2.12}$$

i. e., that the compliance matrix is symmetric and hence has only 21 independent constants. At this point, note that the stiffnesses and compliances are not described with mnemonic notation, but are unfortunately reversed in common usage. The stiffness and compliance components will be referred to as elastic constants (although they could be functions to temperature or moisture content).

With the foregoing reduction from 36 to 21 independent constants, the stress-strain relations are

$$\begin{bmatrix} \sigma_1 \\ \sigma_2 \\ \sigma_3 \\ \tau_{23} \\ \tau_{31} \\ \tau_{12} \end{bmatrix} = \begin{bmatrix} C_{11} & C_{12} & C_{13} & C_{14} & C_{15} & C_{16} \\ C_{12} & C_{22} & C_{23} & C_{24} & C_{25} & C_{26} \\ C_{13} & C_{23} & C_{33} & C_{34} & C_{35} & C_{36} \\ C_{14} & C_{24} & C_{34} & C_{44} & C_{45} & C_{46} \\ C_{15} & C_{25} & C_{35} & C_{45} & C_{55} & C_{56} \\ C_{16} & C_{26} & C_{36} & C_{46} & C_{56} & C_{66} \end{bmatrix} \begin{bmatrix} \varepsilon_1 \\ \varepsilon_2 \\ \varepsilon_3 \\ \gamma_{23} \\ \gamma_{31} \\ \gamma_{12} \end{bmatrix} \quad (2.13)$$

as the most general expression within the framework of linear elasticity. Actually, the relations in Equation (2.13) are referred to as characterizing anisotropic materials (anisotropic means without isotropy) because there are no planes of symmetry for the material properties. An alternative name for such an anisotropic material is a triclinic material (three axes of the material are all oblique to one another). Materials with more property symmetry than anisotropic materials will be described in the next few paragraphs. Proof of the form of the stress-strain relations for the various cases of material property symmetry is given, for example, by Tsai.

If there is one plane of material property symmetry, the stress-strain relations reduce to

$$\begin{bmatrix} \sigma_1 \\ \sigma_2 \\ \sigma_3 \\ \tau_{23} \\ \tau_{31} \\ \tau_{12} \end{bmatrix} = \begin{bmatrix} C_{11} & C_{12} & C_{13} & 0 & 0 & C_{16} \\ C_{12} & C_{22} & C_{23} & 0 & 0 & C_{26} \\ C_{13} & C_{23} & C_{33} & 0 & 0 & C_{36} \\ 0 & 0 & 0 & C_{44} & C_{45} & 0 \\ 0 & 0 & 0 & C_{45} & C_{55} & 0 \\ C_{16} & C_{26} & C_{36} & 0 & 0 & C_{66} \end{bmatrix} \begin{bmatrix} \varepsilon_1 \\ \varepsilon_2 \\ \varepsilon_3 \\ \gamma_{23} \\ \gamma_{31} \\ \gamma_{12} \end{bmatrix} \quad (2.14)$$

where the plane of symmetry is $z = 0$ (or the 1-2 plane). Such a material is termed monoclinic and has 13 independent elastic constants.

If there are two orthogonal planes of material property symmetry for a material, symmetry will exist relative to a third mutually orthogonal plane. The stress-strain relations in coordinates aligned with principal material directions are

$$\begin{bmatrix} \sigma_1 \\ \sigma_2 \\ \sigma_3 \\ \tau_{23} \\ \tau_{31} \\ \tau_{12} \end{bmatrix} = \begin{bmatrix} C_{11} & C_{12} & C_{13} & 0 & 0 & 0 \\ C_{12} & C_{22} & C_{23} & 0 & 0 & 0 \\ C_{13} & C_{23} & C_{33} & 0 & 0 & 0 \\ 0 & 0 & 0 & C_{44} & 0 & 0 \\ 0 & 0 & 0 & 0 & C_{55} & 0 \\ 0 & 0 & 0 & 0 & 0 & C_{66} \end{bmatrix} \begin{bmatrix} \varepsilon_1 \\ \varepsilon_2 \\ \varepsilon_3 \\ \gamma_{23} \\ \gamma_{31} \\ \gamma_{12} \end{bmatrix} \quad (2.15)$$

and are said to define an orthotropic material. Note that there is no interaction between normal stresses $\sigma_1, \sigma_2, \sigma_3$ and shearing strains $\gamma_{23}, \gamma_{31}, \gamma_{12}$ such as occurs in anisotropic materials (by virtue of the presence of, for example, C_{14}). Similarly, there is no interaction between shearing stresses and normal strains as well as none between shearing stresses and shearing strains in different planes. Note also that there are now only nine independent constants in the stiffness matrix.

If at every point of a material there is one plane in which the mechanical properties are equal in all directions, then the material is called transversely isotropic. If, for example, the 1-2 plane is the plane of isotropy, then the 1 and 2 subscripts on the stiffnesses are interchangeable. The stress-strain relations have only five independent constants:

$$\begin{bmatrix} \sigma_1 \\ \sigma_2 \\ \sigma_3 \\ \tau_{23} \\ \tau_{31} \\ \tau_{12} \end{bmatrix} = \begin{bmatrix} C_{11} & C_{12} & C_{13} & 0 & 0 & 0 \\ C_{12} & C_{11} & C_{13} & 0 & 0 & 0 \\ C_{13} & C_{13} & C_{33} & 0 & 0 & 0 \\ 0 & 0 & 0 & C_{44} & 0 & 0 \\ 0 & 0 & 0 & 0 & C_{44} & 0 \\ 0 & 0 & 0 & 0 & 0 & (C_{11}-C_{12})/2 \end{bmatrix} \begin{bmatrix} \varepsilon_1 \\ \varepsilon_2 \\ \varepsilon_3 \\ \gamma_{23} \\ \gamma_{31} \\ \gamma_{12} \end{bmatrix} \quad (2.16)$$

If there is an infinite number of planes of material property symmetry, then the foregoing relations simplify to the isotropic material relations with only two independent constants in the stiffness matrix:

$$\begin{bmatrix} \sigma_1 \\ \sigma_2 \\ \sigma_3 \\ \tau_{23} \\ \tau_{31} \\ \tau_{12} \end{bmatrix} = \begin{bmatrix} C_{11} & C_{12} & C_{12} & 0 & 0 & 0 \\ C_{12} & C_{11} & C_{12} & 0 & 0 & 0 \\ C_{12} & C_{12} & C_{11} & 0 & 0 & 0 \\ 0 & 0 & 0 & (C_{11}-C_{12})/2 & 0 & 0 \\ 0 & 0 & 0 & 0 & (C_{11}-C_{12})/2 & 0 \\ 0 & 0 & 0 & 0 & 0 & (C_{11}-C_{12})/2 \end{bmatrix} \begin{bmatrix} \varepsilon_1 \\ \varepsilon_2 \\ \varepsilon_3 \\ \gamma_{23} \\ \gamma_{31} \\ \gamma_{12} \end{bmatrix} \quad (2.17)$$

The strain-stress relations for the five most common material property symmetry cases are:

Anisotropic (21 independent constants), Monoclinic (13 independent constants), Orthotropic (9 independent constants), Transversely Isotropic (5 independent constants), Isotropic (2 independent constants).

One of the major objectives in studying the strain-stress relations is to be able to conclude what deformation response occurs because of a specific applied stress. The strain-stress relations can be written as

$$\varepsilon_1 = S_{11}\sigma_1 + S_{12}\sigma_2 + S_{13}\sigma_3 + S_{14}\tau_{23} + S_{15}\tau_{31} + S_{16}\tau_{12}$$
$$\vdots$$
$$\gamma_{12} = S_{16}\sigma_1 + S_{26}\sigma_2 + S_{36}\sigma_3 + S_{46}\tau_{23} + S_{56}\tau_{31} + S_{66}\tau_{12} \quad (2.18)$$

Accordingly, for an applied uniaxial stress $\sigma_1 = \sigma$ (all other stresses are zero):

$$\varepsilon_1 = S_{11}\sigma \quad \varepsilon_2 = S_{12}\sigma \quad \varepsilon_3 = S_{13}\sigma$$
$$\gamma_{23} = S_{14}\sigma \quad \gamma_{31} = S_{15}\sigma \quad \gamma_{12} = S_{16}\sigma \quad (2.19)$$

The physical interpretation of these strains is that an originally equal-sided cube has many deformations. Specifically, each side deforms in length differently from any other side (because $S_{11} \neq S_{12} \neq S_{13}$), and each side of the cube undergoes a different shearing deformation (because $S_{14} \neq S_{15} \neq S_{16}$), as depicted imperfectly in Figure 2-4, where the dashed lines represent the undeformed cube and the solid lines represent the deformed cube. Try to imagine yourself in a room that undergoes these deformations! In contrast, an isotropic material would have the same change in side length in the 2- and 3-directions (because $S_{12} = S_{13}$) and no shearing deformation of any side (because $S_{14} = S_{15} = S_{16} = 0$). Thus, for an anisotropic material, significant coupling occurs between the applied stress and the various strain responses.

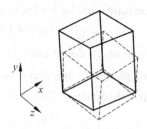

Figure 2-4 Deformation of an anisotropic cube under σ_y

Those various couplings are shown for an arbitrarily stressed body in Figure 2-5 where the physical significance of each compliance is labeled. There, the terms S_{11}, S_{22}, and S_{33} each represent extensional response to an individual applied stress, σ_1, σ_2 and σ_3, respectively, in the same direction. The terms S_{44}, S_{55}, and S_{66} represent shear strain response to an applied shear stress in the same plane. The terms S_{12}, S_{13}, and S_{23} represent coupling between dissimilar normal stresses and normal strains (extension-extension coupling more commonly known as the Poisson effect). The terms S_{14}, S_{15}, S_{16}, S_{24}, S_{25}, S_{26}, S_{34}, S_{35} and S_{36} represent nornal strain response to applied shear stress in a more complex manner than for the preceding compliances (shear-extension coupling). Finally, the terms S_{45}, S_{46}, and S_{56}, represent shear strain response to shear stress applied in another plane (shear-shear coupling). In contrast, the only coupling that exists for an isotropic material is extension-extension coupling. Thus, the deformation response of an anisotropic material even to simple stress states can literally be in every direction and in every plane. Moreover, we will see that S_{11}, S_{22}, and S_{33} are related to the Young's moduli in the 1-, 2-, and 3-directions, respectively. Also, S_{12}, S_{13} and S_{14} will be related to the Poission's ratios and Young's moduli. Finally, S_{44}, S_{55}, and S_{66} will be related to shear moduli in the 2-3, 3-1, and 1-2 planes, respectively.

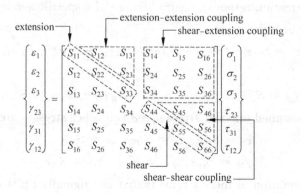

Figure 2-5 Physical significance of the anisotropic stress-strain relations

Words and Expressions

contracted notation		缩约记号
engineering shear strain		工程剪应变
differentiation [ˌdifəˌrenʃi'eiʃən]	n.	微分
compliance [kəm'plaiəns]	n.	柔度
mnemonic [niː'mɔnik]	adj.	记忆的
	n.	记忆方法
triclinic [trai'klinik]	adj.	三斜晶系的
oblique [əb'liːk]	adj.	斜的；倾斜
monoclinic [ˌmɔnə'klinik]	adj.	单斜晶体的
orthotropic [ˌɔːθə'trɔpik]	adj.	正交的
transversely isotropic		横观各向同性
Poisson effect		泊松效应

Reading Material(2): Shape Memory Alloy and Smart Hybrid Composites Advanced Materials for the 21st Century[25]

Introduction

Shape memory alloy (SMA) is a metal which can remember and return to a specific shape after considerable deformation. This function of shape memory alloys was defined as the shape memory effect (SME). Generally, it is believed that the SME results from the thermoelastic martensitic transformation. The schematic micro mechanism of the SME is shown in Fig. 1. M_s, M_f, A_s and A_f are identical to the starting and finishing temperature of martensitic and austenitic transformation, respectively. The martensite will be produced when the parent austenite crystal is cooled below the M_s. At this stage, there will be no macro shape change because of the coordinately twinned deformation, called self-accommodation. Twinned boundaries will move and disappear when the martensite undergoes extra stress at the temperature below M_f, which results in macro deformation. On heating to the A_s temperature, the deformed martensite will resume the original shape of the parent through the reverse transformation from the martensite to the parent austenite phase.

There is another type of shape memory that is termed stress-induced martensite (SIM). The driving force for the transformation is mechanical, as opposed to thermal. When a material is deformed above M_s, martensite can be made stable with the application of stress, but becomes unstable again when the stress is removed, as shown in Fig. 2. The upper plateau corresponds to the formation of martensite under stress, while the lower plateau represents the reversion of the SIM when the stress is released.

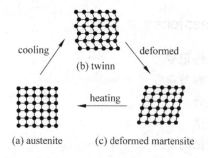

Fig. 1　Schematic of shape memory effect

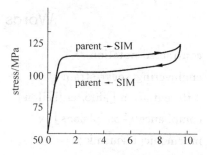

Fig. 2　Stress-strain curve of superelasticity

Application of the SMA

SMAs are widely used as the sensing, actuator and damping instruments. Recently, much work has been done on hybrid structures which incorporated shape memory alloys with other structural or functional materials in our laboratory. These hybrid composites show some unique properties or functions such as self-strengthening, active modal modification, high damping, damage resistance and control so they can provide tremendous potential in many engineering applications.

SMA particulate-reinforced composites

Owing to the mismatch of the thermal expansion coefficient (CTE) between the matrix and filler, a residual thermal stress is introduced into the composite which is fabricated at high temperature and then cooled down to room temperature. It is well established that compressive residual stress in the matrix caused by the higher CTE of the filler than the matrix, is beneficial to the mechanical properties such as the yield stress and fracture toughness. Similarly, if there is a special filler that shrinks in the matrix at use temperature or with increasing applied stress, compressive stress may be introduced into the matrix, thus contributing to the tensile properties of the composite. SMA do exhibit such shrinkage if properly designed. Particulate reinforced MMCs have attracted considerable attention as a result of their feasibility for mass production, promising mechanical properties and potential high damping capacity. In particular, discontinuously reinforced Al alloy MMCs provide high damping and low density and allow undesirable mechanical vibration and wave propagation to be suppressed. The strengthening mechanism of this composite can be described as follows: (1) an as-fabricated composite is heated to shape memorizing temperature, as shown in Fig. 3a; (2) the composite is cooled to martensite phase region (Fig. 3b); (3) it is subjected to tensile prestrain (Fig. 3c); and (4) the last step, the SMA particles are transformed from martensite to austenite by heating the composite above the austenite starting temperature (As). This transformation involves the shape recovery of the SMA particle from the deformed shape in Fig. 3c to the original shape, which is the shape memorized by SMA particles in Fig. 3a. This shape recovery process induced compressive stress in the matrix along the prestrain direction, which in turn enhanced the tension properties and the fatigue life of the composite.

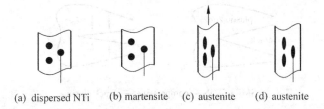

(a) dispersed NTi (b) martensite (c) austenite (d) austenite

Fig. 3 Strengthening of the mechanism of the composite by the SMA particle

Yamada et al. have theoretically studied the strengthening of the Al MMCs by the SME of dispersed TiNi SMA particles, with varying volume fractions and prestrains of the particles. The calculation results have shown that the magnitude and the direction of residual stresses can be controlled composite, the Young's modulus, yield stress by prestraining the and workhardening rate can be increased.

SMA fiber-reinforced composites

In the light of enhancing the tensile properties by using compressive residual stress in the matrix of a composite, SMA fibers are excellent candidate fillers. SMA fibers are of particular interest for their high damping capacity and sensing and actuating functions. Accordingly, SMA fibers/Al MMcs, SMA fibers/polymer or elastomer matrix composites have been developed, and the properties of the composites have been predicted by modeling. Depending on the boundary conditions, fiber pretreatment and distribution, significant changes in stiffness, damping, shape or vibration frequency of the entire composite can be obtained, suggesting the possibility to actively control the static and dynamic properties of composite materials. For a TiNi fiber/Al alloy MMC, experimental results indicate that the mechanical tensile properties and the damping capacity can be significantly improved by the strengthening mechanism. The design concept for the SMA fiber/metal matrix composite is given in Fig. 4.

When SMA fibers were embedded in Al matrix, the composite was prestrained along parallel fiber direction at low temperature, and then heated to the SMA parent phase state, and a compressive residual stress would be introduced into the composite because the SMA fiber has more shrinkage than the Al matrix. This compressive residual stress is very useful for closing the micro-crack of the composite

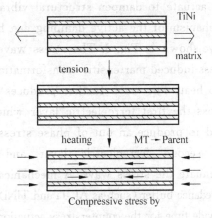

Fig. 4 Strengthening mechanism of SMA-based MMCs

because it can effectively partly decrease environmental stress, which in turn increases the fatigue life of the composite as shown in Fig. 5.

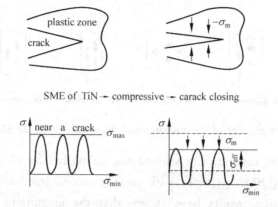

Fig. 5 Residual compressive stress and crack closing

SMA thin film and the ferroelectric ceramic film composites

As a candidate material for mechanical actuators and sensors in micro-electro-mechanical systems, SMA thin films have received considerable attention in recent years because of their desirable mechanical properties, such as exerting the stress of hundreds of megapascals, tolerating strains of more than 3%, working at common TTL voltages, and surviving millions of cycles without failure. However, the limited applications of SMAs are mainly due to their lossy behavior that results in a low speed in response and, therefore, a long cycle lifetime. Ferroelectric ceramics are very sensitive to applied stresses through the piezoelectric effect and have fast response times (of the order of microseconds), but displacements are quite small (of the order of a few micrometers) due to the small strain magnitude ($<10^{-3}$).

By coupling TiNi SMA with a ferroelectric ceramic, the composite material can sense and actuate to dampen structural vibration without the use of an external control. The mechanism of the active damping can be explained by considering an approaching stress wave shown in Fig. 6. The stress wave propagates through the TiNi SMA producing a stress-induced martensitic transformation where some of the mechanical energy converts into heat. The wave further produces a voltage across the first ferroelectric layer which can be used to produce an out of phase stress wave by the second ferroelectric layer and in turn attenuate the stress wave. A mechanical metallic impedance buffer (such as Al, Ti and TiNi) is used to provide time for the counterstress actuation to occur.

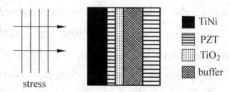

Fig. 6 Schematic illustration of a smart ferroelectric heterostructure for active damping

Words and Expressions

shape memory alloy (SMA) 形状记忆合金
shape memory effect (SME) 形状记忆效应
martensitic transformation 马氏体转变
austenitic transformation 奥氏体转变
martensite ['mɑːtən,zait] *n.* 马氏体
austenite ['ɔːstə,nait] *n.* 奥氏体
austenite crystal 奥氏体晶粒
twinned boundary 孪生边界
phase [feiz] *n.* 相
stress-induced martensite (SIM) 应力诱发马氏体
superelasticity *n.* 超弹性
particulate-reinforced composite 颗粒增强复合材料
thermal expansion coefficient 热膨胀系数
residual thermal stress 残余热应力
prestrain [priː'strein] *n.* 预应变
volume fraction 体积分数
elastomer [i'læstəmə] *n.* 弹性体
ferroelectric [,ferəui'lektrik] *adj.* 铁电的
micro-electro-mechanical 微电机的
tolerating strain 容许应变
piezoelectric [pai,iːzəui'lektrik] *adj.* 压电的
counter stress 对应力；相反应力
heterostructure [hetərəu'strʌktʃə(r)] *n.* 异质结构

Unit Twelve

Fluid Mechanics[30]

  Fluid mechanics deals with the flow of fluids. Its study is important to physicists, whose main interest is in understanding phenomena. They may, for example, be interested in learning what causes the various types of wave phenomena in the atmosphere and in the ocean, why a layer of fluid heated from below breaks up into cellular patterns, why a tennis ball hit with "top spin" dips rather sharply, how fish swim, and how birds fly. The study of fluid mechanics is just as important to engineers, whose main interest is in the applications of fluid mechanics to solve industrial problems. Aerospace engineers may be interested in designing airplanes that have low resistance and, at the same time, high "lift" force to support the weight of the plane. Civil engineers may be interested in designing irrigation canals, dams, and water supply systems. Pollution control engineers may be interested in saving our planet from the constant dumping of industrial sewage into the atmosphere and the ocean. Mechanical engineers may be interested in designing turbines, heat exchangers, and fluid couplings. Chemical engineers may be interested in designing efficient devices to mix industrial chemicals. The objectives of physicists and engineers, however, are not quite separable because the engineers need to understand and the physicists need to be motivated through applications.

  Fluid mechanics, like the study of any other branch of science, needs mathematical analyses as well as experimentation. The analytical approaches help in finding the solutions to certain idealized and simplified problems, and in understanding the unity behind apparently dissimilar phenomena. Needless to say, drastic simplifications are frequently necessary because of the complexity of real phenomena. A good understanding of mathematical techniques is definitely helpful here, although it is probably fair to say that some of the greatest theoretical contributions have come from the people who depended rather strongly on their unusual physical intuition, some sort of a "vision" by which they were able to distinguish between what is relevant and what is not. Chess player, Bobby Fischer (appearing on the television program "The Johnny Carson Show," about 1979), once compared a good chess player and a great one in the following manner: When a good chess player looks at a chess board, he thinks of 20 possible moves; he analyzes all of them and picks the one that he likes. A great chess player, on the other hand, analyzes only two or three possible moves; his unusual intuition (part of which must have grown from experience) allows him immediately to rule out a large number of moves without going through an apparent logical analysis. Ludwig Prandtl, one of the founders of modern fluid mechanics, first conceived the idea of a boundary layer based solely on physical intuition. His knowledge of mathematics was rather limited, as his famous student von Karman (1954) testifies. Interestingly, the boundary layer technique has now become one of the most powerful methods in applied mathematics!

As in other fields, our mathematical ability is too limited to tackle the complex problems of real fluid flows. Whether we are primarily interested either in understanding the physics or in the applications, we must depend heavily on experimental observations to test our analyses and develop insights into the nature of the phenomenon. Fluid dynamicists cannot afford to think like pure mathematicians. The well-known English pure mathematician G. H. Hardy once described applied mathematics as a form of "glorified plumbing" (G. I. Taylor, 1974). It is frightening to imagine what Hardy would have said of experimental sciences!

For mechanical systems, the units of all physical variables can be expressed in terms of the units of four basic variables, namely, length, mass, time, and temperature. The international system of units and commonly referred to as SI units, will be used most of the time. The basic units of this system are meter for length, kilogram for mass, second for time, and Kelvin for temperature. The units for other variables can be derived from these basic units. Some of the common variables used in fluid mechanics, and their SI units, are listed in Table 1.1.

Table 1.1 SI Units

Quantity	Name of unit	Symbol	Equivalent
Length	meter	m	
Mass	kilogram	kg	
Time	second	s	
Temperature	kelvin	K	
Frequency	hertz	Hz	s^{-1}
Force	newton	N	$kg \cdot m \cdot s^{-1}$
Pressure	pascal	Pa	$N \cdot m^{-2}$
Energy	joule	J	$N \cdot m$
Power	watt	W	$J \cdot s^{-1}$

Table 1.2 Common Prefixes

Prefix	Symbol	Multiple
Mega	M	10^6
Kilo	k	10^3
Deci	d	10^{-1}
Centi	c	10^{-2}
Milli	m	10^{-3}
Micro	μ	10^{-6}

To avoid very large or very small numerical values, prefixes are used to indicate multiples of the units given in Table 1.1. Some of the common prefixes are listed in Table 1.2. Strict adherence to the SI system is sometimes cumbersome and will be abandoned in favor of common usage where it best serves the purpose of simplifying things. For example, temperatures will be frequently quoted in degrees Celsius (℃), which is related to kelvin (K) by the relation ℃ = K − 273.15. However, the old English system of units (foot, pound, °F) will not be used, although engineers in the United States are still using it.

Most substances can be described as existing in two states—solid and fluid. An element of solid has a preferred shape, to which it relaxes when the external forces on it are withdrawn. In contrast, a fluid does not have any preferred shape. Consider a rectangular element of solid ABCD (Figure 1.1a). Under the action of a shear force F the element assumes the shape ABC'D'. If the solid is perfectly elastic, it goes back to its preferred shape ABCD when F is withdrawn. In contrast, a fluid deforms continuously under the action of a shear force, however small. Thus, the element of the fluid ABCD confined between parallel plates (Figure 1.1b) deforms to shapes such as ABC'D' and ABC"D"as long as the force F is maintained on the upper plate. Therefore, we say that a fluid flows.

The qualification "however small" in the forementioned description of a fluid is significant. This is because most solids also deform continuously if the shear stress exceeds a certain limiting value, corresponding to the "yield point" of the solid. A solid in such a state is known as "plastic." In fact, the distinction between solids and fluids can be hazy at times. Substances like paints, jelly, pitch, polymer solutions, and biological substances (for example, egg white) simultaneously display the characteristics of both solids and fluids. If we say that an elastic solid has "perfect memory" (because it always relaxes back to its preferred shape) and that an ordinary viscous fluid has zero memory, then substances like egg white can be called viscoelastic because they have "partial memory."

Although solids and fluids behave very differently when subjected to shear stresses, they behave similarly under the action of compressive normal stresses. However, whereas a solid can support both tensile and compressive normal stresses, a fluid usually supports only compression (pressure) stresses. (Some liquids can support a small amount of tensile stress, the amount depending on the degree of molecular cohesion.)

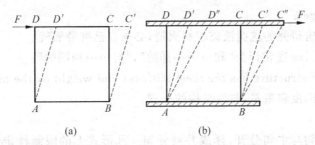

Figure 1.1 Deformation of solid and fluid elements: (a) solid; and (b) fluid

Fluids again may be divided into two classes, liquids and gases. A gas always expands and occupies the entire volume of any container. In contrast, the volume of a liquid does not change very much, so that it cannot completely fill a large container; in a gravitational field a free surface forms that separates the liquid from its vapor.

Words and Expressions

fluid mechanics	流体力学
cellular pattern	空泡
sewage ['sjuːidʒ]	n. 污水,污秽物
fluid coupling	液力联轴节
jelly ['dʒeli]	n. 胶状物
pitch [pitʃ]	n. 沥青

科技英语翻译技巧:定语从句及同位语从句的译法[31]

在英语的各种从句中,定语从句最为复杂,因此翻译时难度也最大。而同位语从句实际上是一种特殊的定语从句,译法有许多相同之处,因此在此与定语从句一起讨论。

1. 限制性定语从句的译法

限制性定语从句和所修饰的先行词的关系十分密切,是先行词在意义上不可缺少的修饰说明语。带有限制性定语从句的句子里,主句的含义是不完整的,要靠从句补充说明,全句概念才能表达清楚。限制性定语从句的翻译往往可以采用以下三种方法。

(1) 合译法

即把英语限制性定语从句译成汉语的"'的'字结构",放在被修饰词之前,把从句和主句合译成汉语的单句。这种方法尤其适合于翻译结构不很长的限制性定语从句。

A molecule may be considered as the smallest particle of matter *that can exist without changing its nature*.

可以认为分子是**在不改变物质性质的情况下能够存在的**物质的最小微粒。

以 as 引导的限制性定语从句往往有比较固定的译法。

(a) such + (名词) + as 或 such as 常译为"像……之类"、"像……(这)那样的"、"……的一种"等。

Such liquid fuel rockets *as* are now being used for space research have to carry their own supply of oxygen.

像现在用于宇宙研究的这类液态燃料火箭,必须自己携带氧气。

(b) the same …as 通常译为"和……一样的","与……相同的"。

The equivalent structure has *the same* stiffness and weight *as* the original one.

该等效结构的刚度和重量,**与原结构的一样**。

(2) 分译法

是指将定语从句与主句分开,译成并列分句。凡形式上的限制性定语从句,除简短者外,一般宜于译成并列分句。限制性定语从句译成并列分句时可分为重复先行词和省略先行词两种形式。

(a) 译成并列分句,重复先行词的含义。有时除了重复先行词的意义之外,还可加上指示代词"这"、"该"、"其",或把关系代词译成人称代词"它"、"它们"等。

A floating object displaces an amount of water *whose weight equals that of the object*.

浮体排开一定量的水,**其重量等于该浮体的重量**。

(b) 译成并列分句,省略先行词

A fuel is a material *which will burn at a reasonable temperature and produce heat*.

燃料是一种物质,**在适当温度下能够燃烧并放出热量**。

(3) 融合法

指把原句中的主句和定语从句融合起来,译成一个独立句子的译法。这种译法特别适用于"there be"结构带有定语从句的句型。

There are some materials which possess *elasticity and viscosity*.

某些材料**既有弹性,又有粘性**。

2. 非限制性定语从句的译法

非限制性定语从句主要采取分译法,作为并列分句进行汉译。

(1) 分译法

非限制性定语从句只对先行词进行描写、叙述或解释,而不加以限制,很自然地多译为并列句的一个分句,甚至译成独立的简单句。

(a) 译成并列分句,重复先行词的含义

A force can be shown by a straight line, *the length of which stands for the magnitude of the force*.

力可以用直线表示,**其长度表示力的大小**。

(b) 译成并列分句,省略先行词

This type of transducer is called strain gage, *which is used to measure strain*.

这种传感器称为应变计,**用来测量应变**。

(c) 译成独立句

Nevertheless the problem was solved successfully, *which showed that the computation was accurate*.

不过问题还是圆满地解决了,**这说明计算是准确的**。

(2) 合译法

当一些较短而且有描述性的非限制性定语从句与主句关系较密切时,也可采用合译法,即译成带"的"的前置定语。

Glass fiber reinforced composite materials, *which are light in weight*, are widely used in engineering structures.

轻质的玻璃纤维增强复合材料在工程结构中得到广泛应用。

3. 带有状语意义的定语从句的译法

有的定语从句跟主句在逻辑上有状语关系,说明原因、结果、目的、时间、条件或让步等。

（1）译成表示原因的分句

Aluminum copper alloy *which when heat-treated has good strength at high temperature* is used for making pistons and cylinder heads for automobiles.

由于铜铝合金经过热处理后具有良好的高温强度,**所以**用来制造汽车发动机的活塞与汽缸头。

（2）译成表结果的分句

Copper, *which is used to widely for carrying electricity*, offers very little resistance.

铜的电阻很小,**所以**广泛地用来传输电力。

（3）译成表示让步的分句

Friction, *which is often considered as a trouble*, is sometimes a help in the operation of machines.

摩擦**虽然**常被认为是一种不利因素,**但**有时却有助于机器的运转。

（4）译成表示条件的分句

For any machine *whose input and output forces are known*, its mechanical advantage can be calculated.

对于任何机器来说,**如果**已知其输入力和输出力,就能计算出其机械效益。

（5）译成表示目的的分句

An improved design of such a large tower must be achieved *which results in more uniformed temperature distribution in it*.

对于这种大型塔的设计必须改进,**以保证**塔内温度分布更为均匀。

（6）译成表时间的分句

Any component *which is deformed as the environmental temperature rise* must behave enough strength to sustain the thermal stress.

当因环境温度升高而变形时,任何部件都必须具有足够的强度承受热应力。

4. 特种定语从句的译法

所谓特种定语从句,是指修饰整个主句或主句部分内容的非限制性定语从句。这种定语从句只能由 which 和 as 引导。

（1）由 which 引导的特种定语从句

这种从句总是位于主句之后,通常说明整个主句,其前有逗号分开。一般采用分译法,which 常译成"这",有时也译成"从而"、"因而"等。

To find the pressure we divide the force by the area on which it presses, *which gives us the force per unit area*.

欲求得压强,需把力除以它所作用的面积,从而得出单位面积上的压力。

(2) 由 as 引导的特种定语从句

在这种定语从句中,as 通常指整个主句的内容或主句的部分内容,其位置十分灵活,不仅可以位于主句之后,还可以位于主句之前,有时也可能位于主句当中,相当于表示说话者态度或看法的插入语。翻译时主句与从句分译,往往把 as 译成"正如……那样"、"这"、"如"、"像"等。

As is mentioned above, the nonlinear differential equation can be solved by numerical method.

如上所述,该非线性微分方程可以用数值方法求解。

5. 定语从句与先行词之间的分隔与译法

定语从句有时会被其他成分隔开,翻译这种定语从句**关键**在于正确理解,通过语法现象和逻辑判断确定定语从句**所修饰的对象**。翻译时总的原则与前述定语从句的译法相同。

(1) 定语从句与先行词之间被定语短语或状语分隔

The concept of energy leads to the principle of the conservation of energy, *which unifies a wide range of phenomena in the physical science*.

对能量的理解导致了能量守恒定律,**该定律统一了物理科学中相当众多的现象**。

(2) 定语从句与先行词之间被谓语分隔。

The day will come *when coal and oil will be used as raw materials rather than as fuels*.

煤和石油用作原料而不是燃料的日子一定会到来。

6. 同位语从句的译法

由于同位语从句在作用上很接近定语从句,因此同位语从句的译法与定语从句基本相同,可采用合译法、分译法和转译法。

(1) 合译法

即把同位语从句译成前置定语,一般在所说明的名词前加个"的"字,有时还可添加"这种"、"这一"、"这个"、"那个"等词,放在同位语从句后面作为同位成分。

The fact *that the gravity of the earth pulls everything towards the center of the earth* explains many things.

地球引力把一切东西都吸向地心这一事实解释了许多现象。

(2) 分译法

采用分译法把同位语从句译成独立句子时,往往要在它的前面加冒号、破折号或"即"字。这种方法尤其适用于较长的同位语从句。

We have come to the conclusion *that Young's modulus of materials decreases as temperature increases*.

我们已得出结论:**材料的杨氏模量随温度的升高而减小**。

(3) 转译法

如果被同位语从句说明的本位语是含有动作意义的名词,如 hope, knowledge, assurance 等,一般可把这类名词译为动词,而将同位语从句译为汉语的主谓词组或动宾词组,作该动词的宾语。

Even the most precisely conducted experiments offer no hope *that the results can be obtained without any error*.

即使进行的是最精确的实验，也不要希望获得无任何误差的实验结果。

Reading Material(1)：Constitutive Equations of Fluids[5]

The Non-viscous Fluid

A nonviscous fluid is one for which the stress tensor is isotropic; i.e., it is of the form

$$\sigma_{ij} = -p\delta_{ij} \tag{7.2-1}$$

where δ_{ij} is the Kronecker delta and p is a scalar called *pressure*. In matrix form, the components of stress in a nonviscous fluid may be displayed as

$$(\sigma_{ij}) = \begin{pmatrix} -p & 0 & 0 \\ 0 & -p & 0 \\ 0 & 0 & -p \end{pmatrix} \tag{7.2-2}$$

The pressure p in an *ideal gas* is related to the density ρ and temperature T by the equation of state

$$\frac{p}{\rho} = RT \tag{7.2-3}$$

where R is the gas constant. For a real gas or a liquid it is often possible to obtain an equation of state

$$f(p,\rho,T) = 0 \tag{7.2-4}$$

An anomaly exists in the case of an *incompressible fluid*, for which the equation of state is merely

$$\rho = const \tag{7.2-5}$$

Thus, the pressure p is left as an arbitrary variable for an incompressible fluid. It is determined solely by the equations of motion and the boundary conditions. For example, an incompressible fluid in the cylinder of a hydraulic press can assume any pressure depending on the force applied to the piston.

Since hydrodynamics is concerned mostly with incompressible fluids, we shall see that pressure is controlled by boundary conditions, whereas the variation of pressure (the pressure gradient) is calculated from the equations of motion.

Air and water can be treated as nonviscous in many problems. For example, in the problems of tides around the earth, waves in the ocean, flight of an airplane, flow in a jet, combustion in an automobile engine, etc., excellent results can be obtained by ignoring the viscosity of the media and treating it as a nonviscous fluid. On the other hand, there are important problems in which the viscosity of the media, though small, must not be neglected. Such are the problems of determining the drag force acting on an airplane, whether a flow is turbulent or laminar, the heating of a reentry spacecraft, the cooling of an automobile engine, etc.

Newton Fluid

A Newtonian fluid is a viscous fluid for which the shear stress is linearly proportional to the rate of deformation. For a Newtonian fluid the stress-strain relationship is specified by the equation

$$\sigma_{ij} = -p\delta_{ij} + \wp_{ijkl} V_{kl} \qquad (7.3\text{-}1)$$

where σ_{ij} is the stress tensor, V_{kl} is the rate-of-deformation tensor, $\wp_{ijkl}$ is a tensor of viscosity coefficients of the fluid, and p is the static pressure. The term $-p\delta_{ij}$ represents the state of stress possible in a fluid at rest (when $V_{kl} = 0$). The static pressure p is assumed to depend on the density and temperature of the fluid according to an equation of state. For Newtonian fluids we assume that the elements of the tensor $\wp_{ijkl}$ may depend on the temperature but not on the stress or the rate of deformation. The tensor $\wp_{ijkl}$ of rank 4, has $3^4 = 81$ elements. Not all these constants are independent. A study of the theoretically possible number of independent elements can be made by examining the symmetry properties of the tensors σ_{ij}, V_{kl} and the symmetry that may exist in the atomic constitution of the fluid. We shall not pursue it here because we know of no fluid that has been examined in such detail as to have all the constants in the tensor $\wp_{ijkl}$ determined. Most fluids appear to be isotropic, for which the structure of $\wp_{ijkl}$ is greatly simplified, as will be seen below. Those readers who are interested in the general structure of $\wp_{ijkl}$ should read Sec. 7.4 and the references referred to therein, because the tensor of elastic constants C_{ijkl} has a similar structure.

If the fluid is *isotropic*, i.e., if the tensor $\wp_{ijkl}$ has the same array of components in any system of rectangular Cartesian coordinates, then $\wp_{ijkl}$ can be expressed in terms of two independent constants λ and μ:

$$\wp_{ijkl} = \lambda \delta_{ij} \delta_{kl} + \mu (\delta_{ik} \delta_{jl} + \delta_{il} \delta_{jk}) \qquad (7.3\text{-}2)$$

and we obtain

$$\sigma_{ij} = -p\delta_{ij} + \lambda V_{kk} \delta_{ij} + 2\mu V_{ij} \qquad (7.3\text{-}3)$$

A contraction of Eq. (7.3-3) gives

$$\sigma_{kk} = -3p + (3\lambda + 2\mu) V_{kk} \qquad (7.3\text{-}4)$$

If it is assumed that the mean normal stress $\frac{1}{3} \sigma_{kk}$ is independent of the rate of dilation V_{kk} then we must set

$$3\lambda + 2\mu = 0 \qquad (7.3\text{-}5)$$

thus the constitutive equation becomes

$$\sigma_{ij} = -p\delta_{ij} + 2\mu V_{ij} - \frac{2}{3} \mu V_{kk} \delta_{ij} \qquad (7.3\text{-}6)$$

This formulation is due to George G. Stokes and a fluid that obeys Eq. (7.3-6) is called a *Stokes fluid*, for which one material constant μ, the coefficient of viscosity, suffices to define its property.

If a fluid is *incompressible*, then $V_{kk}=0$, and we have the constitutive equation for an *incompressible viscous fluid*:
$$\sigma_{ij} = -p\delta_{ij} + 2\mu V_{ij} \qquad (7.3\text{-}7)$$
If $\mu = 0$, we obtain the constitutive equation of the *nonviscous fluid*:
$$\sigma_{ij} = -p\delta_{ij} \qquad (7.3\text{-}8)$$

The presence of the static pressure term p marks a fundamental difference between fluid mechanics and elasticity. To accommodate this new variable, it is often assumed that an *equation of state* exists which relates the pressure p, the density ρ, and the absolute temperature T,
$$f(p,\rho,T) = 0 \qquad (7.3\text{-}9)$$
An *incompressible* fluid specified by Eq. (7.2-5) is again a special case, for which the pressure p is a variable to be determined by the equations of motion and boundary conditions.

Fluids obeying Eq. (7.3-1) or Eq. (7.3-3), whose viscosity effects are represented by terms that are linear in the components of the rate of deformation, are called *Newtonian fluids*. Fluids that behave otherwise are said to be *non-Newtonian*. For example, a fluid whose coefficient of viscosity depends on the basic invariants of V_{ij} is non-Newtonian.

◇◇◇◇◇◇◇◇◇◇◇◇◇◇◇◇◇◇◇◇◇◇◇◇◇◇◇◇◇◇

Words and Expressions

nonviscous	adj.	非粘性，无粘性
ideal gas		理想气体
incompressible fluid		不可压缩流体
hydrodynamics ['haidrəudai'næmiks]	n.	水动力学
combustion [kəm'bʌstʃən]	n.	燃烧，氧化
viscosity [vis'kɔsiti]	n.	粘性
drag [dræg]	n.	阻力
turbulent ['tə:bjulənt]	adj.	湍流的
laminar ['læminə]	adj.	层流
Newtonian fluid		牛顿流体
viscosity coefficient		粘性系数
rate of dilation		膨胀率
equation of state		状态方程
absolute temperature		绝对温度
non-Newtonian fluid		非牛顿流体

◇◇◇◇◇◇◇◇◇◇◇◇◇◇◇◇◇◇◇◇

Reading Material(2): Finite Difference Method[30]

The key to various numerical methods is to convert the partial different equations that govern a physical phenomenon into a system of algebraic equations. Different techniques are available for this conversion. The finite difference method is one of the most commonly used.

Approximation to Derivatives

Consider the one-dimensional transport equation,

$$\frac{\partial T}{\partial t} + u \frac{\partial T}{\partial x} = D \frac{\partial^2 T}{\partial x^2} \quad \text{for} \quad 0 \leqslant x \leqslant L. \tag{11.1}$$

This is the classic convection-diffusion problem for $T(x,t)$, where u is a convective velocity and D is a diffusion coefficient. For simplicity, let us assume that u and D are two constants. This equation is written in nondimensional form. The boundary conditions for this problem are

$$T(0,t) = g \quad \text{and} \quad \frac{\partial T}{\partial x}(L,t) = q, \tag{11.2}$$

where g and q are two constants. The initial condition is

$$T(x,0) = T_0(x) \quad \text{for} \quad 0 \leqslant x \leqslant L, \tag{11.3}$$

where $T_0(x)$ is a given function that satisfies the boundary conditions (11.2).

Let us first discretize the transport equation (11.1) on a uniform grid with a grid spacing Δx, as shown in Figure 11.1. Equation (11.1) is evaluated at spatial location $x = x_i$ and time $t = t_n$. Define $T(x_i, t_n)$ as the exact value of T at the location $x = x_i$ and time $t = t_n$, and let T_i^n be its approximation. Using the Taylor series expansion, we have

$$T_{i+1}^n = T_i^n + \Delta x \left[\frac{\partial T}{\partial x}\right]_i^n + \frac{\Delta x^2}{2} \left[\frac{\partial^2 T}{\partial x^2}\right]_i^n + \frac{\Delta x^3}{6} \left[\frac{\partial^3 T}{\partial x^3}\right]_i^n$$
$$+ \frac{\Delta x^4}{24} \left[\frac{\partial^4 T}{\partial x^4}\right]_i^n + O(\Delta x^5) \tag{11.4}$$

$$T_{i-1}^n = T_i^n - \Delta x \left[\frac{\partial T}{\partial x}\right]_i^n + \frac{\Delta x^2}{2} \left[\frac{\partial^2 T}{\partial x^2}\right]_i^n - \frac{\Delta x^3}{6} \left[\frac{\partial^3 T}{\partial x^3}\right]_i^n$$
$$+ \frac{\Delta x^4}{24} \left[\frac{\partial^4 T}{\partial x^4}\right]_i^n + O(\Delta x^5) \tag{11.5}$$

where $O(\Delta x^5)$ means terms of the order of Δx^5. Therefore, the first spatial derivative may be approximated as

$$\left[\frac{\partial T}{\partial x}\right]_i^n = \frac{T_{i+1}^n - T_i^n}{\Delta x} + O(\Delta x) \quad \text{(forward differece)}$$
$$= \frac{T_i^n - T_{i-1}^n}{\Delta x} + O(\Delta x) \quad \text{(backward differece)}$$
$$= \frac{T_{i+1}^n - T_{i-1}^n}{\Delta x} + O(\Delta x^2) \quad \text{(centered differece)} \tag{11.6}$$

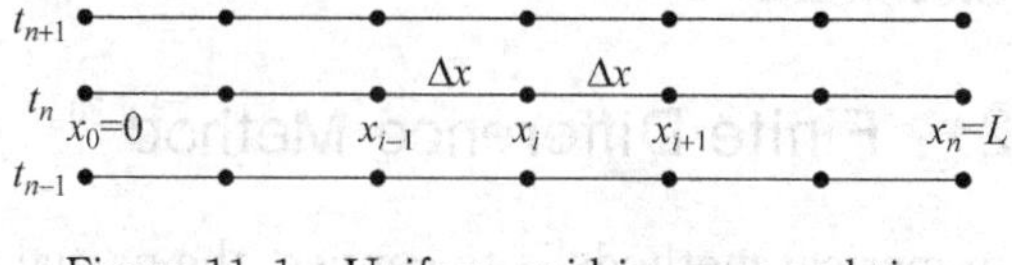

Figure 11.1 Uniform grid in space and time

and the second order derivative may be approximated as
$$\left[\frac{\partial^2 T}{\partial x^2}\right]_i^n = \frac{T_{i+1}^n - 2T_i^n + T_{i-1}^n}{\Delta x^2} + O(\Delta x^2). \tag{11.7}$$

The orders of accuracy of the approximations (truncation errors) are also indicated in the expressions of (11.6) and (11.7). More accurate approximations generally require more values of the variable on the neighboring grid points. Similar expressions can be derived for nonuniform grids.

In the same fashion, the time derivative can be discretized as
$$\left[\frac{\partial T}{\partial t}\right]_i^n = \frac{T_i^{n+1} - T_i^n}{\Delta t} + O(\Delta t)$$
$$= \frac{T_i^n - T_i^{n-1}}{\Delta t} + O(\Delta t)$$
$$= \frac{T_i^{n+1} - T_i^{n-1}}{\Delta t} + O(\Delta t^2) \tag{11.8}$$

where $\Delta t = t_{n+1} - t_n = t_n - t_{n-1}$ is the constant time step.

Discretization and Its Accuracy

A discretization of the transport equation (11.1) is obtained by evaluating the equation at fixed spatial and temporal grid points and using the approximations for the individual derivative terms listed in the preceding section. When the first expression in (11.8) is used, together with (11.7) and the centered difference in (11.6), (11.1) may be discretized by

$$\frac{T_i^{n+1} - T_i^n}{\Delta t} + u \frac{T_{i+1}^n - T_{i-1}^n}{2\Delta x} = D \frac{T_{i+1}^n - 2T_i^n + T_{i-1}^n}{\Delta x^2} + O(\Delta t, \Delta x^2) \tag{11.9}$$

or

$$T_i^{n+1} \approx T_i^n - u\Delta t \frac{T_{i+1}^n - T_{i-1}^n}{2\Delta x} + D\Delta t \frac{T_{i+1}^n - 2T_i^n + T_{i-1}^n}{\Delta x^2}$$
$$= T_i^n - \alpha(T_{i+1}^n - T_{i-1}^n) + \beta(T_{i+1}^n - 2T_i^n + T_{i-1}^n), \tag{11.10}$$

where

$$\alpha = u \frac{\Delta t}{2\Delta x}, \quad \beta = D \frac{\Delta t}{\Delta x^2} \tag{11.11}$$

Once the values of T_i^n are known, starting with the initial condition (11.3), the expression (11.10) simply updates the variable for the next time step $t = t_n + 1$. This scheme is known as an explicit algorithm. The discretization (11.10) is first-order accurate in time and second-order accurate in space.

As another example, when the backward difference expression in (11.8) is used, we will have

$$\frac{T_i^n - T_i^{n-1}}{\Delta t} + u \frac{T_{i+1}^n - T_{i-1}^n}{2\Delta x} = D \frac{T_{i+1}^n - 2T_i^n + T_{i-1}^n}{\Delta x^2} + O(\Delta t, \Delta x^2), \tag{11.12}$$

or

$$T_i^n + \alpha(T_{i+1}^n - T_{i-1}^n) - \beta(T_{i+1}^n - 2T_i^n + T_{i-1}^n) \approx T_i^{n-1} \tag{11.13}$$

At each time step $t=t_n$, here a system of algebraic equations needs to be solved to advance the solution. This scheme is known as an implicit algorithm. Obviously, for the same accuracy, the explicit scheme (11.10) is much simpler than the implicit one (11.13). However, the explicit scheme has limitations.

Convergence, Consistency, and Stability

The result from the solution of the explicit scheme (11.10) or the implicit scheme (11.13) represents an approximate numerical solution to the original partial differential equation (11.1). One certainly hopes that the approximate solution will be close to the exact one. Thus we introduce the concepts of convergence, consistency, and stability of the numerical solution.

The approximate solution is said to be convergent if it approaches the exact solution, as the grid spacings Δx and Δt tend to zero. We may define the solution error as the difference between the approximate solution and the exact solution,

$$e_i^n = T_i^n - T(x_i, t_n) \qquad (11.14)$$

Thus the approximate solution converges when $e_i^n \to 0$ as $\Delta x, \Delta t \to 0$. For a convergent solution, some measure of the solution error can be estimated as

$$\| e_i^n \| \leqslant K \Delta x^a \Delta t^b \qquad (11.15)$$

where the measure may be the root mean square (rms) of the solution error on all the grid points; K is a constant independent of the grid spacing Δx and the time step Δt; the indices a and b represent the convergence rates at which the solution error approaches zero.

One may reverse the discretization process and examine the limit of the discretized equations (11.10) and (11.13), as the grid spacing tends to zero. The discretized equation is said to be consistent if it recovers the original partial differential equation (11.1) in the limit of zero grid spacing.

Let us consider the explicit scheme (11.10). Substitution of the Taylor series expansions (11.4) and (11.5) into this scheme (11.10) produces,

$$\left[\frac{\partial T}{\partial t}\right]_i^n + u\left[\frac{\partial T}{\partial x}\right]_i^n - D\left[\frac{\partial^2 T}{\partial x^2}\right]_i^n + E_i^n = 0 \qquad (11.16)$$

where

$$E_i^n = \frac{\Delta t}{2}\left[\frac{\partial^2 T}{\partial t^2}\right]_i^n + u\frac{\Delta x^2}{6}\left[\frac{\partial^3 T}{\partial x^3}\right]_i^n - D\frac{\Delta x^2}{12}\left[\frac{\partial^4 T}{\partial x^4}\right]_i^n + O(\Delta t^2, \Delta x^4) \qquad (11.17)$$

is the truncation error. Obviously, as the grid spacing $\Delta x, \Delta t \to 0$, this truncation error is of the order of $O(\Delta x, \Delta t^2)$ and tends to zero. Therefore, explicit scheme (11.10) or expression (11.16) recovers the original partial differential equation (11.1) or it is consistent. It is said to be first-order accurate in time and second-order accurate in space, according to the order of magnitude of the truncation error.

In addition to the truncation error introduced in the discretization process, other sources of error may be present in the approximate solution. Spontaneous disturbances (such as the round-off error) may be introduced during either the evaluation or the numerical solution process. A numerical approximation is said to be stable if these disturbances decay and do not affect the solution.

The stability of the explicit scheme (11.10) may be examined using the von Neumann method. Let us consider the error at a grid point,

$$\xi_i^n = T_i^n - \overline{T}_i^n \tag{11.18}$$

where T_i^n is the exact solution of the discretized system (11.10) and $\overline{T}_i^n$ is the approximate numerical solution of the same system. This error could be introduced due to the round-off error at each step of the computation. We need to monitor its decay/growth with time. It can be shown that the evolution of this error satisfies the same homogeneous algebraic system (11.10)

or

$$\xi_i^{n+1} = (\alpha + \beta)\xi_{i-1}^n + (1 - 2\beta)\xi_i^n + (\beta - \alpha)\xi_{i+1}^n \tag{11.19}$$

The error distributed along the grid line can always be decomposed in Fourier space as

$$\xi_i^n = \sum_{k=-\infty}^{\infty} g^n(k)\, e^{ikx_i} \tag{11.20}$$

where $i = \sqrt{-1}$, k is the wavenumber in Fourier space, and g^n represents the function g at time $t = t_n$. As the system is linear, we can examine one component of (11.20) at a time,

$$\xi_i^n = g^n(k)\, e^{ikx_i} \tag{11.21}$$

The component at the next time level has a similar form

$$\xi_i^{n+1} = g^{n+1}(k)\, e^{ikx_i} \tag{11.22}$$

Substituting the preceding two equations (11.21) and (11.22) into error equation (11.19), we obtain,

$$g^{n+1}\, e^{ikx_i} = g^n[(\alpha + \beta)\, e^{ikx_{i-1}} + (1 - 2\beta)\, e^{ikx_i} + (\beta - \alpha)\, e^{ikx_{i+1}}] \tag{11.23}$$

or

$$\frac{g^{n+1}}{g^n} = [(\alpha + \beta)\, e^{-ik\Delta x} + (1 - 2\beta) + (\beta - \alpha)\, e^{ik\Delta x}] \tag{11.24}$$

This ratio g^{n+1}/g^n is called the amplification factor. The condition for stability is that the magnitude of the error should decay with time, or

$$\left|\frac{g^{n+1}}{g^n}\right| \leqslant 1 \tag{11.25}$$

for any value of the wavenumber k. For this explicit scheme, the condition for stability (11.25) can be expressed as

$$\left[1 - 4\beta \sin^2\left(\frac{\theta}{2}\right)\right]^2 + (2\alpha \sin\theta)^2 \leqslant 1 \tag{11.26}$$

where $\theta = k\pi\Delta x$. The stability condition (11.26) also can be expressed as (Noye, 1983),

$$0 \leqslant 4\alpha^2 \leqslant 2\beta \leqslant 1 \tag{11.27}$$

For the pure diffusion problem ($u = 0$), the stability condition (11.27) for this explicit scheme requires that

$$0 \leqslant \beta \leqslant \frac{1}{2} \quad \text{or} \quad \Delta t \leqslant \frac{1}{2}\frac{\Delta x^2}{D} \tag{11.28}$$

which limits the size of the time step. For the pure convection problem ($D=0$), condition (11.27) will never be satisfied, which indicates that the scheme is always unstable and it means that any error introduced during the computation will explode with time. Thus, this explicit scheme is useless for pure convection problems. To improve the stability of the explicit scheme for the convection problem, one may use an upwind scheme to approximate the convective term,

$$T_i^{n+1} = T_i^n - 2\alpha(\overline{T}_i^n - T_{i-1}^n) \tag{11.29}$$

where the stability condition requires that

$$u\frac{\Delta t}{\Delta x} \leqslant 1 \tag{11.30}$$

The condition (11.30) is known as the Courant-Friedrichs-Lewy (CFL) condition. This condition indicates that a fluid particle should not travel more than one spatial grid in one time step.

It can easily be shown that the implicit scheme (11.13) is also consistent and unconditionally stable.

It is normally difficult to show the convergence of an approximate solution theoretically. However, the Lax Equivalence Theorem (Richtmyer and Morton, 1967) states that: *for an approximation to a well-posed linear initial value problem, which satisfies the consistency condition, stability is a necessary and sufficient condition for the convergence of the solution.*

For convection-diffusion problems, the exact solution may change significantly in a narrow boundary layer. If the computational grid is not sufficiently fine to resolve the rapid variation of the solution in the boundary layer, the numerical solution may present unphysical oscillations adjacent to or in the boundary layer. To prevent the oscillatory solution, a condition on the cell Pecl'et number (or Reynolds number) is normally required,

$$R_{cell} = u\frac{\Delta x}{D} \leqslant 2 \tag{11.31}$$

Words and Expressions

finite difference method	有限差分法
algebraic equation	代数方程
transport equation	输运方程；迁移方程
convection-diffusion	对流扩散
convective velocity	对流速度
diffusion coefficient	扩散系数
grid [grid] *n.*	格子

Taylor series expansion		泰勒级数展开
forward difference		向前差分
back difference		向后差分
centered difference		中心差分
second order derivative		二阶导数
truncation error		截断误差
explicit algorithm		显式算法
implicit algorithm		隐式算法
convergence [kən'və:dʒəns]	n.	收敛
convergence rate		收敛速度
consistency [kən'sistənsi]	n.	一致性
round-off error		舍入误差
wavenumber	n.	波数
amplification factor		放大因子,放大倍数
upwind scheme		迎风格式
unconditionally stable		无条件稳定的
necessary condition		必要条件
sufficient condition		充分条件

Unit Thirteen

Rock Mechanics[26]

Rock mechanics was defined by the Committee on Rock Mechanics of the Geological Society of America in the following terms: "Rock mechanics is the theoretical and applied science of the mechanical behavior of rock; it is that branch of mechanics concerned with the response of rock to the force fields of its physical environment". For practical purposes, rock mechanics is mostly concerned with rock masses on the scale that appears in engineering and mining work, and so it might be regarded as the study of the properties and behavior of accessible rock masses due to changes in stresses or other conditions. Since these rocks may be weathered or fragmented, rock mechanics grades at one extreme into soil mechanics. On the other hand, at depths at which the rocks are no longer accessible to mining or drilling, it grades into the mechanical aspects of structural geology.

Historically, rock mechanics has been very much influenced by these two subjects. For many years it was associated with soil mechanics at scientific conferences, and there is a similarity between much of the two theories and many of the problems. On the other hand, the demand from structural geologists for knowledge of the behavior of rocks under conditions that occur deep in the Earth's crust has stimulated much research at high pressures and temperatures, along with a great deal of study of the experimental deformation of both rocks and single crystals.

An important feature of accessible rock masses is that they are broken up by joints and faults, and that pressurized fluid is frequently present both in open joints and in the pores of the rock itself. It also frequently happens that, because of the conditions controlling mining and the siting of structures in civil engineering, several lithological types may occur in any one investigation. Thus, from the outset, two distinct problems are always involved: (i) the study of the orientations and properties of the joints, and (ii) the study of the properties and fabric of the rock between the joints.

In any practical investigation in rock mechanics, the first stage is a geological and geophysical investigation to establish the lithologies and boundaries of the rock types involved. The second stage is to establish, by means of drilling or investigatory excavations, the detailed pattern of jointing, and to determine the mechanical and petrological properties of the rocks from samples. The third stage, in many cases, is to measure the in situ rock stresses that are present in the unexcavated rock. With this information, it should be possible to predict the response of the rock mass to excavation or loading.

Joints are by far the most common type of geological structure. They are defined as cracks or fractures in rock along which there has been little or no transverse displacement. They usually occur in sets that are more or less parallel and regularly spaced. There are also usually several sets oriented in different directions, so that the rock mass is broken up into a blocky structure. This is a main reason for the importance of joints in rock mechanics: they divide a rock mass into different parts, and sliding can occur along the joint surfaces. These joints can also provide paths for fluids to flow through the rock mass.

Joints occur on all scales. Joints of the most important set, referred to as major joints, can usually be traced for tens or hundreds of meters, and are usually more or less planar and parallel to each other. The sets of joints that intersect major joints, known as cross joints, are usually of less importance, and are more likely to be curved and/or irregularly spaced. However, in some cases, the two sets of joints are of equal importance. The spacing between joints may vary from centimeters to decameters, although very closely spaced joints may be regarded as a property of the rock fabric itself.

Joints may be "filled" with various minerals, such as calcite, dolomite, quartz or clay minerals, or they may be "open," in which case they may be filled with fluids under pressure.

Jointing, as described above, is a phenomenon common to all rocks, sedimentary and igneous. A discussion of possible mechanisms by which jointing is produced is given by Price and Pollard and Aydin. Joint systems are affected by lithological nature of the rock, and so the spacing and orientation of the joints may change with the change of rock type.

Another quite distinct type of jointing is columnar jointing, which is best developed in basalts and dolerites, but occasionally occurs in granites and some metamorphic rocks. This phenomenon is of some importance in rock mechanics, as igneous dykes and sheets are frequently encountered in mining and engineering practice. In rocks that have columnar jointing, the rock mass is divided into columns that are typically hexagonal, with side lengths on the order of a few tens of centimeters. The columns are intersected by cross joints that are less regular toward the interior of the body. The primary cause of columnar jointing appears to be tensile stresses that are created by thermal contraction during cooling. At an external surface, the columns run normal to the surface, and Jaeger and others have suggested that in the interior of the rock mass the columns run normal to the isotherms during cooling. The detailed mechanism of columnar jointing has been discussed by Lachenbruch; it has similarities to the cracks that form in soil and mud during drying, and to some extent to cracking in permafrost.

Faults are fracture surfaces on which a relative displacement has occurred transverse to the nominal plane of the fracture. They are usually unique structures, but a large number of them may be merged into a fault zone. They are usually approximately planar, and so they provide important planes on which sliding can take place. Joints and faults may have a common origin, and it is often observed underground that joints become more frequent as a fault is approached.

From the point of view of rock mechanics, the importance of joints and faults is that they cause the existence of fairly regularly spaced, approximately plane surfaces, which separate blocks of "intact" rock that may slide on one another. In practice, the essential procedure is to measure the orientation of all joint planes and similar features, either in an exploratory tunnel or in a set of boreholes, and to plot the directions of their normal vectors on a stereological projection. Some typical examples are shown in the following figures taken from investigations of the Snowy Mountain Hydroelectric Authority in Australia.

Figure 1 is a stereographic projection plot of the normals to the fracture planes in the Headrace Channel for the Tumut 3 Project. The thick lines show the positions of the proposed slope cuts. In this case, 700 normal vectors were measured.

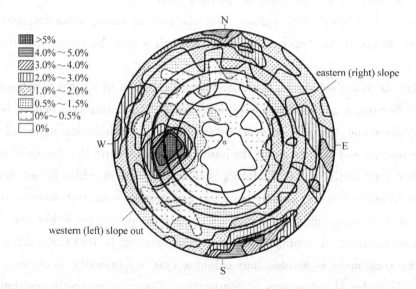

Figure 1　Stereographic plot(lower hemisphere) of normals to fracture planes in Tumut 3 Headrace Channel. The contours enclose areas of equal density of poles

Figure 2 shows the important geological features at the Murray 2 dam site on a different representation. Here, the directions of strike of various features are plotted as a rosette, with the angles of dip of the dominant features at each strike given numerically. The features recorded are joints, sheared zones, and bedding planes, any or all of which may be of importance.

Finally, Fig. 3 gives a simplified representation of the situation at the intersection of three important tunnels. There are three sets of joints whose dips and strikes are shown in Fig. 3.

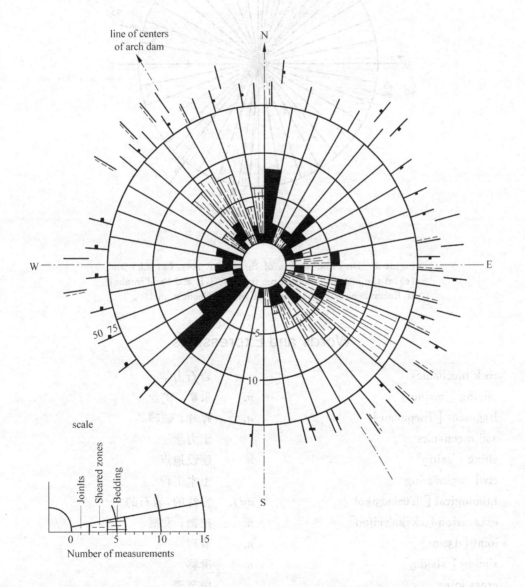

Figure 2 Rosette diagram showing strikes of joints, sheared zones, and bedding planes at the Murray 2 dam site. The predominant dip for each strike is also shown

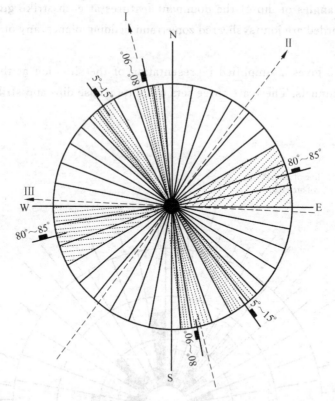

Figure 3 Dips and strikes of three joint sets, (a) (b) and (c), at the intersection of three tunnels: I, Island Bend intake; II, Eucumbene-Snowy tunnel; III, Snowy-Geehi tunnel

Words and Expressions

rock mechanics		岩石力学
mining ['mainiŋ]	n.	采矿；矿业
fragment ['frægmənt]	n.	碎片；破碎
soil mechanics		土力学
siting ['saitiŋ]	n.	建设地点
civil engineering		土木工程
lithological [li'θɔlədʒikəl]	adj.	岩性的，岩石的
excavation [,ekskə'veiʃən]	n.	挖掘；发掘
joint [dʒɔint]	n.	节理
sliding ['slaidiŋ]	n.	滑移
cross joint		横节理
decameter ['dekə,mi:tə]	n.	十米
calcite ['kælsait]	n.	方解石
dolomite ['dɔləmait]	n.	白云石，石灰石

sedimentary [ˌsedi'mentəri]	adj.	沉积的；沉淀性的；沉淀作用造成的
igneous ['igniəs]	adj.	火成的；火的
columnar jointing		柱状节理
basalt [bə'sɔ:lt]	n.	玄武岩
dolerite ['dɔlərait]	n.	辉绿岩，粗粒玄武岩
granite ['grænit]	n.	花岗石
metamorphic [ˌmetə'mɔ:fik]	adj.	变性的；变质的
dyke [daik]	n.	沟；渠；堤坝
mud [mʌd]	n.	泥；泥浆
fault [fɔ:lt]	n.	断层
borehole ['bɔːˌhəul]	n.	钻孔
stereological [stiəri'ɔlədʒi, sterə'ɔlədʒi]	adj.	体视学；立体测量学
bedding plane		层理面
dip [dip]	n.	浸泡；浸；下沉；倾斜
	vt.&vi.	浸泡；浸；下沉；倾斜
strike [straik]	vi.	走向

科技英语翻译技巧：状语从句的译法[31]

英译汉时状语从句的位置尤其重要。状语从句的译法主要应注意状语从句的位置、连词的译法和省略以及状语从句的转译等。一般来说，汉语中，状语从句多半在主句前面，有时放在整个句子当中。此外，汉译时连词常可省略，这在时间、条件状语从句中尤为常见。另一个值得注意的是，不要碰到"when"就译成"当"，碰到"if"就译成"如果"，碰到"because"就译成"因为"，而应酌情进行变化或简化。如：

If water is cold enough, it changes to ice.

水温降到一定程度便会结冰。

另外，科技英语翻译中，有时将时间状语从句转译成条件状语从句，将地点状语从句转译成条件状语从句。

When there is no force on the body, no deformation takes place.

如果物体上没有载荷，就不会发生变形。

1. 时间状语从句的译法

（1）译成相应的时间状语，放在句首

不论原文中表示时间的从句是前置或后置，按汉语习惯，都要译在其主句的前面。

Heat is always given out by one substance and taken in by another *when heat exchange takes place*.

热交换发生时，总是某一物质释放热量，另一物质吸收热量。

（2）译成并列句

有的连词（如 as, while, when 等）引导时间状语从句，在表达主句和从句的谓语动作同时进行时，汉译英时可省略连词，译成汉语的并列句。

The earth turns a round its axis *as it travels around the sun*.

地球一面绕太阳运行,一面绕地轴回转。

(3) 译成条件状语从句

when 等引导的状语从句,若从逻辑上判断具有条件状语的意义,则往往可转译成条件状语从句。

Turn off the switch *when anything goes wrong with the machine*.

如果机器发生故障,就把电门关上。

2. 地点状语从句的译法

(1) 译成相应的地点状语

一般可将地点状语从句译在句首。

Heat is always being transferred in one way or another, *where there is any difference in temperature*.

凡有温差的地方,热都会以这样或那样的方式传输。

(2) 译成条件状语从句或结果状语从句

where 或 wherever 引导的状语从句,若从逻辑上判断具有条件状语或结果状语的意义,则可转译为相应的状语从句。

Where water resources are plentiful, hydroelectric power stations are being built in large numbers.

只要哪里水源充足,就在哪里修建大批的电站。

It is hoped that solar energy will find wide application *wherever it becomes available*.

可以期望,太阳能将得到广泛的利用,以致任何地方都可以使用。

3. 原因状语从句的译法

(1) 译成表"因"的分句

一般说来,汉语表"因"的分句置于句首,英语则较灵活。但现代汉语中,也有放在后面,此时往往含有补充说明的意义。

To launch a space vehicle into orbit, a very big push is needed *because the friction of air and the force of gravity are working against it*.

要把宇宙飞行器送入轨道,需要施加很大推力,**因为空气的摩擦力和地球引力对它起阻碍作用**。

(2) 译成因果偏正复句的主句

这实际是一种省略连词的译法,把从句译成主句。

Because energy can be changed from one form into another, electricity can be changed into heat energy, mechanical energy, light energy, etc.

能量能从一种形式转换成另一种形式,所以电可以转变为热能、机械能、光能等。

4. 条件从句的译法

(1) 译成表示"条件"或"假设"的分句

按照汉语的习惯,不管表示条件还是假设,分句都放在主句的前部,因此英语的条件从句汉译时绝大多数置于句首。

Unless you know the fatigue characteristics of the material, you can not estimate the lifetime of that shaft.

除非已知材料的疲劳特性,否则就无法估计那根轴的寿命。

(2) 译成补充说明情况的分句

不少条件状语从句汉译时可置于主句后面,作补充说明情况的分句。

Iron or steel parts will rust, *if they are unprotected*.

铁件或钢件是会生锈的,**如果不加保护的话**。

5. 让步状语从句

(1) 译成表示"让步"的分句

汉语中让步分句一般前置,但也可后置。

Though we get only a relatively small part of the total power radiated from the sun, what we get is much more than enough for our needs.

虽然我们仅得到太阳辐射总能量的一小部分,但是,与我们的实际需要量相比,这已绰绰有余了。

Energy can neither be created nor destroyed *although its form can be changed*.

能量既不能创造,也不能消失,**尽管其形式可以转变**。

(2) 译成表示"无条件"的条件分句

The imitation of living systems, *be it direct or indirect*, is very useful for devising machines, hence the rapid development of bionics.

对生物的模仿**不管是直接的还是间接的**,对于机械设计都很有用处,因此仿生学才迅速发展。

6. **目的状语从句的译法**

(1) 译成表示"目的"的后置分句

英语的状语从句通常位于句末,汉译时一般采用顺译法。

A rocket must attain a speed of about five miles per second *so that it may put a satellite in orbit*.

火箭必须获得每秒大约五英里的速度**以便把卫星送入轨道**。

(2) 译成表示"目的"的前置分句

汉语里表示"目的"的分句常用"为了"作关联词,置于句首,往往有强调的含意。

All the parts for this kind of machine must be made of especially strong materials *in order that they will not break while in use*.

为了使用时不致断裂,这种机器的所有部件都应该用特别坚固的材料制成。

7. **结果状语从句的译法**

英语和汉语都把表示"结果"的从句置于主句之后,因此这类句子可采用顺译法。注意汉译时应少用连词,或省略连词。

The submarine vessel is so thick *that it can withstand very high external pressure*.

该水下容器**如此的厚,能承受非常高的外部压力**。

Reading Material(1): Special Stress-Strain States of Rock[26]

There are a number of special stress-strain states that are of sufficient importance to make it worthwhile to examine them explicit. In the following discussions, it will be assumed that $0 < \nu < 1/2$, as is always the case in practice.

Hydrostatic Stress, $\sigma_1 = \sigma_2 = \sigma_3 = P$

This is the state of stress that would occur if a rock specimen were surrounded by a fluid under a pressure of magnitude P. The strains are given by

$$\varepsilon_1 = \varepsilon_2 = \varepsilon_3 = P/3k \tag{1}$$

It follows that the volumetric strain is

$$\varepsilon_V = \varepsilon_1 + \varepsilon_2 + \varepsilon_3 = P/k \tag{2}$$

so that $1/k$ can be identified as the compressibility of the rock.

Uniaxial Stress, $\sigma_1 \neq 0$, $\sigma_2 = \sigma_3 = 0$

This is the stress state that arises when a specimen is uniformly loaded in one direction, while its lateral boundaries are free from traction. As well as being commonly used in laboratory testing, this state will also be approximated in practical situations such as in a pillar in an underground mine, for example. The resulting strain state will be a contraction $\varepsilon_1 = \sigma_1/E$ in the direction of σ_1 and an expansion $\varepsilon_2 = \varepsilon_3 = -\nu\sigma_1/E$ in the two perpendicular directions. The fractional change in volume is found to be

$$\varepsilon_V = (1 - 2\nu)\sigma_1/E \tag{3}$$

The volume decreases if the stress is compressive and increases if it is tensile.

Uniaxial Strain, $\varepsilon_1 \neq 0$, $\varepsilon_2 = \varepsilon_3 = 0$

This state is often assumed to occur when, for example, fluid is withdrawn from a reservoir, in which the vertical strain is contractile, whereas lateral strain is inhibited by the rock that is adjacent to the reservoir. The stresses that accompany uniaxial strain are

$$\sigma_1 = (\lambda + 2G)\varepsilon_1, \quad \sigma_2 = \sigma_3 = \lambda\varepsilon_1 = [\nu/(1-\nu)]\sigma_1 \tag{4}$$

In order for the lateral strains to be zero, nonzero lateral stresses must exist. The assumption of uniaxial strain is often used as a simple model for calculating in situ stresses below the Earth's surface

The Case $\sigma_1 \neq 0$, $\varepsilon_2 = 0$, $\sigma_3 = 0$

This state corresponds to an applied stress in one direction, with zero stress and zero strain in two mutually orthogonal directions that are each perpendicular to the direction of the applied load.

$$\varepsilon_1 = (1 - \nu^2)\sigma_1/E, \quad \sigma_2 = \nu\sigma_1, \quad \varepsilon_3 = -[\nu/(1-\nu)]\varepsilon_1 \tag{5}$$

Biaxial Stress or Plane Stress, $\sigma_1 \neq 0, \sigma_2 \neq 0, \sigma_3 = 0$

The strains in this case are found to be

$$\varepsilon_1 = (\sigma_1 - v\sigma_2)/E, \quad \varepsilon_2 = (\sigma_2 - v\sigma_1)/E, \quad \varepsilon_3 = -v(\sigma_1 + \sigma_2)/E \tag{6}$$

Plane stress occurs when a thin plate is loaded by forces acting in its own plane. It also occurs locally at any free surface, because the normal and shear stresses vanish on a free surface, and so the outward normal to a free surface is necessarily a direction of principal stress corresponding to $\sigma_3 = 0$. In plane stress, there is an expansion in the out-of-plane direction if $\sigma_1 + \sigma_2 > 0$ and a contraction if $\sigma_1 + \sigma_2 < 0$. When the biaxial stress state is one of pure shear, then $\sigma_1 + \sigma_2 = 0$ and the lateral strain is zero. The fractional volume change in plane stress is

$$\varepsilon_V = (1 - 2v)(\sigma_1 + \sigma_2)/E \tag{7}$$

The stress-strain relations for plane stress conditions can be written as

$$\sigma_1 = \frac{4G(\lambda + G)}{(\lambda + 2G)}\varepsilon_1 + \frac{2G\lambda}{(\lambda + 2G)}\varepsilon_2 \tag{8}$$

$$\sigma_2 = \frac{2G\lambda}{(\lambda + 2G)}\varepsilon_1 + \frac{4G(\lambda + G)}{(\lambda + 2G)}\varepsilon_2 \tag{9}$$

It is important to note that this "two-dimensional" version of Hooke's law cannot be obtained from the three-dimensional form by simply ignoring the terms that contain the subscript "3."

Biaxial Strain or Plane Strain, $\varepsilon_1 \neq 0, \varepsilon_2 \neq 0, \varepsilon_3 = 0$

The stresses in this case are found to be

$$\sigma_1 = (\lambda + 2G)\varepsilon_1 + \lambda\varepsilon_2 \quad \sigma_2 = (\lambda + 2G)\varepsilon_2 + \lambda\varepsilon_1, \tag{10}$$

$$\sigma_3 = \lambda(\varepsilon_1 + \varepsilon_2) = \frac{\lambda}{2(\lambda + G)}(\sigma_1 + \sigma_2) = v(\sigma_1 + \sigma_2) \tag{11}$$

In order for the out-of-plane strain to be zero, a nonzero out-of-plane stress whose magnitude is given by (11) is needed in order to counteract the Poisson effect due to the two in-plane stresses. The inverse form of Hooke's law for plane strain is

$$\varepsilon_1 = \frac{(1 - v^2)}{E}\sigma_1 - \frac{v(1 + v)}{E}\sigma_2 \tag{12}$$

$$\varepsilon_2 = \frac{(1 - v^2)}{E}\sigma_2 - \frac{v(1 + v)}{E}\sigma_1 \tag{13}$$

If the x- and y-axes are not principal axes, then give

$$\varepsilon_{xx} = \frac{(1 - v^2)}{E}\tau_{xx} - \frac{v(1 + v)}{E}\tau_{yy}, \tag{14}$$

$$\varepsilon_{yy} = \frac{(1 - v^2)}{E}\tau_{yy} - \frac{v(1 + v)}{E}\tau_{xx}, \tag{15}$$

$$\varepsilon_{xy} = \frac{(1 + v)}{E}\tau_{xy} = \frac{1}{2G}\tau_{xy} \tag{16}$$

The assumption of plane strain is very often invoked when analyzing the stresses around boreholes or elongated underground openings.

Combined Formulae for Plane Stress and Plane Strain

If λ is replaced by $2G\lambda/(\lambda+2G)$ in (10), then the resulting equations will be identical to (8) and (9). This suggests the possibility that the stress-strain relations for plane stress and plane strain could be written in a form that is applicable to both situations. Indeed, both sets of stress-strain relations can be written as

$$\varepsilon_1 = \frac{(\kappa+1)}{8G}\sigma_1 + \frac{(\kappa-3)}{8G}\sigma_2 \tag{17}$$

$$\varepsilon_2 = \frac{(\kappa-3)}{8G}\sigma_1 + \frac{(\kappa+1)}{8G}\sigma_2 \tag{18}$$

where "Muskhelishvili's coefficient," κ, is defined as

$$\kappa = 3 - 4\upsilon \text{ for plane strain} \tag{19}$$

$$\kappa = \frac{3-\upsilon}{1+\upsilon} \quad \text{for plane stress} \tag{20}$$

The correctness of (17) and (18) can be verified by substituting the appropriate value of κ and recalling that $E = 2G(1+\upsilon)$. The general forms of (17) and (18) that are applicable in nonprincipal coordinate systems are

$$\varepsilon_{xx} = \frac{(\kappa+1)}{8G}\tau_{xx} + \frac{(\kappa-3)}{8G}\tau_{yy} \tag{21}$$

$$\varepsilon_{yy} = \frac{(\kappa-3)}{8G}\tau_{xx} + \frac{(\kappa+1)}{8G}\tau_{yy} \tag{22}$$

$$\varepsilon_{xy} = \frac{(1+\upsilon)}{E}\tau_{xy} = \frac{1}{2G}\tau_{xy} \tag{23}$$

It is useful to be able to convert solutions for plane stress into the corresponding solutions for plane strain, as many solutions in the literature are written out explicitly for one case or the other, but usually not for both cases. This is done most readily if the solutions are written in terms of G and υ, in which case a solution for plane strain maybe converted to the case of plane stress by replacing $3-4\upsilon$ with $(3-\upsilon)/(1+\upsilon)$, which is to say, by replacing υ with $\upsilon/(1+\upsilon)$. Similarly, plane stress solutions may be converted to plane strain solutions by making the inverse substitution, which is to say, replacing υ with $\upsilon/(1+\upsilon)$.

Constant Strain along the z-axis

It is assumed here that w is independent of x and y, that both μ and υ are independent of z, and that

$$\varepsilon_{zz} = \frac{\partial w}{\partial z} = \varepsilon (= \text{constant}) \tag{24}$$

Under these circumstances $\varepsilon_{xz} = \varepsilon_{yz} = 0$,

$$E\varepsilon_{xx} = (1-\upsilon^2)\tau_{xx} - \upsilon(1+\upsilon)\tau_{yy} - E\upsilon\varepsilon, \tag{25}$$

$$E\varepsilon_{yy} = (1-v^2)\tau_{yy} - v(1+v)\tau_{xx} - Ev\varepsilon, \qquad (26)$$

$$2G\varepsilon_{xy} = \tau_{xy} \qquad (27)$$

These equations provide a simple generalization of the plain strain equations, (21)-(23) and are often used when considering the stresses around under-ground tunnels.

Words and Expressions

volumetric strain		体积应变
compressibility		可压缩性
uniaxial stress		单轴应力
uniaxial strain		单轴应变
contractile [kən'træktail]	adj.	可压缩的
reservoir ['rezəvwɑː]	n.	蓄水库
biaxial stress		双轴应力
plane stress		平面应力
biaxial strain		双轴应变
plane strain		平面应变
out-of-plane		面外
in-plane		面内

Reading Material(2): Soil Mechanics[27]

The reproduction of the rock carving of a ploughman on the cover of Soil & Tillage Research is ample proof that implement design actually pre-dates soil mechanics! What then is the belated contribution made by soil mechanics theory to the development of agricultural tillage tools? In examining this question it is worthwhile remembering that soil mechanics is not the only discipline that has helped to mould modern agriculture as we know it today, and much wider considerations must be taken into account in the analysis. Soil mechanics is a comparatively young discipline and, as its quest for an understanding of the mechanical behaviour of soils made headway, the findings helped to augment the empiricism inherent in the process of tillage-tool design.

The discipline of soil mechanics evolved at the turn of this century, as a specialised branch of applied mechanics and was associated exclusively with the solution of problems in civil engineering, with the main effort directed at obtaining a better understanding of the long-term stability of large structures interacting with saturated soils. In contrast, in a typical soil-machine system short-duration loads are applied to small areas and the soil, which is not necessarily saturated, is invariably brought to failure. The need to deal with these significant differences has led to the development of the new discipline of soil-machine mechanics, which deals with soil-machine interactions in the agricultural and earth-moving industries and in certain aspects of military engineering such as the performance of off-road vehicles. The recognition of these special exigencies has culminated in the formation of the ISTVS and ISTRO, both societies having their own thriving learned journals.

In agriculture the end objective of machine operations on the soil is to ensure the best possible environment for the growth and proliferation of the roots of crops. This biological component is perhaps the key constituent in the entire soil-machine system in agriculture and the discipline of soil-machine mechanics must encompass a study of plant root growth.

The basic structural blocks, which constitute the discipline of soil-machine mechanics, are set out in the organization chart in Fig. 1. Soil-vehicle mechanics is mainly concerned with off-road mobility and traction of vehicles and the sequel to which activity results in compaction problems in the soil. On the other hand, soil-implement mechanics deals with implement draught and soil-disturbance zones and is usually associated with soil loosening.

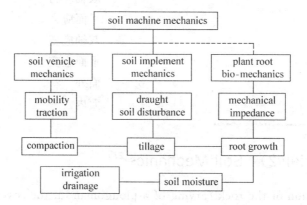

Fig. 1 General organization chart

As shown in Fig. 2 the engineering input into the system comes from two separate aspects of soil mechanics designated classical soil mechanics and critical-state soil mechanics. The former subject handles the analysis of soil forces on machine elements, helps to identify the soil-disturbance zones induced by soil failure and deals with the problems of scouring of tool surfaces. A rigid perfectly-plastic soil-failure model is used in this approach, and the stresses at failure are related by the simple linear Mohr-Coulomb failure criterion. This model takes no account of the strains in the soil and is thus incapable of saying anything about soil-volume changes taking place during the loading process. This aspect is dealt with by critical-state soil mechanics which models the volume-change behaviour of soil to applied stresses. The paper attempts to review the main developments in soil-implement mechanics in the light of these two models with a brief reference to their relevance in plant root bio-mechanics.

The evaluation of all earth pressure problems involves the following basic factors:

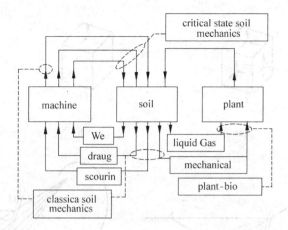

Fig. 2 The main pathways traced by the interactions between machines, soil and plant roots and the models used in their analysis

(1) a knowledge of external loads and their displacements; (2) estimation of internal stresses and associated displacements; (3) a failure criterion for the soil; (4) a suitable failure mechanism. In practice it is difficult to formulate a failure mechanism which will simultaneously satisfy the remaining 3 conditions in any but the simplest problems. There are thus two compromise solution techniques in current use: (1) limit analysis methods which accept any arbitrary failure mechanism in which the energy input from the displacements of the external loads must be entirely dissipated by the internal stresses and their associated displacements. No account is taken of equilibrium conditions; (2) the slip-line method where a failure mechanism is constructed to contain a stress field which is in equilibrium with the external loads and the stresses nowhere violate the failure criterion, in this case no account is taken of energy dissipation or displacements. The methods discussed in this paper fall almost exclusively into the latter category and this choice is dictated by the need to obtain order of magnitude predictions to extremely complex problems. Usually practical experience or simple experiments form the basis on which the failure mechanism is constructed.

The most general stress field induced by soil-machine interactions is three-dimensional. As shown in Fig. 3a there are normal and shear stresses on all 6 faces of an elemental cube of soil, and the development of admissible failure mechanisms is fraught with considerable difficulty. However, the two-dimensional stress system shown in Fig. 3b is easier to deal with. The presence of the body force W introduces certain complications but, as will be shown later, this is not a problem in most soil-machine systems. Prior to examining the details of this method in classical soil mechanics it should be stated that in a vast majority of instances only passive pressure is encountered and hence the discussion will dwell only on this form of earth pressure.

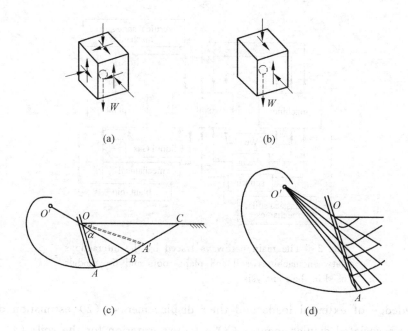

Fig. 3 (a) Stress system in three-dimensional soil failue; (b) stress system in two-dimensinal soil failure; (c) logarithmic-spatial solution; (d) slip-line field at machine-soil interface in logarithmic-spatial solution

Words and Expressions

ploughman ['plaumən]	n.	庄稼汉
predate [pri:'deit]	vt.	在日期上早于
tillage ['tilidʒ]	n.	耕种，耕作
headway ['hedwei]	n.	前进；航行速度
saturated soil		饱和土
earth-moving		运土的
military engineering		军事工程学
off-road		越野的
exigency [ek'sidʒənsi]	n.	紧急
culminate ['kʌlmineit]	vi.	达到顶点
proliferation [prə,lifə'reiʃən]	n.	增殖；扩散
sequel ['si:kwəl]	n.	结局；后果
critical state		临界状态
scouring ['skauəriŋ]	n.	擦洗；冲刷
Mohr-Coulomb failure criterion		摩尔-哥伦布破坏准则

Unit Fourteen

Structural Optimization[28]

The Basic Idea

A structure in mechanics is defined by J. E. Gordon as "any assemblage of materials which is intended to sustain loads." Optimization means making things the best. Thus, structural optimization is the subject of making an assemblage of materials sustain loads in the best way. To fix ideas, think of a situation where a load is to be transmitted from a region in space to a fixed support as in Fig. 1. We want to find the structure that performs this task in the best possible way. However, to make any sense out of that objective we need to specify the term "best". The first such specification that comes to mind may be to make the structure as light as possible, i. e., to minimize weight. Another idea of "best" could be to make the structure as stiff as possible, and yet another one could be to make it as insensitive to buckling or instability as possible. Clearly such maximizations or minimizations cannot be performed without any constraints. For instance, if there is no limitation on the amount of material that can be used, the structure can be made stiff without limit and we have an optimization problem without a well defined solution. Quantities that are usually constrained in structural optimization problems are stresses, displacements and/or the geometry. Note that most quantities that one can think of as constraints could also be used as measures of "best," i. e., as objective functions. Thus, one can put down a number of measures on structural performance-weight, stiffness, critical load, stress, displacement and geometry-and a structural optimization problem is formulated by picking one of these as an objective function that should be maximized or minimized and using some of the other measures as constraints.

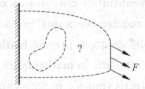

Figure 1 Structural optimization problem. Find the structure which best transmits the load F to the support

The Design Process

The measures on structural performance indicated above are purely mechanical, e. g., we did not consider functionality, economy or esthetics. To make clear the position of structural optimization in relation to such, usually not mathematically defined, factors, we give a short indication of the main steps in the process of designing a product in general, as described by Kirsch. At least in an ideal world these steps are as follows:

1. Function: What is the use of the product? Think of the design of a bridge: how long and broad should it be, how many driving lanes, what loads can be expected, etc. ?

2. Conceptual design: What type of construction concept should we use? When we are to construct a bridge we need to decide if we are to build a truss bridge, a suspension bridge or perhaps an arch bridge.

3. Optimization: Within the chosen concept, and within the constraints on function, make the product as good as possible. For a bridge it would be natural to minimize cost; perhaps indirectly by using the least possible amount of material.

4. Details: This step is usually controlled by market, social or esthetic factors. In the bridge case, perhaps we need to choose an interesting color.

The traditional, and still dominant, way of realizing step 3 is the iterative-intuitive one, which can be described as follows. (a) A specific design is suggested. (b) Requirements based on the function are investigated. (c) If they are not satisfied, say the stress is too large, a new design must be suggested, and even if such requirements are satisfied the design may not be optimal (the bridge may be overly heavy) so we still may want to suggest a new design. (d) The suggested new design is brought back to step (b). In this way an iterative process is formed where, on mainly intuitive grounds, a series of designs are created which hopefully converges to an acceptable final design.

For mechanical structures, step (b) of the iterative-intuitive realization of step 3, is today almost exclusively performed by means of computer based methods like the Finite Element Method (FEM) or Multi Body Dynamics (MBD). These methods imply that every design iteration can be analyzed with greater confidence, and probably every step can be made more effective. However, they do not lead to a basic change of the strategy.

The mathematical design optimization method is conceptually different from the iterative-intuitive one. In this method a mathematical optimization problem is formulated, where requirements due to the function act as constraints and the concept "as good as possible" is given precise mathematical form. Thus, step 3 in the design process is much more automatic in mathematical design optimization than in an iterative-intuitive approach.

Clearly, not all factors can be usefully treated in a mathematical design optimization method. A basic requirement is that the factor need to be measurable in mathematical form. This is usually easy for mechanical factors but difficult for, say, esthetic ones.

Three Types of Structural Optimization Problems

In this text, x will almost exclusively represent some sort of geometric feature of the structure. Depending on the geometric feature, we divide structural optimization problems into three classes:

- Sizing optimization: This is when x is some type of structural thickness, i. e. , cross-sectional areas of truss members, or the thickness distribution of a sheet. A sizing optimization problem for a truss structure is shown in Fig. 2.
- Shape optimization: In this case x represents the form or contour of some part of the boundary of the structural domain. Think of a solid body, the state of which is described by a set of partial differential equations. The optimization consists in choosing the integration domain for the differential equations in an optimal way. Note that the connectivity of the structure is not changed by shape optimization: new boundaries are not formed. A two-dimensional shape optimization problem is seen in Fig. 3.
- Topology optimization: This is the most general form of structural optimization. In a discrete case, such as for a truss, it is achieved by taking cross-sectional areas of truss members as design variables, and then allowing these variables to take the value zero, i. e. , bars are removed from the truss. In this way the connectivity of nodes is variable so we may say that the topology of the truss changes, see Fig. 4. If instead of a discrete structure we think of a continuum-type structure such as a two-dimensional sheet, then topology changes can be achieved by letting the thickness of the sheet take the value zero. If pure topological features are optimized, the optimal thickness should take only two values: 0 and a fixed maximum sheet thickness. In a three-dimensional case the same effect can be achieved by letting x be a density-like variable that can only take the values 0 and 1. Figure 5 shows an example of topology optimization.

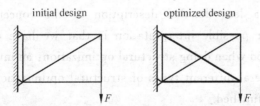

Figure 2 A sizing structural optimization problem is formulated by optimizing the cross-sectional areas of truss members

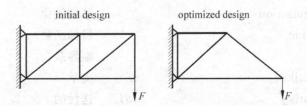

Figure 3 A shape optimization problem. Find the function $\eta(x)$, describing the shape of the beam-like structure

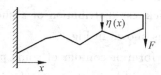
Figure 4 Topology optimization of a truss. Bars are removed by letting cross-sectional areas take the value zero

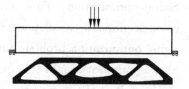
Figure 5 Two-dimensional topology optimization. The box is to be filled to 50% by material. Where should the material be placed for optimal performance under loads and boundary conditions shown in the upper picture? The result is shown in the second picture. Calculations performed by Borrvall

Ideally, shape optimization is a subclass of topology optimization, but practical implementations are based on very different techniques, so the two types are treated separately in this text and elsewhere. Concerning the relation between topology and sizing optimization, the situation is the opposite: from a fundamental point of view they are very different, but they are closely related from practical considerations.

When the state problem is a differential equation, we can say that shape optimization concerns control of the domain of the equation, while sizing and topology optimization concern control of its parameters.

The fact that there exist several types of structural optimization problems seems to have two different interpretations. The first one is that the boundary between step 2 and step 3 is flexible: topology optimization, which is the most general type of structural optimization, requires a less detailed description of the concept than, e.g., shape optimization. The other possible interpretation is that we have only partially left the intuitive-iterative method when doing structural optimization: an intuitive ingredient is left and it is likely that several different types of structural optimization problems need to be solved before step 3 is finished.

Words and Expressions

optimization [ˌɔptimaiˈzeiʃən]	n.	优化
structural optimization		结构优化
objective function		目标函数
critical load		临界载荷
esthetics [esˈθetiks]	n.	美学
iterative [ˈitərətiv]	adj.	迭代的
Multi Body Dynamics (MBD)		多体动力学
measurable [ˈmeʒərəbəl]	adj.	可测量的
sizing optimization		尺寸优化

shape optimization		形状优化
integration [ˌinti'greiʃən]	n.	积分
topology optimization		拓扑优化

科技英语翻译技巧：长句的译法[31]

长句常见的翻译方法有：化整为零，分译法；纲举目张，变序法；逆流而上，逆序法。此外，某些长句也可能根据原文的顺序，保持不变，一气呵成，依次译出，即递序而下，顺序法。现分别举例说明。

1. 分译法

原句包含多层意思，而汉语习惯一个小句表达一层意思。为了使行文简洁，将整个长句译成几个独立的句子，顺序基本不变，保持前后的连贯。

Steel is usually made where the iron ore is smelted, so that the modern steelworks forms a complete unity, taking in raw materials and producing all types of cast iron and steel, both for sending to other works for further treatment, and as finished products such as joists and other consumers.

[初译] 通常在炼铁的地方就炼钢，所以现代炼钢厂从运进原材料到生产供送往其他工厂进一步加工处理并制成如工字钢及其他商品钢材的成品而形成一整套的联合企业。

这种译文令人感到，读起来佶屈聱牙，看起来，概念不清。究其原因，囿于英语结构形式，忽略汉语自身规律。试将原文拆散为三个独立的小句译成汉语。steel is … smelted 为第一小句；so that … steel 为第二小句；both for … consumers 为第三小句。原文中，通过 both … and 连接的两个介词短语在译文中可扩展成句子。

[改译] 通常炼铁的地方也炼钢。因此，现代炼钢厂是一个配套的整体，从运进原料到生产各种类型的铸铁与钢材；有的送往其他工厂进一步加工处理，有的就制成成品，如工字钢及其他一些成材。

The loads a structure is subjected to are divided into dead loads, which include the weights of all the parts of the structure, and live loads, which are due to the weights of people, movable equipment, etc.

[初译] 一个结构物受到的荷载可分为包括结构物各部分重量的静载和由于人及可移动设备等的重量引起的活载。

从理解原文的角度看，译文传达了原意，符合"信"的原则。但由于汉语习惯用小句，这46个字的长句很难一气读完，有欠"达、雅"。如采用化整为零，分译法，则可收醒目易读之效。

[改译] 一个结构物受到的荷载可分为静载与活载两类。静载包括该结构物各部分的重量。活载则是由于人及可移动设备等的重量而引起的荷载。

2. 变序法

原句结构复杂，可按汉语由远及近的顺序从中间断句，层层展开，最后画龙点睛，突出主题。

An "alloy" steel is one which, in addition to the contents of carbon, sulphur and phosphorus, contains more than 1 per cent of manganese, or more than 0.3 per cent of silicon, or some other elements in amounts not encountered in carbon steels.

［初译］合金钢是一种钢。除掉炭、硫、磷以外，还含有多于1%的锰或多于0.3%的硅或者一些碳素钢中不包括的其他元素。

以上译文采用了分译法。但"合金钢是一种钢"这句话毫无价值，没有再现作者的原意。而且与后半部分脱节，失去逻辑上的严密性。试从 in addition to … 译起，最后回到句首，展示主要信息，既可衔接紧密，又能突出主题。

［改译］如果一种钢除含有炭、硫、磷以外，还含有多于1%的锰或多于0.3%的硅或者一些碳素钢中不包含的其他元素，那么这种钢便是"合金钢"。

The reason that a neutral body is attracted by a charged body is that, although the neutral body is neutral within itself, it is not neutral with respect to the charged body, and the two bodies act as if oppositely charged when brought near each other.

［初译］中性物体被带电物体吸引的原因在于，虽然中性物体本身是不带电的，但对带电体来说，它不是中性。当这两个物体彼此接近时，就会产生带有相反电荷的作用。

上述译文不恰当地采用了顺序分译法，以致译文内部衔接松弛，破坏了作者所提出的概念的完整性。从 although … 到句尾，都是说明"中性物体被带电体吸引的原因"，这一整体不容分割。试从 although 引导的让步状语从句入手，将原文前置的主要信息在译文中后置，画龙点睛。

［改译］虽然中性物体本身是不带电的，但对于带电体来说，它并非中性；当这两个物体彼此接近时，就会产生极性相反的电荷的作用。这就是中性物体被带电体吸引的原因。

3. 逆序法

由于英语惯用前置性陈述，先果后因；而汉语相反，一般先因后果，层层递进，最后综合，点出主题。处理这类句子，宜于先译全句的后部，再依次向前，逆序译出。

The construction of such a satellite is now believed to be quite realizable, its realization being supported with all the achievements of contemporary science, which have brought into being not only materials capable of withstanding severe stresses involved and high temperatures developed, but new technological processes as well.

［初译］制造这样的人造卫星确信是可能的，因为可以依靠现代科学的一切成就。这些成就不仅提供了能够承受高温高压的材料，而且也提供了新的工艺过程。

原文由三部分构成：主句，作原因状语的分词独立结构，修饰独立结构的定语从句。根据汉语词序，状语特别是原因状语在先，定语前置，故从 which … 入手，再译出 its realization … 最后才译出 The construction … realizable。

［改译］现代科学的一切成就不仅提供了能够承受高温高压的材料，而且也提供了新的工艺过程。依靠现代科学的这些成就，我们相信完全可以制造出这样的人造卫星。

In reality, the lines of division between sciences are becoming blurred, and science is again approaching the "unity" that it had two centuries ago—although the accumulated knowledge is enormously greater now, and no one person can hope to comprehend more than a fraction of it.

［初译］事实上，各学科之间的分界线变得模糊不清，科学再次近似于两百年前那样的

"单一整体"——虽然现在积累起来的知识比以往多得多,而且任何个人也只可望了解其中的一小部分。

翻译一是要传达原旨,二是要符合汉语习惯。上述译文虽然达旨,但是西化汉语。应遵照汉语的习惯,将由 although 引出的让步状语从句提前,逆序而上为好。

[改译] 虽然现在积累起来的知识要多得多,而且任何个人也只可望了解其中的一小部分,但事实上,各学科之间界线却变得模糊不清,科学再次近似于两百年前那样的"单一整体"。

4. 顺序法

英语原句的结构的顺序与汉语相同,层次分明,译成汉语时可顺序推进,一气呵成。

All commercial iron and steel contains iron as chief constituent, but the percentages of carbon and other elements and the methods by which iron and steel is produced, as well as the processes to which they may be subjected, so change the characteristic properties that there are many distinct forms of iron and steel, some of which have properties so different as to appear like different metals.

[译文] 所有商用钢铁都以其含铁为主要成分,但由于碳和其他元素的含量不同,钢铁冶炼方法以及加工过程不同,从而改变了它们的特性,以至于有多种不同的钢铁,其中有些钢铁的特性极不相同,看上去就像不同的金属一样。

The development of rockets has made possible the achievement of speeds of several thousand miles per hour; and what is more important it has brought within reach of these rockets heights far beyond those which can be reached by aeroplanes, and where there is little or no air resistance, and so it is much easier both to obtain and to maintain such speed.

[译文] 火箭技术的进展已使速度可达每小时几千英里,而更为重要的是,这种进展已使火箭所能达到的高度大大超过了飞机所能达到的高度,在这样的高度上,几乎没有或根本没有空气阻力,因而很容易达到并保持火箭的那种高速度。

Reading Material(1): Research Directions in Computational Mechanics[21]

Computational mechanics: a core discipline in computational science and engineering

Theoretical and applied mechanics (TAM) is the branch of applied science concerned with the study of mechanical phenomena: the behavior of fluids, solids, and complex materials under the actions of forces. Few disciplines have had a greater impact on the industrialized world, enabling technological developments in virtually every area that affects our lives, security, and well being.

Computational mechanics (CM) is that sub-discipline of TAM concerned with the use of computational methods and devices to study events governed by the principles of mechanics. It is the fundamentally important part of computational science and engineering concerned with the use of computational approaches to characterize, predict, and simulate physical events and engineering systems governed by the laws of mechanics. Computational mechanics has had a profound impact on science and technology over the past three decades. It has transformed much of classical Newtonian theory into practical tools for prediction and understanding of complex systems. These are used in the simulation and design of current and future advances in technology throughout the developed and developing world. These have had a pervasive impact on manufacturing, communication, transportation, medicine, defense and many other areas central to modern civilization. By incorporating new models of physical and biological systems based upon quantum, molecular and biological mechanics, computational mechanics has an enormous potential for future growth and applicability.

Not surprisingly, successful research in CM is usually interdisciplinary in nature, reflecting a combination of concepts, methods, and principles that often span several areas of mechanics, mathematics, computer sciences, and other scientific disciplines as well. As will soon become evident in this exposition, tomorrow's research in CM will be broader than ever before, spanning many new technologies and scientific fields.

Our goal here is to provide a perspective of the major research areas in CM that will be the focus of inquiry during the next decade: what are the research directions in the CM and what are the opportunities for industrial, governmental, university researchers, and those who would implement and apply the research results in computational mechanics?

Reliability of computational mechanics

The question of reliability of computer-generated predictions is one of great concern to specialistsin CM. Without some confidence in the accuracy of simulations, their value is obviously diminished. Today, remarkably accurate and reliable simulations are obtained routinely in many application areas while others are, at best, qualitative and capable of depicting only trends in physical events.

This concern for reliability has led to the creation of a challenging technological area labeledsimply validation and verification: the creation, study and documentation of tools for assessing the predictability of CM-based methods and programs. Validation has to do with determining the appropriateness of the scientific principles and mathematical models used to develop a simulation tool. Verification has to do with determining if the final tool can indeed function as it was intended and if it can correctly produce results consistent with the models upon which it is based.

Validation methods include, when possible, actual comparisons of CM predictions with observations, physical tests and experiments. Even then, such comparisons can be made for only a limited range of parameters and generally not the full range of possibilities embraced by general computational modeling schemes. Modern validation methods also seek todefine the limits of various modeling schemes and, ideally, to provide insight as to when these limits are reached and can be overcome.

Verification methods involve the use of benchmark tests developed by experienced analysts over years of work, or implementation of software engineering methods to minimize coding errors and optimize computational performance and program design.

With the rapidly expanding use of CM throughout many areas of science and engineering, "V and V" has become a critical component of today s research in CM. New V and V tools are on the horizon that could dramatically increase the reliability of sophisticated computation modeling. Some of these tools are mentioned later in this exposition.

Computational mechanics: the next decade and the next millennium

It may be confidently said that virtually every aspect of our day-to-day lives is affected in some way by CM. Still, the subject is undergoing rapid change and development and many open issues remain.

During the next decade, the field of CM will undergo dramatic changes that will require computational mechanics capabilities not available today. An unprecedented growth in activity and importance is expected that may have been unimaginable only a few years ago. Also, in the next millennium, a paradigm shift in the computational sciences is essential if the needs of industry are to be met.

Perhaps the most remarkable aspect of our vision of CM in the next decade is that CM research will require new interactions of computational methods and devices with a variety of supporting technologies, including imaging, various tomographic modalities, visualization, testing, and laboratory experimentation. In the new CM, "mechanics" will interact with theories of quantum mechanics, molecular dynamics, materials science, biomedical and biological systems, and other disciplines. It will involve the study of microscopic phenomena taking place in pica seconds. A myriad of technological tools need to be integrated into the mechanical analysis, not only for studying engineering materials, but also to study biological systems, submicron devices, and robots. These far-reaching applications will impact predictability, our life styles and personal health and longevity.

Funding sources: computer versus computational science

In general, the subtle difference between the terms "computer science" and "computational science", are not recognized but the distinct differences in these disciplines has had a significant impact on the distribution of resources for fundamental research. Computer science refers to the science and technology pertinent to the computer, the computational device with which computation is done. Computational science, on the other hand, addresses the development of modeling techniques, algorithms, software, and for specific problems in science and engineering. There has been a tendency to promote investment in computer science as the necessary tool with which good computational science can be done, but there has been no comparable support by traditional funding agencies has emerged in the important computational sciences necessary to do important applications. A good example is PITAC, the President's Information Technology Advisory Committee (in the United States), largely populated by computer scientists as opposed to computational scientists, which after a study of over a year, recommended that federal government invest over a billion dollars into new research in "information technology", principally pure computer science, networking, and hardware. In explaining the value of this program to the US Congress, however, the great benefits of such an investment for doing computational science were stressed, but few funds were allocated to the latter. Similar situations exist in Europe and Asia.

In order to meet the needs of industry, renewed emphasis on the computational sciences, and, particularly, CM, is needed. This is not to say that some impressive investments have not been made in this discipline. Indeed, very ambitious programs are underway that will raise the bar in computational modeling. These include the ASCI program (Accelerated Scientific Computation Initiative) which is aimed at displacing traditional nuclear testing and storage procedures with highly-tuned, computer simulations. It remains to be seen whether many of the goals of ASCI are attainable, but the program undoubtedly will create some important advances in CM and related sciences. Such programs also foster a broadening and generalization of all fields supporting computational science, and intrinsically advance supporting technologies to make meaningful simulations possible.

In the pages below, we outline flbriey a number of areas with significant research opportunities in CM:
- Virtual design
- Multi-scale phenomena, including bridging of molecular to atomistic to continuum models
- Model selection and adaptivity
- Very large-scale parallel computing
- Biomedical applications, including predictive surgery, application of mechanics to the study of cells, bones, nerves, and other biological systems
- Controlling uncertainty: probabilistic methods

Model selection and adaptivity

Throughout all the mathematical and computational sciences, the first and most primitive step in computer modeling is the selection of the mathematical and computational model itself. Modle selection is a largely heuristic process, based on the judgement and experience of the modeler, and on testing and experimentation. But it is frequently purely a subjective endeavor: different analysts may select different models to describe the same physical phenomena. The selection of the model, by which we ordinarily mean the selection of the partial differential, integral or ordinary diffrential equations, the algorithms, the physical, geometrical and topological characteristics, boundary and initial conditions, etc., is quite often the single most important step in obtaining valid computer simulations of physical events.

In recent years, considerable progress has been made in determining theoretical and computational techniques that aid in model selection. A variety of techniques are under study. Some of these involve embedding a given class of models into a larger class of more sophisticated models in which finer and more detailed representations of the behavior of physical system may be possible. Once such a datum is identified, a notion of modeling error can be made precise, and by various measures, such modeling error can be controlled by adaptive modeling processes. Areas in which adaptive modeling have great promise include the study and characterization of composite materials, unsteady turbulentflows, multiphase flows of fluids, etc. Other techniques for model adaptivity involve the use and integration of test and imaging data, feedback from experiments and measurements, and various combinations of these methodologies.

Model selection is a crucial element in automating engineering analysis and applications are unlimited; the subject could conceivably embrace classes of models including diverse spatial and temporal scales, enabling the systematic and controlled simulation of events modeled using atomistic or molecular models to continuum models. Model selection, model error estimation, and model adaptivity are exciting areas of CM and promise to provide an active area of research for the next decade and beyond.

Error estimation and adaptivity

The notion of computing estimates of numerical error in computer simulations is not new; serious work in this subject began in the 1980's, and today the notion of a posteriori error estimation is a common topic in university research environments. Error estimation provides a quantitative measure for determining the quality of numerical simulations; it provides a basis for adapting characteristics of discrete models (for example, meshes or approximation orders) so as to improve the quality of results.

To date, most of a posteriori estimation has been confined to a fairly narrow class of problems, largely drawn from linear theory; it has not been fully utilized in the more complex computer simulations used in industry and government laboratories.

It is predicted that a posteriori error estimation and adaptivity will become a common ingredient in all significant computer simulations in CM during the next decade. With a renewed and invigorated interest in reliability of simulations, the calculation of estimates of error in simulations will be as natural a feature of the simulation as any other estimate of physical quantities of interest. An important advance in this area has been the recent discovery of methods to determine upper and lower bounds of local approximation error, so that in any given simulation, once a particular model is selected, computable bounds giving upper and lower limits to computed quantities of interest could be a natural by-product in every simulation. This is a fertile area of research, one in which significant work will be done during the next decade.

Computational mechanics: conclusions

CM has become a central enabling discipline that has led to greater understanding and advances in modern science and technology. It has been the basis of numerous important developments in recent years and will continue to be crucial to industrial development and competition, to safety and security, and to understanding the diverse physical and biological systems occurring in nature and in society. Many research problems in CM await resolution and will provide significant challenges for research in the future. If "the past is prologue", then, in the future, we may anticipate even greater contributions of CM to the advancement of knowledge and to the benefit of a global society.

Words and Expressions

computational mechanics		计算力学
theoretical and applied mechanics		理论与应用力学
sub-discipline		分支学科
interdisciplinary [ˌintəˈdisiplinəri]	adj.	学科间的;学科交叉的
reliability [riˌlaiəˈbiliti]	n.	可靠性,可靠度
benchmark test		基准测试
optimize [ˈɔptimaiz]	vt. & vi.	优化
paradigm [ˈpærədaim]	n.	范例
tomographic [təuˈmɔgrəfi]	n.	X线断层摄影术;X线体层照相术
modality [məuˈdæliti]	n.	样式;形式;形态
quantum mechanics		量子力学
molecular dynamics		分子动力学
myriad [ˈmiriəd]	n.	无数;极大数量
	adj.	无数的;极大数量的
submicron [ˌsʌbˈmaikrɔn]	n.	亚微细米;亚微细粒
longevity [lɔnˈdʒeviti]	n.	长寿;寿命
virtual design		虚拟设计
multi-scale		多尺度
large-scale parallel computing		大规模并行计算
heuristic [hjuəˈristik]	adj.	启发式的;探索的
partial differential equation		偏微分方程
ordinary differential equation		常微分方程
integral equation		积分方程
turbulent flow		湍流流动

multiphase flow		多相流
feedback ['fiːdbæk]	n.	反馈
error estimation		误差估计
adaptivity [ədæp'tivəti]	n.	适应性
posteriori error estimation		后验误差估计

Reading Material(2): New Directions in Mechanics[29]

Structures form spontaneously at all size scales. Electrons, protons and neutrons form atoms. Atoms form clusters and molecules. These building blocks form mesostructures; examples range from the classic Guinier-Preston zones in aluminum-copper alloys, to ubiquitous lipid bilayers, and to more recently discovered strain-induced quantum dots. Daoud and Williams have edited a lucid introduction to objects under the rubric of soft matter, such as block copolymers, surfactants, colloids, emulsions, and liquid crystals. Other self-assembled mesostructures include nanohole arrays formed by the anodic oxidation of aluminum, droplet lattices formed from a liquid film, dealloying nanoporous structures, and magnetic dots on an insulating substrate. We are, of course, aware of larger self-assembled structures: animals and plants, rivers and mountains, stars and galaxies.

Life, the most complex self-assembly currently known, by its very existence offers inspiration. The ultimate self-assembled structures will be multifunctional, simultaneously transporting energy, matter and information. Fluidics will be an integral part of those structures, in addition to solid state components. The structures will have the attributes of self-preservation: healing, self-sensing, and replication. They will be adaptive and tunable, and be programmed to self-de-assemble. Hierarchical organization is needed to achieve these goals.

Self-assembly and directed self-assembly will be an increasingly significant part of the technology that mass-produces devices that harvest energy, sense trace amounts of matter, and manipulate information. Molecular cars may one day be self-assembled and outperform the protein motors in nature, with higher energy transduction effciency and greater versatility. The state of the art is of course not so advanced: the gap between quantum dots and life is huge. This gap can only be filled by inspiration and perseverance in years to come.

Edisonian-type investigations have been driving many, if not all, of the most exciting advances in this important area of research. Neither our understanding nor our control of self-assembly is adequate to map out the road to the ultimate structures that will, one day, achieve selectivity and functionality of the kind that is already achieved routinely by the lowliest forms of living organisms. While many systems self-assemble, too few have led, by rational design, to profoundly new technological uses. It is an exciting time when both Edisonian and mechanistic approaches can make great progress.

We next describe several current research topics in which the mechanistic approach plays a significant role in understanding and exploiting mesoscale self-assembly and fluidics. In the space available, we will only describe a few examples. A notable omission is strain-induced quantum dots, a subject to which mechanics has made crucial contributions. Also missing is a more general topic: nanofabrication; see, e. g., Decher and Schlenoff (2003) and Heller and Guttman (2002). Several mechanical-based fabrication processes have shown astonishing capabilities. For example, Chou et al. (1995) showed that embossing print can replicate nanoscale features, which can then be used as templates to make functional structures, such as nanoscale transistors. The revelation has inspired worldwide activities to retool this ancient technology, embossing print, for modern uses. As another example, Alaca et al. (submitted) have developed a method to introduce a controlled pattern of cracks, which can be used as fluid channels or as templates to form nanowires. Mechanics has long played a significant role in manufacturing technologies, such as metal forming, ceramic sintering, and polymer molding. Nanofabrication involves deformation, fracture, and mass transport at the nanoscale, and will be a persistent challenge to mechanics in the coming decade.

Evaporation-induced Self-assembly (EISA)

Evaporation-induced self-assembly (EISA) illustrates the enormous versatility of self-assembly (Fig. 1). Start with a dilute aqueous solution of alcohol, amphiphile and Si-precursor. Allow water and alcohol to evaporate. When amphiphile exceeds a critical concentration, micelles form in lamellar, hexagonal and cubic phases. The micelles are the templates for silica structures by condensation reactions. EISA can be implemented in many ways: spin coating, spray drying and dip coating. During dip coating, for example, evaporation is extremely fast at the leading edge (the top). The assembly progresses by nucleation at the top and growth toward the bottom, like a zipper. Large defect-free domains of various phases emerge. EISA is a deceptively easy route to highly intricate structures. By including other ingredients in the aqueous solution, one can explore an enormous range of nanocomposites.

EISA poses a great challenge to fundamental understanding. Viewed from this angle, the dip coating is a complex process. New length scales emerge as the structures form. Such a process can not be described by conventional constitutive relations. The viscosity, evaporation rate, solution vapor surface tension are all complex functions of the concentrations. EISA can be visualized as a trajectory in the equilibrium phase diagram of an amphiphile-ethanol-water system. This first-order approach provides insight into which structures may be encountered. However, the two interfaces, liquid/vapor and liquid/substrate, can modify the relative stability of various structures. So can kinetic factors such as shear and concentration gradients across the films. Incidentally, the liquid/substrate interface presents a good illustration of directed assembly. By controlling the substrate, one may harness the inherent self-assembling tendencies of the solution and steer the structure formation process into desirable directions.

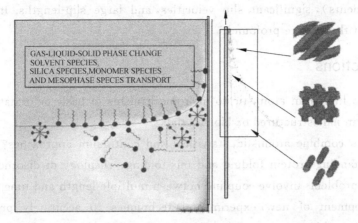

Fig. 1 Schematic illustrating evaporation-induced self-assembly (EISA) for the dip-coating process. A substrate is dipped into an aqueous solution of surfactant and silica precursor. Surface tension causes a thin film to adhere to the substrate as it is pulled upwards. Fast evaporation at the leading edge of the film causes rapid concentration of the surfactant, which produces three-dimensional structures inside the thin film. These "soft" organic structures then serve as templates for the inorganic architectures of various symmetries.

Modeling of amphiphile self-assembly is an active field. An obvious challenge is the significant time and length scale variations during self-assembly. One needs to capture molecular level detail in some form, in order to capture the effects of amphiphile size, for instance. One must also allow for larger length scale phenomena in order to represent, say, the formation of periodic structure, the role of interfaces, shear, or the concentration gradients. To fully model the dip coating process requires the implementation of a multilength scale strategy that reaches from molecular to continuum.

Various molecular modeling approaches are currently pursued to study aspects of self-assembly, including molecular dynamics (MD), Monte Carlo (MC), and density functional theory (DFT), as well as hybrid forms of these. Some of these studies involve lattice models while others are off-lattice. A new approach, introduced by Fraaije (1999), involves a coupling of DFT with transport equations. This mesoscopic approach has been very successful in modeling actual processes, illustrating the role of process variables such as shear as well as the need for coarse-graining of molecular features. A coupling of MC (or DFT) with concentration gradients and chemical reactions has also been introduced, further expanding the arsenal of the process variables available.

With relative ease, EISA can be used to apply coatings to other materials. An interesting application involves mimicking the Lotus Leaf. High solid-liquid interfacial energies, in conjunction with rough surface topographies, cause high contact angles, rolling and bouncing of liquid droplets, and self-cleaning of particle contaminants. When a fluid channel has such a super-hydrophobic coating, one observes increased flow rates (reduced friction coefficients), significant slip velocities, and large slip-lengths. Implications for energy-efficient fluidics are profound.

Future directions

- How to link from atomistic to micromechanisms in basic deformation modes and failure in nanostructured or biomaterials?
- How to combine atomistic, statistical and continuum approaches? For example, understanding protein folding and mis-folding; rheology of disordered networks. These problems involve coupling between multiple length and time scales.
- Development of new experimental techniques to accurately probe dynamical evolution of bionanomaterial response
  - improvement in temporal and spatial resolution (protein machine);
  - to discriminate single versus ensemble molecular events at surfaces/interfaces.
- Interconnection between experiment and theory/simulation is crucial to answering the open questions in nanobiomaterials.
- Nanomechanics at the interface between liquids and solids with biomolecules is critical for materials and mechanics research, especially for new biomaterials synthesis, friction and dissipation, and energy conversion. Possibility of fabrication and replication of nanostructures, e. g. , using self-assembly.

Words and Expressions

cluster ['klʌstə]	n.	群;群集
mesostructure	n.	细观结构;中构造
ubiquitous [juːˈbikwitəs]	adj.	到处存在的
lipid ['lipid]	n.	脂质;油脂
strain-induced quantum dot		应变诱发量子点
rubric ['ruːbrik]	n.	类;标题;红色的
block copolymer		嵌段共聚物
surfactant [səːˈfæktənt]	n.	表面活性剂
	adj.	表面活性剂的
colloid ['kɔlɔid]	n.	胶体
	adj.	胶状的
emulsion [iˈmʌlʃən]	n.	乳胶液;感光乳剂
liquid crystal		液晶
nanohole	n.	纳米空洞
droplet ['drɔplit]	n.	小滴;微滴
lattice ['lætis]	n.	格子;点阵

dealloying [ˌdiːəˈlɔiiŋ]	n.	脱合金成分腐蚀
magnetic dot		磁点
fluidics [ˈfluːidiks]	n.	应用流体学；射流技术
tunable [ˈtjuːnəbl]	adj.	可调谐的
hierarchical [ˌhaiəˈrɑːkikl]	adj.	按等级划分的
hierarchical organization		分层结构
outperform [ˌautpəˈfɔːm]	vt.	优于；超额完成
perseverance [ˌpəːsiˈviərəns]	n.	不屈不挠；毅力
lowly [ˈləuli]	adj.	贫贱的；地位低下的
mechanistic [ˌmekəˈnistik]	adj.	机械学的；机械的
nanofabrication	n.	纳米加工
embossing [imˈbɔːs]	vt.	压纹；模压加工
nanoscale	n.	纳米尺度
retool [riːˈtuːl]	vi. & vt.	重组；重新装备
nanowire	n.	纳米线
sintering [ˈsintəriŋ]	vi.	烧结
aqueous [ˈeikwiəs]	adj.	水的；水成的
amphiphile	n.	两亲物；两亲性分子
micelle [maiˈsel]	n.	微团；胶束
nanocomposite	n.	纳米复合材料
dip coating		浸涂
amphiphile	n.	两亲物
ethanol [ˈeθəˌlɔn, ˈeθəˌnəul]	n.	乙醇
substrate [ˈsʌbstreit]	n.	基片；基底
inorganic [ˌinɔːˈgænik]	adj.	无机的；非自然生长的
harness [ˈhɑːnis]	n.	马具；管理；控制
molecular dynamics (MD)		分子动力学
Monte Carlo (MC)		蒙特卡罗
density functional theory (DFT)		密度泛函理论
off-lattice		非格子
coarse-grain		粗粒的；大粒度的
contaminant [kənˈtæmənənt]	n.	杂质；污染物
super-hydrophobic		超疏水
nanostructure	n.	纳米结构
protein folding		蛋白质折叠
mis-folding		错折叠
bionanomaterial	n.	生物纳米材料
nanomechanics	n.	纳米力学

附录：常用专业词汇和用语汇总表

A

absolute temperature		绝对温度
abutment [ə'bʌtmənt]	n.	桥墩；桥基；桥台
acceleration [æk,selə'reiʃən]	n.	加速度
accelerometer [æk,selə'rɔmitə]	n.	加速度计
action-at-a-distance		远距离作用
active gage		工作片
acoustic emitter		声发射器
acute angle		锐角
adaptivity [ədæp'tivəti]	n.	适应性
aerospace engineering		航空工程
aggregate ['ægrigit]	n.	偏析，聚合体
algebraic equation		代数方程
Almansi strain		阿曼西应变
allowable stress		许用应力
alternator ['ɔːltəneitə]	n.	交流发电机
amorphous [ə'mɔːfəs]	adj.	无定性的；非晶形的，无一定方向的
amphiphile	n.	两亲物；两亲性分子
amphiphile	n.	两亲物
amplitude ['æmplitjuːd]	n.	幅值
amplification factor		放大因子，放大倍数
amplitude stress		幅值应力
amplitude of vibration		振动幅值；振幅
anelastic [,ænil'æsti]	adj.	滞弹性的
aneurysm ['ænjurizəm]	n.	动脉瘤
anisotropic [æn,aisə'trɔpik]		各向异性的
anisotropy [,ænai'sɔtrəpi]	n.	各向异性
apparatus [,æpə'reitəs]	n.	仪器；装置
apparent stress		表观应力
appearance [ə'pirəns]	n.	出现，显露，外观
aqueous ['eikwiəs]	adj.	水的；水成的
arch [aːtʃ]	n.	拱
arm [aːm]	n.	臂

artificial heart valve		人工心脏瓣膜
assembly [ə'sembli]	n.	组集,集合
Atomic Force Microscope		原子力显微镜
autocatalytic [ˌɔːtəukætə'litik]	adj.	自动催化的
austenite ['ɔːstəˌnait]	n.	奥氏体
austenite crystal		奥氏体晶粒
austenitic transformation		奥氏体转变
average stress		平均应力
axil force		轴向力

B

back difference		向后差分
backing ['bækiŋ]	n.	衬底;基底
bar [bɑː]	n.	杆;条;横木;栅
basalt [bə'sɔːlt]	n.	玄武岩
basis function		基函数
Bauschinger effect		包辛格效应
beam [biːm]	n.	梁,桁,横梁
bedding plane		层理面
benchmark test		基准测试
bend [bend]	vt.&vi.	弯曲,折弯
bending moment		弯矩
bending stress		弯曲应力
biaxial strain		双轴应变
biaxial stress		双轴应力
biharmonic [baihɑː'mɔnik]	adj.	双调和的
bionanomaterial	n.	生物纳米材料
block copolymer		嵌段共聚物
bobbin ['bɔbin]	n.	线轴
body force		体力
bolt [bəult]	n.	螺栓
bomb blast		炸弹爆炸
borehole ['bɔːhoul]	n.	钻孔
boron ['bɔːrɔn]	n.	硼
boundary condition		边界条件
boundary integral		边界积分
brake drum		制动鼓;鼓式制动器
brass [brɑːs]	n.	黄铜,黄铜色
brittle fracture		脆性断裂

brittle fracture mechanics		脆性断裂力学
buckle ['bʌkl]	vi.	屈曲
bushing ['buʃiŋ]	n.	绝缘套,轴衬

C

calcite ['kælsait]	n.	方解石
calibration [ˌkæli'breiʃən]	n.	标定
calibration constant		标定常数
cantilever ['kæntiliːvə]	n.	悬臂;支架
carbon steel		碳钢
Cartesian coordinate		笛卡儿坐标
cast iron		铸铁
catastrophically [ˌkætə'strɔfikli]	adv.	灾难性地
cavitation [ˌkævi'teiʃən]	n.	气穴;成洞
cellular pattern		空泡
centered difference		中心差分
central crack		中心裂纹
centripetal acceleration		向心加速度
centroidal axis		形心轴,质心轴
chaotic [kei'ɔtik]	adj.	混乱的;混沌的
chord [kɔːd]	n.	弦;弦杆
civil engineering		土木工程
cleavage ['kliːvidʒ]	n.	分裂;裂隙
clay soil settle		粘土土层沉降
closed form		闭型
cluster ['klʌstə]	n.	群;群集
civil engineering		土木工程
coarse-grain		粗粒的;大粒度的
collapse [kə'læps]	vi.	破坏,塌陷
collinear [kə'linjə]	adj.	同线的;共轴的
collision [kə'liʒən]	n.	相撞,碰撞
colloid ['kɔlɔid]	n.	胶体
	adj.	胶状的
column ['kɔləm]	n.	柱体,圆柱
columnar jointing		柱状节理
combustion [kəm'bʌstʃən]	n.	燃烧,氧化
complex frequency response		复频响应
compliance [kəm'plaiəns]	n.	柔度
composite material		复合材料

compressibility		可压缩性
compressive stress		压应力
computational mechanics		计算力学
concomitant [kən'kɔmitənt]	adj.	伴随的；共存的
concrete ['kɔnkri:t]	n.	混凝土,凝结物
conservation of momentum		动量守恒
consistency [kən'sistənsi]	n.	收敛性
constraint [kən'streint]	n.	约束
contaminant [kən'tæmənənt]	n.	杂质；污染物
continuum mechanics		连续介质力学
contractile [kən'træktail]	adj.	可压缩的
contracted notation		缩约记号
contour ['kɔntuə]	n.	轮廓,等高线
convection-diffusion		对流扩散
convective velocity		对流速度
convergence [kən'və:dʒəns]	n.	收敛
convergence rate		收敛速度
coolant ['ku:lənt]	n.	冷冻剂
Coriolis acceleration		科氏加速度
corrosion [kə'rəuʒən]	n.	腐蚀,侵入
corrosion resistance		耐蚀性；抗腐蚀性
couple-stress		偶应力
couple ['kʌpl]	n.	力偶
	vt.	偶合
curvature ['kə:vətʃə]	n.	弯曲；曲率
corrugate ['kɔrugeit]	vt.&vi.	起皱纹
complex truss		复式桁架
compound truss		复氏桁架
coplanar [kəu'pleinə]	adj.	共平面的
concurrent [kən'kʌrənt]	adj.	同时发生的
configuration [kən,figju'reiʃən]	n.	构型,结构,形态
critical form		危形
complementary function		余函数
critical damping		临界阻尼
conjugate ['kɔndʒə,geit]	adj.	共轭的
constituent [kən'stitjuənt]	adj.	本质的,本构的
constitutive theory		本构理论
constitutive equation		本构方程
constantan ['kɔnstəntæn]	n.	一种铜与镍的合金

contrived variational principle		约束变分原理
corrosion fatigue		腐蚀疲劳
counter stress		对应力；相反应力
crack [kræk]	vt.&vi.	裂开,爆裂,断裂
	n.	裂纹
crack front		裂纹前沿
crack initiation		裂纹起始；起裂
crack nucleation		裂纹成核
crack propagation		裂纹扩展
crack tip		裂尖
creep [kri:p]	vi.	蠕变
	n.	蠕变
creep fatigue		蠕变疲劳
creep fracture		蠕变断裂
criterion [krai'tiəriən]	n.	标准；准则
critical state		临界状态
critical load		临界载荷
cross-bracing		交叉撑条
cross joint		横节理
cross section		横截面
crook [kruk]	vi.	弯曲,成钩状
crookedness ['krukidnis]	n.	弯曲；扭曲
crush [krʌʃ]	vt.&vi.	压碎；折皱
crystal lattice		晶格
cull [kʌl]	vt.	剔除
	n.	剔除
culminate ['kʌlmineit]	vi.	达到顶点
cycle number		循环次数
cyclic loading		循环载荷
cyclic stress		循环应力
cylinder head		汽缸盖

D

damage ['dæmidʒ]	n.	损伤 vt. 损坏
damping ['dæmpiŋ]	adj.	阻尼
damping factor		阻尼系数
dashe line		虚线
dead weight		静止重量；自重；净重
dealloying [,di:ə'lɔiiŋ]	n.	脱合金成分腐蚀

decameter ['dekə,miːtə]	n.	十米
defect [di'fekt]	n.	缺陷
deflect [di'flekt]	vt.&vi.	偏斜,转向
deflection [di'flekʃən]	n.	挠曲,挠度,偏斜
deform [di'fɔːm]	vt.&vi.	变形
deformation [,diːfɔː'meiʃən]	n.	变形
degree of freedom		自由度
degree of redundancy		冗余度
denominator [dɪ'nɔmə,neɪtə]	n.	分母
density functional theory (DFT)		密度泛函理论
derivative [di'rivətiv]	n.	导数
determinate [di'təːminit]	adj.	确定的,静定的
determinate structure		静定结构
deviatoric plane		偏平面
deviatoric stress		偏应力
die [dai]	n.	冲模,钢模
die-cast housing		压铸壳
differential equation		微分方程
differentiation [,difə,renʃi'eiʃən]	n.	微分
differential operator		微分算符
diffusion coefficient		扩散系数
digital image correlation		数字图像相关
dimensionless [də'menʃənləs]	adj.	无量纲
dip [dip]	n.	浸泡；浸；下沉；倾斜
	vt.&vi.	浸泡；浸；下沉；倾斜
dip coating		浸涂
Dirac delta function		狄拉克δ函数
direction cosine		方向余弦
Dirichlet condition		狄利克来条件
discipline [,disiplin,'disəplin]	n.	学科
discrete		离散的
dislocation [,dislə'keiʃən]	n.	位错
displacement [dis'pleismənt]	n.	位移
displacement function		位移函数
dissipation principle		耗散定理
divergence [dai'vəːdʒəns]	n.	散度,分歧,分离
dolerite ['dɔlərait]	n.	辉绿岩,粗粒玄武岩
dolomite ['dɔləmait]	n.	白云石,石灰石
drag [dræg]	n.	阻力

droplet ['drɔplit]	n.	小滴；微滴
ductile ['dʌktail]	adj.	韧性的，柔软的
ductility [dʌk'tiliti]	n.	韧性
Duhamel's integral		杜哈美积分
dummy resistor		假电阻；仿真电阻
duty cycle		负载循环；工作周期
dyke [daik]	n.	沟；渠；堤坝
dynamics [dai'næmiks]	n.	动力学；力学；动态
dynamic crack growth		动态裂纹扩展

E

earth-moving		运土的
eccentricity [,eksen'trisiti]	n.	离心；偏心率
elastic [i'læstik]	adj.	弹性的
elastic limit		弹性极限
elastic-perfectly plastic		理想弹塑性
elastic-plastic		弹塑性的
elastic wave		弹性波
elasticity [,elæs'tisəti]	n.	弹性
elasticity matrix		弹性矩阵
elastomer [i'læstəmə]	n.	弹性体
elastoplastic [i'læstəplæstik]	n.	弹塑性
elasto-viscoplastic		弹粘塑性的
electrical resistance strain gage		电阻应变计
element ['elimənt]	n.	构件，要素，成分
elongate ['i:lɔŋgeit]	vt.&vi.	拉长；伸长；延长
elongation [,i:lɔŋ'geiʃən]	n.	伸长，延长
embossing [im'bɔ:s]	vt.	压纹；模压加工
emulsion [i'mʌlʃən]	n.	乳胶液；感光乳剂
encapsulation [in,kæpsju'leiʃən]	n.	包装；封装
energy release rate		能量释放率
engine block		发动机缸体
engineering shear strain		工程剪应变
epoxy [ep'ɔksi]	n.	环氧树脂
equation of continuity		连续性方程
equation of state		状态方程
equilibrium [,i:kwi'libriəm]	n.	平衡，均衡
equilibrium equation		平衡方程
equivalent nodal force		等效节点力

error estimation		误差估计
esthetics [es'θetiks]	n.	美学
etch [etʃ]	vt.	蚀刻
ethanol ['eθənɔl,'eθənəul]	n.	乙醇
Euler-Lagrange equation		欧拉-拉格朗日方程
excavation [,ekskə'veiʃən]	n.	挖掘；发掘
excitation [ek'saitətiv]	n.	激励
exigency [ek'sidʒənsi]	n.	紧急
experimental stress analysis		实验应力分析
explicit algorithm		显式算法
extensometer [,eksten'sɔmitə]	n.	伸长计；引伸计
external force		外力
externally statically determinate		外部静定
extreme position		极端位置

F

failure ['feiljə]	n.	破坏,失效
fallacious [fə'leiʃəs]	adj.	谬误的；不合理的
fashion ['fæʃən]	vt.	制造,使成形
	n.	时尚
fatigue [fə'ti:g]	n.	疲劳
	vi.&vt.	(使)疲劳
fatigue curve		疲劳曲线
fatigue failure		疲劳破坏
fault [fɔ:lt]	n.	断层
felt pad		毛毡坐垫
ferroelectric [,ferəui'lektrik]	adj.	铁电的
fiber reinforced composite		纤维增强复合材料
fibrous ['faibrəs]	adj.	纤维的
finite element		有限单元
finite difference method		有限差分法
fixed-end		固定端
flange [flændʒ]	n.	凸缘；边缘；轮缘
flexible ['fleksəbl]	adj.	柔度的,可弯曲的,柔韧的
flexure ['flekʃə]	n.	弯曲,曲率,挠度
flow [fləu]	vi.	流动
fluidics ['flu:idiks]	n.	应用流体学；射流技术
fluid coupling		液力联轴节
fluid mechanics		流体力学

flux [flʌks]	n.	流量；熔化
foil strain gauge		箔式应变计
folded plate		褶皱板
force [fɔːs]	n.	力；力量
forced vibration		强迫振动
formula ['fɔːmjulə]	n.	公式
formulate ['fɔːmjuleit]	vt.	公式化,用公式描述
forward difference		向前差分
fracture ['fræktʃə]	n.	断裂
	vi. & vt.	(使)断裂
fracture mechanics		断裂力学
fracture toughness		断裂韧性
frame [freim]	n.	框架
free-cutting alloy		易切削合金
free vibration		自由振动
frequency of vibration		振动频率
friction force		摩擦力
fringe [frindʒ]	n.	条纹
fragment ['frægmənt]	n.	碎片；破碎
functional ['fʌŋkʃnəl]	n.	泛函

G

gage factor		应变灵敏度系数
gas turbine engine		汽轮机
geology [dʒi'ɔlədʒi]	n.	地质学,地质情况
gigahertz ['gigəhəːts]	n.	十亿赫兹,千兆赫
gradient ['greidiənt]	n.	梯度,倾斜度
grain [grein]	n.	晶粒
granite ['grænit]	n.	花岗岩,花岗石
graphite ['græfait]	n.	石墨
grid [grid]	n.	格子
Griffith's problem		Griffith 问题
gusset ['gʌsit]	n.	角板；三角形衬料
gust [gʌst]	n.	阵风

H

hanger ['hæŋə]	n.	挂钩,悬挂物
hardening characteristic		硬化特性
hardening rule		强化准则,强化定律

hardness ['hɑːdnis]	n.	硬度，硬性
harmonic [hɑːˈmɔnik]	adj.	简谐的
harmonic force		谐力
harmonic motion		简谐振动
harness [ˈhɑːnis]	n.	马具；管理；控制
headway [ˈhedwei]	n.	前进；航行速度
heat conduction equation		热传导方程
heterodyning [ˈhetərəuˌdainiŋ]	n.	外差作用
heterogeneity [ˌhetərɔdʒiˈniːiti]	n.	非均匀性
heterostructure [hetərəuˈstrʌktʃə(r)]	n.	异质结构
heuristic [hjuəˈristik]	adj.	启发式的；探索的
hierarchical [ˌhaiəˈrɑːkikl]	adj.	按等级划分的
hierarchical organization		分层结构
high-cycle fatigue		高周疲劳
high-frequency component		高频分量
high-strength		高强度
holder [ˈhəuldə]	n.	固定器；支架
holography [həuˈlɔgrəfi]	n.	全息照相技术
holy grail		圣杯；圣盘
homogeneous [ˌhɔməˈdʒiniəs]	adj.	同质的，均匀的，齐次的
	n.	谐波
homogeneous equation		齐次方程
Hooke's law		胡克定律
hostile environment		恶劣环境
hydrodynamics [ˈhaidrəudaiˈnæmiks]	n.	水动力学
hydrostatic pressure		静水压力
hysteresis [ˌhistəˈriːsis]	n.	滞后(现象)，滞后作用
hysteresis loop		迟滞环；滞后回线

I

ideal gas		理想气体
identity matrix		单位矩阵
igneous [ˈigniəs]	adj.	火成的；火的
imaginary part		虚部
imaging method		成像法
implicit algorithm		隐式算法
impregnate [imˈpregneit]	vt.	注入，使充满
	adj.	充满的
impress [imˈpres]	n.	印象；特征；传送

	vi.	印象；传送
impulse-response function		脉冲响应函数
inasmuch [inəz'mʌtʃ]	adv.	由于；因为
incompressible fluid		不可压缩流体
indeterminate [,indi'tə:minit]	adj.	不确定的,超静定的
indeterminate structure		超静定结构
indiscriminately [indi'skriminitli]	adv.	无差别；任意地
inertia [in'ə:ʃiə,in'ə:ʃə]	n.	惯性
infinitesimal [,infini'tesiməl]	adj.	无限小的
initial displacement		初始位移
initial residual stress		初始残余应力
initial velocity		初始速度
initial yield surface		初始屈服面
inorganic ['inɔ:'gænik]	adj.	无机的；非自然生长的
in-plane		面内
I-shaped steel		工字钢
instability [,instə'biliti]	n.	不稳定
insulating backing		绝缘基
integral ['intigrəl]	n.	积分；整数
integral equation		积分方程
integration [,inti'greiʃən]	n.	积分
interferometry [,ɪntəfə'rɔmɪtə]	n.	干涉测量法
interior cycle		内循环
internal force		内力
internal variable		内变量
internally statically indeterminaten		内部静定
interpolation function		插值函数
interdisciplinary [,intə:'disiplinəri]	adj.	学科间的；学科交叉的
invariant [in'vɛəriənt]	n.	不变量
	adj.	无变化的,不变的
irreducible formulation		不可约型公式
isothermal ['aisəu'θə:məl]	adj.	等温的
	n.	等温线
isotropic [,aisə'trɔpik]	adj.	各向同性的
isotropic hardening		各向同性强化
isotropy [ai'sɔtrəpi]	n.	各向同性
iterative ['itərətiv]	adj.	迭代的

J

jaw [dʒɔ:]	n.	虎钳

jelly ['dʒeli]	n.	胶状物
J integral		J 积分
joint [dʒɔint]	n.	节理

K

kinematic hardening		运动强化
kinematics [,kinə'mætiks]	n.	运动学；动力学
kinetic energy		动能
kinetic friction		动摩擦

L

Lagrangian [lə'grɑːndʒiən]	adj.	拉格朗日的
Lagrange method		拉格朗日方法
Lagrange multiplier		拉格朗日乘子
Lame constants		拉梅常数
lamina ['læmənə]	n.	薄板；薄片
laminar ['læminə]	adj.	层流
laminate ['læmineit]	n.	薄板；层压板；层板
lamination [,læmi'neiʃən]	n.	制成薄板；薄板；层状体
landslide ['lændslaid]	n.	滑坡
Laplace operator		拉普拉斯算符
large-scale parallel computing		大规模并行计算
lateral force		横向力
lattice ['lætis]	n.	格子；点阵
layer ['leiə]	n.	层
least energy dissipation principle		最小能量耗散原理
lifetime ['laiftaim]	n.	寿命
linear elastic fracture mechanics		线性弹性断裂力学
linear interpolation		线性插值
linearized theory		线性化理论
lipid ['lipid]	n.	脂质；油脂
liquid crystal		液晶
lithological [li'θɔlədʒikəl]	adj.	岩性的,岩石的
Lode parameter		Lode 参数
longevity [lɔn'dʒeviti]	n.	长寿；寿命
longitudinal ['lɔndʒi'tjuːdinəl]	adj.	纵向的,经度的
longitudinal shear (or antiplane) mode of cracking		裂纹纵向剪切(反对称)模式
longitudinal strain		纵向应变

low-carbon steel		低碳钢
low-cycle fatigue		低周疲劳
lowly ['ləuli]	adj.	贫贱的；地位低下的

M

machinability [məʃi:nə'biliti]	n.	可切削性；机械加工性
macro-mechanics		宏观力学
macroscopic crack		宏观裂纹
magnetic dot		磁点
magnesium ['mæg'ni:ʃiəm]	n.	镁
mandrel ['mændrəl]	n.	心轴；拉延
martensite ['mɑ:tən,zait]	n.	马氏体
martensitic transformation		马氏体转变
masonry ['meisnri]	n.	石造建筑；石造工程
mass-spring-damper system		质量-弹簧-阻尼系统
material derivative		物质导数
mathematical statement		数学表达式，数学描述
matrix ['meitriks]	n.	矩阵；基体（材料）
matrices [复数] ['meitrisi:z]		
mean free path		平均自由程
measurable ['meʒərəbəl]	adj.	可测量的
mechanics [mi'kæniks]	n.	力学
mechanics of fluids		流体力学
mechanistic [,mekə'nistik]	adj.	机械学的；机械的
member ['membə]	n.	构件
meso-mechanics		细观力学
mesostructure	n.	细观结构；中构造
metallurgical [,metə'lə:dʒikl]	adj.	冶金的
metal forming		金属成型
metamorphic [,metə'mɔ:fik]	adj.	变性的；变质的
method of weigted residual		加权残值法
micelle [mai'sel]	n.	微团；胶束
microcavitation	n.	微空隙
microcrack ['maikrəukræk,'maikrəu,kræk]	n.	微裂纹
micro-electro-mechanical		微机电的
micro-mechanics		微观力学
microscopic ['maikrə'skɔpik]	adj.	显微的，微观的
microvoid [,maikrəu'vɔid]	n.	微孔
military engineering		军事工程学

mining ['mainiŋ]	n.	采矿；矿业
mis-folding		错折叠
mixed formulation		混合型公式
mnemonic [ni:'mɔnik]	adj.	记忆的
	n.	记忆方法
modal analysis		模态分析
modality [məu'dæliti]	n.	样式；形式；形态
modulus ['mɔdjuləs]； moduli [复数]['mɔdʒə‚lai]	n.	模量，系数
modulus of elasticity		弹性模量
modulus of volume expansion		体积膨胀模量
Mohr-Coulomb failure criterion		摩尔-哥伦布破坏准则
moire [mwɑ:]	n.	云纹
moire interferometry		云纹干涉法
molecular dynamics (MD)		分子动力学
moment of inertia		惯性矩
momentum [məu'mentəm]	n.	动量，冲量
monolithic [‚mɔnə'liθik]	adj.	独石的；单体的；整体的
monotonic [mɔnəu'tɔnik]	adj.	单调的；单斜晶体的
Monte Carlo (MC)		蒙特卡罗
mount [maunt]	vt.	安装
mud [mʌd]	n.	泥；泥浆
Multi Body Dynamics (MBD)		多体动力学
multiphase flow		多相流
multiplier ['mʌltəplaiə]	n.	乘数
multi-scale		多尺度
myriad ['miriəd]	n.	无数；极大数量
	adj.	无数的；极大数量的

N

nanocomposite	n.	纳米复合材料
nanofabrication	n.	纳米加工
nanohole	n.	纳米空洞
nano-mechanics		纳米力学
nanoscale	n.	纳米尺度
nanostructure	n.	纳米结构
nanowire	n.	纳米线
natural frequency		固有频率
natural variational principle		自然变分原理

Navier's equation		纳维方程
necessary condition		必要条件
necking zone		紧缩区域
Neumann condition		纽曼条件
neutral axis		中性轴
Newtonian fluid		牛顿流体
Newton's first law		牛顿第一定律
Newton's second law		牛顿第二定律
nitrocellulose ['naitrəu'seljuləus]	n.	硝化纤维素
nodal displacement		节点位移
nondimensional ['nɔndi'menʃənəl]	n.	无量纲
	adj.	无量纲（的）
nonhomogeneous ['nɔnhɔmə'dʒi:njəs]	adj.	非均质的；非齐次的；多相的
nonlinearity [,nɔnlini'æriti]	n.	非线性
non-cyclic load		非循环载荷
nonhomogeneous ['nɔnhɔmə'dʒi:njəs]	adj.	非均匀的
nonstationary ['nɔn'steiʃənəri]	adj.	不稳定的；非定常的
nondestructive evaluation		无损评价
nonviscous	adj.	非粘性，无粘性
non-Newtonian fluid		非牛顿流体
normal force		法向力
notwithstand [,nɔtwiθ'stændiŋ]	prep.	尽管；虽然
numerator ['nu:mə,reɪtə]	n.	分子

O

objective function		目标函数
oblique [əb'li:k]	adj.	斜的；倾斜
offshore structure		离岸结构
off-lattice		非格子
off-road		越野的
opening mode of cracking		裂纹张开模式
operator ['ɔpə,reitə]	n.	算符
optimization [,ɔptimai'zeiʃən]	n.	优化
optimize ['ɔptimaiz]	vt.&vi.	优化
optimum ['ɔptiməm]	adj.	最优的
ordinary integral		寻常积分
ordinary differential equation		常微分方程
organic [ɔ:'gænik]	adj.	有机的；有机物质
orthotropic [,ɔ:θə'trɔpik]	adj.	正交的

oscillation [ˌɔsiˈleiʃən]	n.	振荡
ostensibly [ɔsˈtensəbli]	adv.	表面上地；外表上地
out-of-plane	n.	面外
outperform [ˌautpəˈfɔːm]	vt.	优于；超额完成
overstress [ˈəuvəˈstres, ˌəuvəˈstres]	n.	过应力
oxidize [ˈɔksiˌdaiz]	vt. & vi.	（使）氧化

P

paradigm [ˈpærədaim]	n.	范例
partial differential equation		偏微分方程
particular integral		特积分；特解
particulate [pəˈtikjulit]	adj.	微粒的
particulate-reinforced composite		颗粒增强复合材料
pendulum [ˈpendjuləm]	n.	单摆，摆锤
period of vibration		振动周期
permanent deformation		永久变形
perseverance [ˌpəːsiˈviərəns]	n.	不屈不挠；毅力
phase [feiz]	n.	相
phase angle		相位角
phenolics [fiˈnɔliks]	n.	酚醛树脂
photoelastic [fəutəuiˈlæstik]	adj.	光弹性的
photoelastic coating		光弹性涂层
photoelastic stress analysis		光弹性应力分析
piezoelectric [paiˌiːzəuiˈlektrik]	adj.	压电的
pile [pail]	n.	柱，桩，堆
pinned end		销轴支承
pin joint		铰接；关节接头
piston [ˈpistən]	n.	活塞
pitch [pitʃ]	n.	沥青
pixelate	vt.	使……像素化；将……分解成像素
plane-strain		平面应变
plane stress		平面应力
plastic [ˈplæstik]	adj.	塑性的
plastic flow		塑性流动
plastic wave		塑性波
plasticity [plæsˈtisiti]	n.	塑性
ploughman [ˈplaumən]	n.	庄稼汉
pneumatic [njuːˈmætik]	adj.	气动的；充气的
Poisson effect		泊松效应

Poisson's ratio		泊松比
polar coordinate		极坐标
polarize ['pəulə,raiz]	vi.&vt.	(使)极化
polycrystalline [pɔli'kristəlain]	n.	多晶体
polymer ['pɔlimə]	n.	聚合物
post [pəust]	n.	柱
posteriori error estimation		后验误差估计
potential energy		势能
predate [priː'deit]	vt.	在日期上早于
prestrain [priː'strein]	n.	预应变
primary structure		主要结构
primary unknowns		主要未知量
principal material axis		材料主轴
principal stress		主应力
printed circuit technique		印刷电路技术
product		乘积
proliferation [prə,lifə'reiʃən]	n.	增殖；扩散
proportional limit		比例极限
protein folding		蛋白质折叠
pseudo-stochastic		伪随机的
pulsating load		脉动载荷
pulse excitation		脉冲激励
pump [pʌmp]	n.	泵
punch [pʌntʃ]	vt.	钻孔
pure shear		纯剪切

Q

quadratic [kwə'drætik]	adj.	二次的
quadratic functional		二次泛函
quantum mechanics		量子力学
quasi-static		准静态, 拟静态

R

rate-dependednt		率相关的
rate of dilation		膨胀率
Rayleigh wave		瑞利波
reaction [ri'ækʃən]	n.	支反力
reactor piping		反应堆管道
red blood cell		红血球

redundant constraint		多余约束
reference axis		参考坐标系
reinforced concrete		增强混泥土，钢筋混凝土
reliability [ri,laiə'biliti]	n.	可靠性，可靠度
reloading [riː'ləudiŋ]	vt. & vi.	重复加载
rendition [ren'diʃən]	n.	解释；演奏；投降
repertoire ['repətwɑː]	n.	全部节目；全部技能
Representative Volume Element (RVE)		代表性体积单元
reservoir ['rezəvwɑː]	n.	蓄水库
residual thermal stress		残余热应力
resinous ['rezinəs]	adj.	树脂的
resin-coated	adj.	树脂涂层的
resonance ['rezənəns]	adj.	共振
response [ri'spɔns]	n.	响应，反应，回答
resultant [ri'zʌltənt]	adj.	合成的，组合的
resultant momentum		合力矩
retool [riː'tuːl]	vi. & vt.	重组；重新装备
reversible [ri'vəːsəbl]	adj.	可逆的
rib [rib]	n.	肋
rigid-body		刚体
rigid frame		刚架
rigidity [ri'dʒiditi]	n.	刚度，刚性
rise time		上升时间
rivet ['rivit]	n.	铆钉；铆接
rock foundation		岩石基
rock mechanics		岩石力学
rosette [rəu'zet]	n.	玫瑰花形物
rotate [rəu'teit]	vi.	转动，旋转
rotation [rəu'teiʃən]	n.	转动，旋转
round-off error		舍入误差
rubric ['ruːbrik]	n.	类；标题；红色的

S

sag [sæg]	n.	弧垂，垂度
saturated soil		饱和土
scalar ['skeilə]	n.	数量；标量
Scanning Electron Microscope (SEM)		扫描电子显微镜
scanning mode		扫描方式
Scanning Tunneling Microscope		扫描隧道电子显微镜

second order derivative		二阶导数
scouring ['skauəriŋ]	n.	擦洗；冲刷
seed [si:d]	vt.	催云化雨
sedimentary [ˌsedi'mentəri]	adj.	沉积的；沉淀性的；沉淀作用造成的
seismic wave		地震波
seismological [ˌsaizmə'lɔdʒikl]	adj.	地震学上的
seismology [saiz'mɔlədʒi]	n.	地震学
sequel ['si:kwəl]	n.	结局；后果
sewage ['sju:idʒ]	n.	污水，污秽物
shadow moire		影栅云纹
shape function		形状函数
shape memory alloy (SMA)		形状记忆合金
shape memory effect (SME)		形状记忆效应
shape optimization		形状优化
shearing strain		剪切应变
shearing stress		剪切应力
shock spectrum		冲击谱
shock wave		冲击波；激波
shrinkage		收缩；减少；损耗
silicone gel		硅凝胶
silly putty		弹性橡胶泥
SI metric system		国际单位制
simply supported beam		简支梁
simple truss		简支桁架
simultaneous [ˌsaiməl'teinjəs]	adj.	同时发生的；同步的
simultaneous equation		联立方程
single-DOF		单自由度
singularity [ˌsiŋgju'læriti]	n.	奇异性
sintering ['sintəriŋ]	vi.	烧结
sinusoidal function		正弦函数
siting ['saitiŋ]	n.	建设地点
sizing optimization		尺寸优化
slab [slæb]	n.	平板；厚板
slenderness ['slendənis]	n.	细长；细长度
sliding ['slaidiŋ]	n.	滑移
slip [slip]	n.	滑移
slip plane		滑移面
soil foundation		土基础
soil mechanics		土力学

solder ['sɔldə]	n.	焊接剂；接合剂
solid mechanics		固体力学
specified displacement		给定位移
specified surface traction		给定面力
speckle interferometry		散斑干涉法
spring constant		弹簧常数
spring-supported		弹簧支撑
stability [stə'biliti]	n.	稳定，稳定性
stainless steel		不锈钢
statical indeterminancy		静不定
static equilibrium		静力平衡
static fatigue		静态疲劳
static friction		静摩擦
statics ['stætiks]	n.	静力学
stationarity [steiʃə'næriti]	n.	稳定性；稳态
stationary ['steiʃənəri]	adj.	稳定的；不动的
steady-state		稳态
steel-framed		钢架
step excitation		阶跃激励
stereological [stiəri'ɔledʒi, sterə'ɔledʒi]	adj.	体视学；立体测量学
stereoscopic [,steriəs'kɔpik]	adj.	有立体感的
stiffen ['stifn]	vt. & vi.	刚化；使坚硬
stiffness ['stifnis]	n.	刚度
stocky ['stɔki]	adj.	矮壮的；结实的
strain [stren]	n.	应变
strain energy		应变能
strain gage		应变计
strain-induced quantum dot		应变诱发量子点
strain rate		应变率
strength [strenθ]	n.	强度
strength-to-weight ratio		比强度
stress [strɛs]	n.	应力
stress concentrator		应力集中点
stress concentration		应力集中
stress corrosion cracking		应力腐蚀起裂
stress distribution		应力分布
stress gradient		应力梯度
stress-induced martensite（SIM）		应力诱发马氏体
stress intensity factor		应力强度因子

stress-matrix		应力矩阵
stress ratio		应力比
stress-strain diagram		应力应变图
stress tensor		应力张量
stress wave		应力波
stretch [stretʃ]	vt. & vi.	伸展,拉紧,延伸
strike [straik]	vi.	走向
structural optimization		结构优化
structural steel		结构钢
sub-discipline		分支学科
subdomain	n.	子域
submicron ['sʌb'maikrɔn]	n.	亚微米;亚微细粒
	adj.	表面活性剂的
substrate ['sʌbstreit]	n.	基片;基底
sufficient condition		充分条件
super-hydrophobic		超疏水
superelasticity	n.	超弹性
superposition [ˌsju:pəpə'ziʃn]	n.	叠加,重叠,叠合
support [sə'pɔ:t]	n.	支撑
surface force		表面力
surface traction		表面力
surfactant [sə:'fæktənt]	n.	表面活性剂
symmetric [si'metrik]	adj.	对称的

T

tangent matrix		切线矩阵
Taylor series expansion		泰勒级数展开
T-beam		T 型梁
tectonophysics [ˌtektənəu'fiziks]	n.	构造物理学,地壳构造物理学
tensile stress		拉应力
tensile strength		拉伸强度
tensile-testing machine		拉伸试验机
tensile test specimen		拉伸试样
tension ['tenʃən]	n.	张量,张力,拉力
tensor ['tensə]	n.	张量
tensor-transformation		张量转换
theoretical and applied mechanics		理论与应用力学
thermal camera		热感照相机
thermal expansion coefficient		热膨胀系数

thermal stress		热应力
thermo-fatigue		热疲劳
thermography [θəˈmɔgrəfi]	n.	温度记录法；热熔印刷
thermomechanics [θəːməumiˈkæniks]	n.	热力学
thermosetting resin		热固性树脂
thrust [θrʌst]	vt.&vi.	抛掷
tillage [ˈtilidʒ]	n.	耕种，耕作
time derivative		时间导数
time lag		时间滞后
titanium [taiˈteiniəm]	n.	钛
tolerating strain		容许应变
tomographic [təuˈmɔgrəfi]	n.	X线断层摄影术；X线体层照相术
topography [təˈpɔgrəfi]	n.	地质,地形学
topology optimization		拓扑优化
trade-off	n.	权衡；取舍
transducer [trænsˈdjuːsə]	n.	传感器
transient term		暂时项；衰减项
transport equation		输运方程；迁移方程
Transmission Electron Microscope (TEM)		透射电子显微镜
transverse shear mode of cracking		裂纹横向剪切模式
transversely isotropic		横观各向同性
Tresca yield criterion		特雷斯卡屈服准则
trial and error		试错
trial function		试函数
triaxiality[traiæksiˈæliti]	n.	三轴；三维
triclinic [traiˈklinik]	adj.	三斜晶系的
true stress		真实应力
truncation error		截断误差
truss [trʌs]	n.	桁架
turbulent flow		湍流流动
tunable [ˈtjuːnəbl]	adj.	可调谐的
turbulent [ˈtəːbjulənt]	adj.	湍流的
twinned boundary		孪生边界
two-span beam		双跨梁

U

ubiquitous [juːˈbikwitəs]	adj.	到处存在的
ultimate tensile strength		最大拉伸强度
ultrasonics [ˌʌltrəˈsɔniks]	n.	超声波,超声学

unbalance [ˌʌnˈbæləns]	n.	不平衡
unconditionally stable		无条件稳定的
undamped [ʌnˈdæmpt]	adj.	无阻尼的
uniaxial strain		单轴应变
uniaxial stress		单轴应力
uniaxial tension		单轴拉伸
unit impulse		单位脉冲
unload [ˈʌnˈləud]	vt.&vi.	卸载
upwind scheme		迎风格式

V

vacuum deposition technique		真空淀积技术
variable [ˈvɛəriəbl]	n.	变量
	adj.	可变的
variational principle		变分原理
vector [ˈvektə]	n.	矢量；向量
vibration [vaiˈbreiʃən]	n.	振动,震动
vibratory [ˈvaibrətəri]	adj.	振动的
Vierendeel truss		空腹桁架；弗伦第尔桁架
virtual design		虚拟设计
visco-elastic		粘弹性的
viscoelastic wave		粘弹性波
viscoelasticity [ˈviskəuilæsˈtisiti]	n.	粘弹性
visco-plastic		粘塑性的
viscoplastic potential		粘塑性势
viscosity [visˈkɔsiti]	n.	粘性
viscosity coefficient		粘性系数
viscous [ˈviskəs]	adj.	粘性的
viscous damping		粘性阻尼
von Mises yield criterion		冯米泽斯屈服准则
volume fraction		体积分数
volumetric strain		体积应变

W

wavenumber	n.	波数
wear resistance		耐磨性,耐磨度
web [web]	n.	腹板
weld [weld]	vt.&vi.	焊接
	n.	焊接

weldability [weldə'biliti]	n.	焊接性；可焊性
Wheatstone bridge		惠斯通电桥
whisker ['hwiskə]	n.	金须
wire strain gauge		金属丝应变计
work [wə:k]	n.	功
workability [,wə:kə'biliti]	n.	可使用性；施工性能；可加工性
woven fiber		编织纤维
wraparound ['ræpə,raund]	adj.	围绕的；围绕物
wrought [rɔ:t]	adj.	锻造的；加工的；精细的

Y

yield criterion		屈服准则
yield function		屈服函数
yield point		屈服点
yield strength		屈服强度

Z

zinc [ziŋk]	n.	锌

参 考 文 献

[1] Spiegel M R. Theory and problems of Theoretical Mechanics[M]. 6th Ed. New York: McGraw-Hill,1980.
[2] Morin D. Introduction to Classical Mechanics with Problems and Solutions[M]. New York: Cambridge University Press,2008.
[3] Taylor J R. Classical Mechanics[M]. California: University Science Books,2005.
[4] Mott R L. Applied Strength of Materials[M]. New Jersey: Pearson/Prentice Hall,2008.
[5] Fung Y C. A first Course in Continuum Mechanics[M]. 3rd Ed. New Jersey: Prentice Hall,1994.
[6] RiceJ R. Solid Mechanics[M]. 2nd Edition. Massachusetts: Cambridge,2010.
[7] Timoshenko S P,Goodier J N. Theory of Elasticity[M]. 3rd Edition. New York: McGraw-Hill,1970.
[8] Kolsky H. Stress Waves in Solids[J]. Journal of Sound and Vibration,1964(1): 88-110.
[9] Karnovsky I A,Lebed O. Advanced Methods of Structural Analysis[M]. New York: Springer,2009.
[10] Leet K,Uang M C,Gilbert A. Fundamentals of Structural Analysis[M]. 3rd Edition. Tennessee: McGraw-Hill,2008.
[11] Timoshenko S P,Young D H. Theory of Structures[M]. 2nd Ed. New York: McGraw-Hill,1965.
[12] Thomson W T, Dahleh M D. Theory of Vibration with Applications[M]. 5th Edition. New Jersey: Prentice-Hall,1997.
[13] Chopra A K. Dynamics of Strucure Theory and Applications to Earthquake Engineering[M]. 3rd Edition. Beijing: Tsingua University Press,2009.
[14] Doltsinis I. Elements of Plasticity[M]. Boston: WIT Press,2000.
[15] Chakrabarty J. Applied Plasticity[M]. 2nd Edition. New York: Springer,2010.
[16] Chaboche J L. A Review of Some Plasticity and Viscoplasticity Constitutive Theories[J]. International Journal of Plasticity,2008(24) 1642-1693.
[17] Window A L. Strain Gauge Technology[M]. 2nd Edition,New York: Elsevier Applied Science,1992.
[18] Shukla A,James W D. Experimental Solid Mechanics[M]. Tennessee: College House Enterprises,2010.
[19] Knauss W G. Perspectives in Experimental Solid Mechanics[J]. International Journal of Solids and Structures,2000(37): 251-266.
[20] Zienkiewicz O C,Taylor R L,Zhu J Z. The Finite Element Method: Its Basis and Fundamentals[M]. 6th Edition. London: Butterworth-Heinemann Book Company,2005.
[21] Oden J T, Belytschko T,Babuska I,Hughes T J R. Research Directions in Computational Mechanics [J]. Computer Methods in Applied Mechanics and Engineering,2003(192): 913-922.
[22] Bolotin V V. Mechanics of Fatigue[M]. Florida: CRC Press,1999.
[23] Rice J R. Fracture Mechanics[J]. Applied Mechanics Review,1985,38(10).
[24] Jones R M. Mechanics of Composite Materials[M]. 2nd Edition. Pennsylvania: Taylor & Francis,1999.
[25] Yang D. Shape Memory Alloy and Smart Hybrid Composites Advanced Materials for the 21st Century[J]. Materials and Design,2000(21): 503-505.
[26] Jaeger J C, Neville G, Cook W, Robert W Z. Fundamentals of Rock Mechanics[M]. 4th Edition. Massachusetts: Wiley-Blackwell,2007.
[27] Hettiaratchi D R P. Theoretical Soil Mechanics and Implement Design[J]. Soil & Tillage Research,

1988(11):325-347.

[28] Christensen P W, Klarbring A. An Introduction to Structural Optimization[M]. New York: Springer,2009.

[29] Kassner M E, Nemat-Nasser S, Suo Z, etc. New Directions in Mechanics[M], Mechanics of Materials,2005(37):231-259.

[30] Kundu P K,Cohen I M. Fluid Mechanics[M]. 3rd Edition. New York: Elsevier Academic Press,2004.

[31] 韩其顺,王学铭.英汉科技英语翻译教程[M].上海:上海外语教育出版社,1997.

[32] Weissberg R, Bucker S. Writing up Research[M]. New Jersey: Prentice-Hall,1990.

[33] Sekine H,Yan B,Yasuho T. Numerical simulation study of cracked aluminum panels repaired with a FRP composite patch with combined BEM/FEM[J]. Engineering Fracture Mechanics,2005(72):2549-2563.

[34] Hu N,Wang X,Fugunaga H,et. al. Damage assessment of structures using modal test data[J]. Internatioanl Journal of Solids and Structures,2001(38):3111-3126.

[35] Yan B,Lin X, Luo W,Chen Z,Liu ZQ. Numerical study on dynamic swing of suspension insulator string in overhead transmission line underwind load[J]. IEEE Transactions on Power Delivery,2010,25(1):248-259.